A Falling Star

A Falling Star

☆

A True Story of Romance

—— *by* ——

Betty Leslie-Melville

MACMILLAN PUBLISHING COMPANY

NEW YORK

Macmillan Publishing Company
866 Third Avenue, New York, N.Y. 10022
Collier Macmillan Canada, Inc.

Library of Congress Cataloging-in-Publication Data
Leslie-Melville, Betty.
A falling star.
1. Leslie-Melville, Betty—Biography—Marriage.
2. Leslie-Melville, Jock—Biography—Marriage.
3. Authors, American—20th century—Biography.
I. Title.
PS3562.E83Z465   1986   813'.54 [B]   85-23728
ISBN 0-02-583980-2

Macmillan books are available at special discounts for bulk purchases for sales promotions, premiums, fund-raising, or educational use. For details, contact:

Special Sales Director
Macmillan Publishing Company
866 Third Avenue
New York, N.Y. 10022

10 9 8 7 6 5 4 3 2 1

Designed by Mary Cregan
Printed in the United States of America

To Jock, of course.

☆

I had never written a book without Jock before, but now I had to try to write this book, the sixth, alone. I was so scared. But then, amidst our papers, I found many pages we had already written together before he got sick. So, once again, many thanks to Jock, for, as before, without him this book would never have been written.

A Falling Star

☆

Chapter 1

O UR wish on a falling star came true in a lovely love story.

Just after Jock and I had met on the beach of the Indian Ocean in Kenya, we each made a secret wish, unknown to the other, on a star that streaked across the African sky, that we would be together forever. It wasn't forever, but it was for twenty magical, scintillating, exuberant years full of mutual joy and adventure and accomplishment—a love most of us dream of but experience only briefly, if at all. It was as if the falling star had turned us into a modern-day prince and princess and spun our lives into an idyllic fairy tale in never-never land. We were eternally in love with one another and with our wondrous life, until . . .

But let me start from the beginning.

It was July 1963 and I was at Malindi, a picturesque little fishing village on the Indian Ocean that once was an Arab sultanate and slaving post. I was staying at the Sindbad Hotel for the summer, and on finishing dinner one evening with friends, I spied, standing at the bar, the tall, lean, handsome young man with his arm in a leather sling whom I had often seen in Nairobi. I'd noticed him walking on the street, having coffee in the Thorn Tree, and one night dancing in the Equator Club (to rock 'n' roll sung in French by an African piano player who always stood up to play). Our eyes had met, but each time I had quickly looked away, embarrassed that I found him so alluring.

Now again we locked glances for a moment and every time I stole another look, I found his eyes on me. My stomach got up and went for a walk. Finally I asked my companions if anyone knew that man over there. One did, rather well, and he went and invited him to join our table. "This is Jock Leslie-Melville. Jock, I'd like you to meet Betty Bruce." Sitting down next to me, he looked at me with blue blue eyes and smiled a brilliant smile. He dazzled me. Everyone spoke the usual banalities at first, then the conversation turned to primitive tribes.

Speaking in an easy, educated British accent, his voice as mellifluous as a bush lark's, he said to the group, "My cousin teaches the Nandi, that very primitive tribe way up there in that remote northern region of Kenya. Well, the newly acquired mobile cinema was coming from Nairobi to show the Nandi their first film, so at dusk they all arrived at the marketplace in their antelope skins and carrying their ever-present spears, and stood under trees and watched the film. It was a John Wayne movie. Of course, they couldn't understand a word of English, but they got the idea that Wayne was the good guy and the Indians the bad. Toward the end of the film, when 4,000 Indians were left but only six of John Wayne's men, the Nandi grew very tense and terribly concerned about Wayne's safety, because unknown to him an Indian was creeping up behind him with his tomahawk at the ready, and just as he swung his arm upward to bring it down on poor John Wayne's head, a Nandi warrior raised his spear and threw it at the Indian. It went straight through the Indian's heart—and demolished the new screen." Everyone at the table laughed, then Jock commented, "It's a good thing it wasn't a play."

We talked only a few more minutes before departing, but we met again the next morning on the beach. "May I join you?" he asked with that lovely smile and lowered himself next to me onto the beach towel. Adjusting his arm in his sling, he explained, "Polio—it left my arm useless. I'm very self-conscious about it, especially when I'm shirtless and can't cover it up."

"But I think your sling is sexy," I exclaimed.

"Then I'll never be uneasy about my infirmity again."

His presence added even more brilliance to the already brilliant day. I felt intoxicated by him, and some wise sage's words flashed through my mind: "to experience that thunderclap of unreasoning instant infatuation"; so I asked, "Last night you said you had always been in Kenya. How did you come to live here?"

Egged on and on by me, he told his story: Jock's grandfather was the Earl of Leven and Melville, but was killed in a steeplechase; the second son inherited the title, the estates, and so forth; the third son was Jock's father. He was aide-de-camp to the King of Greece, played polo for England (with a handicap of nine), and because he was an adventurer, decided in 1919 to farm in Kenya.

On the ship to East Africa, he met Jock's mother, Mary, who had just been married the week before. She had been forced into the marriage in the most Victorian of ways by her stern mother, who chose the man because he was "appropriate," which meant, Jock said, that she could "see the Governor's plumes upon him one day." The day they were married, he had to leave for a remote region in Uganda to resume his job in the colonial administration, and Mary was to follow by ship a week later. On board she fell desperately in love with a dashing figure—Jock's father, the Honorable David Leslie-Melville.

However, when the ship landed in Mombasa, she dutifully went to join her husband in the furthest corner of Uganda, proceeding by road as far as it went, where porters and gun bearers awaited. They were dressed in their usual garb of skins with lion rampant on their hats, and she set off walking with them for five days, averaging about twenty-five miles per day.

Her husband appeared even more dreary than she had remembered, and two weeks was all that she could endure— she knew she had to end their marriage, so she decided to run away. Secretly she told the leader of the porters that she and her Bwana were due to leave the next morning at dawn, and at 5:30 A.M. she crept out of her tent and whispered to the leader that the Bwana was ill and would not accompany them after all; then she retraced her journey. But on the trip she contracted malaria, and in addition to being extremely ill, the missionary doctor gave her an overdose of quinine that thickened her eardrums and left her deaf. She sent a message by cleft stick to Jock's father, and he responded to the damsel who truly was in much distress, and rushed to the rescue. He nursed her to health, and when her marriage was annulled they married.

They lived on his farm on the steep western slopes of the Aberdare Mountains, fifteen miles north of the Equator in the infamous area known as the Happy Valley, which later was the epicenter of the grisly Mau Mau uprising. Jock told me how he was raised there, and how he remembered his father hunting hounds, which was done perfectly in Kenya, complete with pink coats, except the fox was replaced by a jackal. He told me that one day when he was four years old and his mother was off playing polo, his father, alone on the farm, had an attack of appendicitis and drove himself on dreadful dirt roads (which during the rains kept them captive, unable to leave at all for three months) for eight hours to a hospital in Nairobi, but died of a burst appendix during the operation.

Jock and his mother and sister stayed on the farm—a dairy farm. Jock's father had brought the first Jersey cows to East Africa. Jock spoke Swahili before English, didn't wear shoes or go to school until he was eight years old, and went off with the cook's son to have tribal scars cut into his cheeks until his mother discovered his plan and stopped him. Throughout his youth he played endlessly in the forest and came to know every tree and gully. Later, when the terrible Mau Mau occurred, knowing the forest so well, he led the soldiers through it to find the caves and other secret places where the Mau Mau hid.

"The emergency is over now, isn't it?" I asked.

"Yes, it was officially over in 1959. You know there are so many misconceptions about Mau Mau. People have been led to believe it was a blood bath of whites, when in fact only thirty-two white civilians were killed by Mau Mau. It was a civil war among the Kikuyu tribe." Jock poured some lemon squash from a thermos he had brought along and handed me a cup.

I sensed he did not want to talk about Mau Mau any longer, so I asked, "So you went to school here?" I was considering enrolling my children in Kenyan schools.

"Yes, but after primary school here I went to England and went to Eton, then Sandhurst."

"The military academy—did you stand in front of Buckingham Palace in your funny hat?"

"For a while, when I was in the Coldstream Guards." He smiled and I was able to get a glance at something that had intrigued me—two white dots on his two top front, already very white teeth. "Then I was lucky to be appointed aide to the Colonial Governor and could return here."

"What does an aide do?"

"Oh, all kinds of things—generally arranging the Governor's safaris and being with him all the time to remind him of his appointments and . . ."

"He had appointments on safari?"

"Oh, I forgot you're American. Not safari the way you use it—as a sojourn in the bush to look at animals, 'safari' in Swahili means 'journey'—you take a safari to church, to political meetings, any trip. However, when the Queen Mother arrived, I was her personal escort on both kinds of safaris."

"Was she nice?"

"Absolutely charming." He took a sip of his drink. "Anyway, I've always seen and been in sympathy with the onrushing tide that is about to bring independence to the colony, so after my stint with the Governor, I joined up with Sir Michael Blundell and Sir Wildfrid Havelock and other enlightened Brits and helped organize Kenya's first multiracial political party, and currently I'm at Parliament working for them."

"What kind of work?" I asked.

"Oh, I write speeches for Daniel Moi—he'll be President

of Kenya one day, a wonderful man—but I've talked more than enough. Now it's your turn to tell me the story of your life."

"It's so dull compared to yours."

"But I insist." His bright blue eyes matched the cloudless sky.

"Okay—I was born in Baltimore, to a middle-class family. My father died when I was ten and left my mother and me with very little, so to help out I had to sell eggs. I hated selling eggs. I had to go from door to door soliciting customers. Then every Tuesday the farmer, Mr. Grubecker, brought the eggs, and I had to count them out, bag them, then deliver them on my bicycle. When I'd knock on a door and someone would call out asking who's there, I'd have to answer, 'The egg lady.' It was humiliating. I hated two people in the world, Mr. Grubecker and Hitler. And I hated Mr. Grubecker more.

"I was ready for boys, and my girlfriends blackmailed me into doing their homework for them—if I didn't they'd tell all the boys I sold eggs, God forbid. But it was probably the best thing that ever happened to me: I learned I can always sell eggs. Then at twelve I got a job doing marionette shows at children's parties, and then when I was fifteen I got a job selling lingerie in a department store on Thursday nights and Saturdays, but I got fired after my first day, then . . ."

"Why?" Jock interrupted.

"I had lied about my age and they found out. In Maryland you have to be sixteen to work, so they told me to come back when I was, and I did. And in my final year of high school, since there was no money for college, every day after school I went to Johns Hopkins Hospital, learning to be a research technician, and got a job there. It was interesting, as any job is at first. I learned about hormones. We'd change a rooster to a chicken every other day, and the lab next to mine was the epilepsy lab and everyone working there was an epileptic, so I learned a lot about that disease too." (Little did I know, sitting there on the beach with Jock that day, how useful this knowledge would be years later.)

"That job lasted about six months and ended—by mutual

consent—because I could never bring myself to slit the throats of the experimental mice as directed, but instead, surreptitiously, I put them to sleep peacefully with chloroform, and ruined all the experiments. I must have set medical science back six months."

His smile melted me. I took a gulp of the lemon drink and continued, "After that I taught nursery school, then opened my own nursery school, got married and had three children—two sons and a daughter.

"Where are they?" Jock asked.

I pointed to the ocean. "Out there, trying to surf." I waved.

Jock turned and waved too. "What brought you here?"

"Crazy story." I laughed. "Actually, it goes back to that early nursery school job. One of my co-workers was a young woman named Helen—she was spunky and smart and we became close friends. Because she was engaged to a Roman Catholic, she had to take a six-week instruction course in his faith before they could marry. At the end of the course she told me, 'I'm not going to marry Joe after all.'

" 'Why not?' I asked her, surprised. 'Don't you like Catholicism?'

" 'On the contrary,' she answered. 'I'm going to be a nun.' "

"Good God!" Jock exclaimed.

"That's just what I said. So Helen became a Catholic, waited the required two years, and became a nun. She joined the Sisters of Africa, and wrote letters to me telling me all about Tanganyika. I had always been fascinated with Africa—I don't know why, a hangover from Tarzan, maybe. I had never been out of the States, never been on an airplane, as a matter of fact, but the idea of going to visit my good friend became an obsession with me. So I got a part-time job modeling in lunchtime fashion shows and saved my money. When I had enough, I asked my husband if he would come with me. 'Damned if I am going to spend two weeks in a convent,' was his answer."

"So you came here alone?" Jock asked.

"No, another friend of mine in Baltimore said she was not going to sit around the rest of *her* life listening to me talk about *my* trip to Africa. So we conned our mothers and husbands into taking care of our children for two weeks, and Bebe and I set off together."

"Tell me all about it, every detail," Jock said as he ran the sand through his fingers. "What was your first impression?"

"Well, I was surprised how beautiful and civilized Nairobi was. I expected Tarzan swinging on vines, not Woolworth's and modern hotels and all that traffic. Anyway, Helen's convent was six hundred miles inland on Lake Tanganyika across from the Congo, near Ujiji—you know, where Stanley met Livingston. We booked a flight on a small plane—we were the only two passengers among a cargo of cigarettes—to Tabora, the last airstrip, and planned to go the last two hundred miles by train. The good nuns in Tabora had been alerted by Helen, so they welcomed us and told us apologetically that there was only one train a week to Ujiji and it had gone through just the night before, but they would be pleased to put us up at their convent until the next train.

"Well, we had only two weeks so Bebe said, 'Thank you but we'll just rent a car and drive there.' The nuns laughed. There were only two things wrong with that idea—there were no cars, and in any case there were no roads. But then the nuns did mention that there was a freight train due through that very night. So after dark, Bebe and I got out on the tracks and flagged down the freight train, and the engineer, an Indian, let us ride in his caboose all the way to Ujiji, twelve hours through the bush."

"Good God!" Jock said again and laughed, and I was able to get another glance at the two white dots on his teeth. "Go on."

"Helen greeted us joyously, and that turned out to be one of the few times we were actually with her during our entire stay. The rules of her order forbade the sisters from having meals with outsiders, and they weren't permitted to speak with anyone for more than an hour a day. I whispered to her, 'I wouldn't be a nun for a million dollars,' and she whispered back, 'Neither would I.' She loves being a nun. Anyway she'd arranged a room for us, a cubbyhole with just two cots and a wooden table, with the legs set in tin cans to frustrate the termites from eating the entire table. The window was curtainless, and outside the bemused Africans climbed trees to stare in at us. Clearly we were a source of wonderment, even fear, to them, and we soon found out it was because of our hair—the women of that tribe all shaved their heads and the nuns then still wore full habits that revealed no hair, so we must have looked like tarantulas to them.

"But we soon overcame their anxieties. We knew none of their language, of course, but we found out how to bridge the communication gap—we danced with them, copying them, then we taught them our 'Twist.' "

"Yes," Jock commented, "they would have liked that. Go on, I'm riveted."

"The next ten days we spent riding bicycles with the nuns over rutted, sandy paths and through bush to the surrounding villages, where they taught schools and administered to the sick. We ate hippo meat—tastes like greasy hamburger—and strange fruits and vegetables we'd never heard of. It was the most stirring experience I'd ever had. And I fell in love with Africa."

"Everyone does." Jock smiled. "Africa is a disease, you know. As early as the eighteenth century, an explorer said, 'He who drinks of African waters shall return.' "

I paused. "Yes, it's true. I knew I'd return, and I did."

"How did you manage that?" Jock asked as we moved out of the equatorial sun under an umbrella of thatch. He was so tall and lean.

"It wasn't easy. When I got back, my husband said, 'Well, at least you've got that out of your system.'

"I said, 'I hate to tell you, but it's only just begun.' My husband was a banker—and hated the banking business. But I knew that he would love Africa. It took me two years of nagging to get him to agree to come here. We had no money, but finally I convinced him to borrow some, and in 1960 we sailed here with the children, five days across the Atlantic and twenty-eight days from London, practically steerage class, and spent three months exploring East Africa. Then we returned to the States, and were the first Americans to organize non-hunting safaris."

"So that's what you're doing here—taking Americans on safari?"

"Not exactly. I've just done a documentary in Tanganyika on leprosy, and another on Ethiopia. My husband's on safari." I didn't want to tell Jock any more about my current personal life, so I changed the subject. "Are you here on holiday?"

"No, I'm here recuperating from cerebral meningitis," he answered matter-of-factly.

"Cerebral meningitis! That's terrible!"

"Not really," he laughed. "I've had typhoid fever, tick typhus, malaria five times." With a wry smile he added, "And contagious abortion—that's what it's called in cattle, but it's called brucellosis in man. And then I was totally paralyzed for two years with polio . . ."

"Two years!" I interrupted.

"Ummm, and oddly enough, when I first got it I was lying in the hospital unable to move, when the radio in my room announced Dr. Jonas Salk's discovery of a vaccine—just too late for me. But eventually everything came back but this arm of mine."

Just then the children came running up to us. "Rick, Dancy, McDonnell, this is Mr. Leslie-Melville." They shook his hand and Jock said, "Come on, I'll teach you all how to surf properly."

He turned to me, "Do you want to join us?"

I wanted to run my fingers through his great mass of hair, I wanted to kiss his lips, so I said, "I don't like the ocean much, I'll just watch." I wanted to watch him. *God, he is beautiful.*

When they came out of the ocean, he said he was going back to his hotel down the beach for lunch, but suggested we all go goggling when the tide was right. So at 2 P.M. we all climbed into a *ngalawa*, a canoe hollowed out from a tree, and were poled out to the Marine Preserve and, wearing our flippers and goggles and snorkles, slid over the side into the silent Technicolored world under water. I felt I was in a museum of art, where all the paintings came alive and moved. Coral formed cities of skyscrapers and castles through which paisley fish and zebra fish and angel fish and polka-dot fish and iridescent ones and big and little ones and schools of fish scooted in and out.

We snorkeled for a few hours, then sat on the beach and listened as Jock told us the names of the fish we described to him and explained about the twelve-foot tide and how each day you goggled one hour later.

"Will you take us again tomorrow?" asked seven-year-old McDonnell, bless him.

"I'd love to. See you all at 3 P.M. tomorrow."

"Then why don't you have lunch at the Sindbad with us?" invited fourteen-year-old Rick, bless him.

"Come early so we can surf again," said nine-year-old Dancy. Bless them all.

The children thanked him and ran off, and Jock turned to me, his great mass of hair blowing in the breeze. "Nice children. There's dancing tonight here. Would you join me?"

"I'd love to." So he called for me at nine and we went to the Moon Garden, where the band was playing under a full moon and a starry sky.

"You're an excellent dancer," he said after our first dance, which was a Twist.

"I love to dance—in my next life I'm going to be a chorus girl. In Baltimore I danced in quite a few musicals—*Can Can* and *Pajama Game,* and *Kismet*—I've always loved to dance. My mother told me when I was two years old she took me downtown one day and on the street was an organ grinder with a monkey. A circle of people had gathered around to watch the monkey, and I got in with him and upstaged him dancing, so Mother sent me for dancing lessons when I was three. Later I taught tap dancing for a while, but my most interesting dancing experience was at a veterans' mental hospital." Our drinks arrived.

Jock clicked his drink to mine. "Cheers. Mental hospital? How did that happen?"

"When I had that job modeling, one of the other models

was a Catholic who had joined some program with the Catholic War Veterans at Perry Point, the government hospital for mentally disturbed and shellshocked veterans. She asked if any of us would go with her every Friday night to dance with them. I was the only one who volunteered—and I loved it. The guards would take us to a ward, lock us in, and we would dance with the patients. Some of them became quite good friends. I remember one man who was never without his flyswatter, which he carried in a brown paper bag—we always danced with his little package—and one night after we had been talking and laughing together quite a few weeks, he said to me, 'Lady, they think I'm crazy, but I *know* you're crazy.' "

Jock laughed. "Did you ever have any problems?"

"Only once—one of the patients suddenly thought I was his sister, whom he must have hated, because while we were dancing, all of a sudden he grabbed my arm, twisted it behind my back, and started screaming at me. The other patients ran to my aid even before the guard could get there. You know, I think if we released all the people in mental hospitals and put all the 'sane' people in, we'd hardly notice the difference in the world."

"Umm . . . How long did you go there?"

"Oh, every Friday night for about two years . . . until I came here."

"Tell me more about it—I'm intrigued."

"But I talk all the time."

He gestured for me to go on.

"Well, a funny thing did happen one night. Once a year they had a big dance for everyone who was well enough to get a pass out of their ward and go to the main building for the Christmas party. At this dance they had all the women patients there, too—the Wacs and Waves—but they needed some men from outside to dance with them. I asked my husband if he would come, but being very shy and nervous he didn't want to. But I shamed him into it, saying it was his civic and patriotic duty. So reluctantly he went.

"There were chairs on each side of the room and he went to the women's side and asked someone to dance, which she did, but immediately after his first dance I saw him go to the men's side and just sit down with the patients. I went over to him and asked why he wasn't dancing again. 'Betty,' he said, disturbed, 'I told her I liked her dress, and she said she was glad I did, that she couldn't make up her mind which of two dresses to wear, so she wore both of them. I didn't know what to say. I'm just no good here.' So he just sat there the rest of the evening. A Red Cross lady passed cakes and Dixie cups . . ."

" 'Dixie cups?' " Jock asked.

"Little cardboard cups of ice cream. She passed them around to all the patients, some of whom just took the cake and smashed it in their foreheads, and when she got to Dan she asked him patronizingly, 'And would you like some ice cream and cake?' He took it and sat there and ate it along with all the other inmates.

"At 10 P.M., when the dance was over, the guards blew their whistles and called, 'Everyone in Ward A line up,' and they'd get in line and shuffle out. Then they'd call for Ward B and so on, and when the last ward was leaving, I winked at a guard I knew and gestured to Dan. He caught on and walked up to him, grabbed him by the arm, pulled him up, and said, 'Okay, buddy, come on, get in line.'

" 'Oh, I'm just a visitor here,' Dan said quickly.

" 'Sure you are, buddy. That's what they all say . . . come on.'

" 'Betty! Betty!' Dan called desperately, as the guard was leading him into the line . . . and then the guard laughed and let him go, but Dan never went back to Perry Point again."

Jock laughed. "I don't believe I'm as good a dancer as your mental patients, but would you like to dance again?"

It was a slow dance this time, and when he took me in his arms I melted. The song was "Just in Time" and, listening to the appropriate words, I felt bewitched.

All evening we talked and danced. It was magical. He walked me to my cottage and said he'd see me for lunch tomorrow.

I felt transformed into another person. It was as if he had invaded my whole being. Did he feel this too? He gave no indication that he did—he talked of nothing personal—was it because he thought I was married? After all, I had told him I was. Visions of him danced in my head the rest of the night, and I thought tomorrow would never come.

But it did, and he appeared on the beach and sat beside me and we talked until the children spotted him and dragged him into the ocean with them. I felt drunk on him. We all had lunch and goggled again, and Jock said, "Tonight is my last night—will all of you be my guests at dinner here and then we'll go to the film?"

His last night. I felt sick. After dinner we went to the patio where every Sunday night a film was projected on a bedsheet that waved in the breeze, which he called "ripple vision"; and the Technicolor was so faded, he called it "fungus color." Toward the end of the movie, Jock touched my hand and pointed out the Southern Cross. Just then a falling star streaked across the starlit African sky.

"Make a wish," he whispered to me, and later we learned that we both had wished the same thing—that we might be together forever.

He walked us to our cottage and bid his goodbyes to the children; they went off to bed and we stood by the door.

"I'm off at dawn," Jock said.

"Back to the salt mines?"

"I beg your pardon?" he asked, not understanding the American expression.

"Back to Parliament?"

"Yes. Will you be in Nairobi any time soon?"

"Oh, I fly up from time to time."

"When does your husband come back?"

"He returns from safari tomorrow, but," I added, wanting him to know now, despite the fact that I hadn't even told the children, "we're separated." Then I took a breath and tried to sound casual as I asked the question I had been wanting to ask since we first met. "Are you married?"

"I was, but for a very short time. I'm waiting for my divorce to be final now."

I felt like a Christmas tree that had just been lit up. He shook my hand and said goodbye, but his eyes said a lot more.

Chapter 2

I HAD surprised myself by my wish. It wasn't until that moment my feelings actually translated themselves into words that I admitted to myself what I had felt all along—I was in love with him. First my eyes had fallen in love with his aristocratic sculptured face with its bright blue eyes, lovely smile, and his tall and lean body. Then my mind was captured by his wit, his knowledge of East Africa, and his involvement in his good political cause, so unlike most of the colonials. My soul was filled with admiration for his enthusiasm for life, his lack of self-pity, and his determined victory over his illnesses. My heart had fallen right in line and was charmed by his charm and easy elegance. Sure as a witch doctor, Jock had cast his spell upon me, and I realized I was not only in like with him, but I was also hopelessly in love.

All the next day I walked the beach aimlessly, picturing Jock and hearing the things he had said. Rashly I wrote a letter to him, saying how much I had enjoyed meeting him and how I hoped we would see each other soon again (meaning I was in love with him), and gave him news of the children and other unnecessary things to disguise what was really an aggressive letter of love.

At the same time, unknown to me, he was writing to me, saying how he had enjoyed meeting me and how he would like to see me again. Our letters crossed. Again I was thrilled. So, like all females, I confided in my good friend Jane, who was at the coast with me and who also met Jock.

"I've gone crazy," I told her. "I'm out of control. I've just got to see Jock again. I've got to renew my certainty that I am in love with him, or get over this obsession with him and settle down to sanity again."

"You are crazy."

"I know, I know, but love is a form of insanity, you know that."

"I know what you are feeling for Jock is not love, it's sex—you're just physically attracted to him, that's all."

"Jane, I wouldn't be physically attracted to him if I didn't like his mind, his character, his humor—the things he says, the things he does . . . Look, you've got to telephone him and tell him you're having a party in Nairobi next week and invite him . . ."

"But I'm not having a par—"

"Yes you are. That's what friends are for." So she called Jock at Parliament and performed her ruse.

"All right," she told me, "he asked if you would be there and I told him yes, you were flying up, and he said he'll meet you at the airport."

I was ecstatic. I left the children with friends and boarded the plane, which I felt was propelled by my exuberant emotions. All the way to Nairobi I rehearsed all the clever and charming things I planned to say to Jock at the party—and flew into what was to become my new life.

When Jock and I saw each other at the airport, the bells rang and never stopped.

I felt it and knew he did, too, yet his British reserve made him say only, "Mother just sold the farm and has bought a house in Karen; I'm staying with her temporarily, but she's on safari now—so first we are going there."

As we walked toward his car, I asked, "Isn't Karen the area named after Baroness Karen von Blixen, who wrote my favorite book, *Out of Africa?*"

"Yes. Do you realize how clever her pen name Isak Dinesen is? In Swahili, Isak is 'work' spelled backwards. She was a close friend of my mother's. In fact, we have a lot of her furniture; when she left the country she gave it to us."

We arrived at a sprawling white stucco house and I admired the pink and purple bougainvillea spilling from the tiled rooftop. "It's named after Count de Bougainville, who discovered the wonderful flowers," Jock told me. Drinking sundowners (cocktails), we sat alone on the terrace, except for a parrot in its cage and four horses grazing peacefully on the lawn, and watched the orange sun lowering behind the Ngong Hills, the scent of roses and wild gardenias all about us. We talked and talked and finally Jock stood and put his hand out to me. "It's getting dark, let's go in." As I stood, he gathered me in his arms and kissed me and kissed me and kissed me.

"Oh God," he said, "from the moment I saw you I had to meet you, and from the moment I met you I had to touch you—the first time I touched you was when I pointed out the Southern Cross—you electrify me, and now the world just changed colors." Then he went to the telephone and told Jane we wouldn't be at the party.

No one over fifteen should have felt the way we did.

The next morning, on the way to the airport, Jock asked, "Will you come back next weekend?" I accepted eagerly, because I knew I was lost.

The next day his letter arrived:

> We said goodbye an hour ago and already I feel gloomy. By the time you get this I will be feeling better, because a day of your absence will have passed and your return will be closer. It will be like sitting out with our coffee that night after supper in Malindi and waiting for the moon—the sky gets fractionally lighter every second and the anticipation grows. The moon emerging from the sea will be your stepping out of the plane in Nairobi. And then I will be whole again.
>
> Despite a tremendous amount of things going on in Nairobi, I know that nothing will happen until Friday when life will once again become just that—life.
>
> Jock

That weekend we drove up-country to Jock's good friend Kim Manderville—Viscount Manderville, who would become the Duke of Manchester when his father, the current Duke, died. All weekend I felt as if I had flown to the moon. I was falling more and more in love with Jock. I couldn't find anything about him to dislike. But we were with other people constantly—luncheons, dinners, and game runs, and although when we were alone he was kissing me and saying things like if he had one wish it would be doing exactly what he was doing now, the subject of love had not arisen. Time it did. So when I walked out on the tarmac to board my plane back to Malindi, I looked up at Jock, who was standing above me on the waving base and said, "Incidentally, I'm in love with you," and kept on walking.

The next day I got what he later told me was his first letter of love:

> Yes I am in love with you. And what it is to be in love with you, to have you to look forward to. You are so loved by me because you are the only person in the world who is anything like you. I know what Christopher Columbus felt when he discovered a new world.
>
> But sometimes I am seized by a panic. What would life be like had I never met you? Or worse, if we had met and then parted, but with the knowledge of each other? One does not really know what one has missed until one has experienced it. The idea of you floating around on the same planet but our not being together is the kind of nightmare that is far worse than Frankenstein.
>
> I feel in love, and desolate and empty and lost without you. The whole of life revolves around you, and without you I have no reason to do anything and no joy. The only answer is for you to stay with me always and then I shall keep you chained up so that you can never go away . . .
>
> Jock

That following weekend he drove me right from the plane to a special place in the Ngong Hills, which commanded a view of Mount Kilimanjaro looming clear and proud in front of us, and the Great Rift Valley, that spectacular geographic wonder, to our right, and to our left we could see the two volcanic cavities—Suswa and Longnot mountains. And standing there, he kissed me and spoke the magic words "I love you." There was a pause, then he looked into my eyes and added, "I've never told anyone that before." After we kissed again, he held me close and whispered in my ear, "So this is what they mean by love, what they sing about and write about. I've never known it. I've never been in love before."

"What do you mean, you've never been in love before? What about your wife?"

He spread a blanket and we sat. "I wasn't in love with her. I had known her for a long time, we were good friends. I guess I thought I'd never fall in love, so I asked her to marry me. But we both realized very soon it was a mistake. However, it did last a long time though—three months. She went back to England." He put his arm around me.

"Who is she?" I asked, pulling a blade of long golden grass and putting it in my mouth.

"She's The Lady Zinnia—but I don't want to talk about her. I want to talk about us. I love you I love you I love you."

I knew who The Lady Zinnia was, daughter of the Earl of Londesborough, and one of the wealthiest women in England.

"The law in Kenya is that you can't even apply for a divorce until you have been married for three years. My time will be up in June and I'll be free in July."

"My divorce will be final in July too!"

He grabbed the grass from my mouth, put his hand on my chin, and held my face close to his. "Will you marry me the next day?"

I knew anything else was impossible, so I kissed him yes. He crushed me to him, and we kissed and kissed and then just stared into each other's eyes and smiled. We were exuberant.

He reached into the pocket of his bush jacket and pulled out a little box. "Let me put your engagement ring on," and around my neck he clasped a gold chain with a lovely little gold giraffe with ruby eyes, eating a tiny leaf of turquoise and diamonds. The intensity of delight that day made us feel we were soaring. Sitting high up on Africa's red soil, we ate the picnic lunch Jock had brought, and as we talked and kissed we watched the mighty Maasai far below, coming and going from their manyattas, which from that distance looked like tiny toy igloos. We watched the giraffe and antelope, which share their world with the Maasai, bounding about on the plains so far below they looked like mechanical toys. We sat in our lovely place in the Ngong Hills until the sun turned pink and blue as it began to set.

"Mother is back from safari. Let's go tell her."

"Don't you think she should spend one evening with me before you tell her you're going to marry me?"

"Of course not." He pulled me up and kissed me again. "I've never been happier."

Neither had I.

As we drove toward Karen, I asked Jock, "How am I going to be polite about that parrot of hers? You said she loves it, but I hate birds."

"But this one is an African Grey from the Congo. My father got it from a zoo in Nairobi which folded. It has a spectacular vocabulary of swear words in Swahili, Kikuyu, Hindustani, and English." He was very proud of it.

"But I really do hate birds, their beady little eyes and their lice-filled feathers. I merely hate birds, but I loathe bats. Remember at the coast when we were all talking about fears and I told you my only fear is death? Well, I lied—I'm phobic about bats too. I panic and crawl under tables and scream. . . . Do you still love me?"

He smiled. "Why bats?"

"Oh, I guess a shrink would say it's because of the only time I ever saw my father frightened. When I was three years old, he was hollering and running excitedly up and down the hallway in front of my bedroom, swinging a tennis racket at a bat, obviously scared. I know my fear is totally irrational, but that doesn't make it go away. Do you have any phobias?"

"Yes, one—I'll admit it—chameleons."

"Chameleons? Those harmless little things that change colors?"

He almost shivered. "I know. It's irrational, too, but growing up with the Kikuyu it was inculcated in me by their legend."

I leaned over and kissed him and the car almost went off the road. "Tell me their legend."

"Their legend says when man first walked the earth he was very upset because he could not remember yesterday nor could he imagine tomorrow. Seeing this, God sent a chameleon to earth with the message that tomorrow would always come, that there would be no death. Then a few days later God became peeved with man, so he sent another message with an egret, saying that one day the tomorrows would end and there would be death. Then God said that whichever message got there first would be the true one. The chameleon, such a slow and lazy thing, arrived just before the egret, but he was interested only in catching bugs with his long tongue to eat and did not give the message to man. When the egret arrived and started to speak, the chameleon tried to sputter out his message but there were too many bugs on his tongue for him to speak, so instead of giving his message to man, he merely turned from one color to another. And so man got the message from the egret instead, and since then there has been death and all people die."

"Good a reason as any I've ever heard. And if you're not nice to me I'll put chameleons in your bed." I snuggled up to him. "But surely you're not afraid now that you're older and educated and . . ."

"You're still afraid of bats, aren't you? There's an old Kikuyu proverb that says, 'A scalded cat fears even cold water.' "

"Yes, that's true. . . . Does she let the parrot out of the cage?"

"Yes, but it can't fly. We had its wings clipped. I'll tell you an amazing story—true, too. One day when it was strutting on the lawn a buzzard spotted it, swooped down, grabbed the parrot in its talons and carried it aloft. The parrot shrieked

'Kamau!' the name of his friend, our cook. Kamau dashed out of the kitchen, yelled at the buzzard one hundred feet up, and hurled a stone at it. The buzzard dropped the parrot, which fell to the ground with a great thud but survived the kidnapping."

"What a lovely parrot," I lied to Jock's mother, trying to impress her. "How old is he?" I asked, feigning interest.

"One hundred nine. And it isn't a he, it's a she. We thought it was a he for ten years, then he laid an egg."

"Your house is lovely. And Jock told me you were a close friend of Karen Blixen's and he showed me some of the furniture she gave you when she left the country . . ."

"How would you know about Karen?" Jock's mother asked.

"Well, she is my favorite author, she wrote *Out of Africa* and . . ."

"Oh, that's right. Karen did write a book. I must read it one of these days. Now tell me, you're American? I like. . . ."

"Mother," Jock interrupted her, glowing, "Betty and I are going to be married."

"*Married!*" she gasped.

Oh God, she hates me, I thought, even though I smiled at her rotten parrot. Well, did you expect her to be over-joyed at her only son marrying a poor American with three kids?

"Why don't you just live together?" She was adamant.

I had often heard the expression "Are you married or do you live in Kenya?" and now I knew what it meant. Could I explain to her that I was a puritanical American with a hangover from Sunday school, that my mother told me if I ever went to bed with anyone before I was married God would strike me dead with lightning—and I believed it.

Jock saved me from commenting. "We're getting married when our divorces are final—next July."

And we did.

Or at least I think we did. We were married in his mother's drawing room by the African District Commissioner. "What marriage laws are you going to be wed by," he asked, "Muslim, Hindu, Christian, pagan, or Jewish?" I feared Jock, who claimed to be an agnostic leaning toward atheism, was going to say pagan but, although he looked uncomfortable, he answered Christian. So the ceremony began:

"Do you, Betty, know that if you take another husband while this one is still alive, or if you haven't divorced, it will be bigamy?"

"Yes, I know that."

"Do you, Jock, know that if you take another wife while this one is still alive, or if you haven't divorced, it will be bigamy?"

"Yes, I know that."

"I now pronounce you man and wife."

And that was it. Some Christian ceremony.

Right after the champagne, we climbed into our Land Rover with the black Labrador puppy we had named Shirley Brown, crossed the Great Rift Valley that splits Africa from the Dead Sea to Mozambique, climbed 10,000 feet high into the Mau Forest, which we were told was the largest cedar forest in the world, and arrived at the remote little house we had acquired and called our Hansel and Gretel cottage. It had no electricity or refrigeration. There was a wood-burning stove for cooking and a roaring cedar fire to keep our stone house warm and make it smell like Christmas all year long. Even though we were almost on the Equator, because of the altitude it was very cold. Frost covered our world in the morning and in the evening if it hailed we gathered the hailstones for our sundowners. Candles lighted our way inside; it was fun taking a bath by candlelight (it also prevented us from seeing the slimy little fish swimming around in the muddy bathwater pumped up from the stream below.) We spent a lovely week there fishing for trout in the nearby stream, taking long exploratory walks with Shirley Brown in the lichen-filled forest alive with Colobus monkeys, leopard, and buffalo. The Maasai owned the land and occasionally we would see them, but no one else. Our nearest neighbor was six miles away, and the nearest village, therefore telephone, was thirty-two miles.

Nights we clung together in the unspoiled stillness and made love. Our wish on the falling star had come true.

Chapter 3

O N our way back to Nairobi, we were driving along on the floor of the Great Rift Valley when an impala darted out of the bush onto the dirt road and we struck it head on. With reflexes swifter than a leopard's, Jock jumped out of the Land Rover, unsheathed his knife, and slit the writhing beast's throat. Stunned, I protested. "Why didn't we take it to a vet?"

"Betty, it would be useless," he replied, getting back into the car and driving on. "The nearest vet is a hundred miles off and he would have done the same thing. The poor thing had two broken legs and bad internal injuries. Why let it suffer? And you've got to promise me you'll do the same for me if ever I become incapacitated or terminally ill."

"We're all terminal . . ."

"You know what I mean. Will you promise?" His blue eyes were very serious.

"All right," I answered unconvincingly, "but I told you I have a terrible dread of death. I am very good at coping with life, but I am miserable at coping with death. I guess it's because of my father's death. I worshipped him, and he me. He spoiled me and would never let me be disciplined. 'She'll need that spirit one day,' was his excuse for letting me do whatever I wanted. When he got sick I thought it was like chicken pox or measles, the only kind of sickness I knew. I never thought of death—I guess most ten-year-olds don't; and when they told me he had died, I'll never forget that electric shock of terror that started in my feet and went right up through my head . . . the most horrid feeling I've ever known. And the rest of it was dreadful too."

Jock stopped the car, turned off the ignition, and held me close. "Tell me."

"My father was Catholic, my mother Quaker, so my sister and I were raised Episcopalians. When my father died, his family—good Catholics—came down from Massachusetts for the funeral. They insisted he be 'laid out' in the house, and I remember our maid insisting I go downstairs and see the body. To this day I remember vividly her dragging me down the stairs, and me screaming and clutching the railings of the banister one by one, fighting to hang on to each rail— unsuccessfully. Sometimes I still dream about clutching those banister rails. . . ." Jock kissed my forehead.

"I also remember after the funeral thinking I had to take over. My mother, though she wasn't, appeared helpless to me. So I saw an APARTMENT FOR RENT sign up the street, went in, asked to see it, asked how much the rent was, was electricity included—all that. I told the people we'd take it, my mother would be back in a half-hour to pay. To their surprise my mother was back in a half-hour and paid, and to this day they still talk about how the little girl wearing a long snow cap rented the apartment."

Jock reached for our cool box and handed me a soft drink. "Go on."

I took a swig and continued. "Although my father was a doctor, and we had a nice big house and a maid, he was only forty-eight when he died, and his illness had eaten up all the money, so my mother had to work for the first time in her life. She got a job selling dresses in a department store, and on my way home from school every day I'd buy the food and have dinner ready for her.

"Then when I was in high school my grandmother came to live with us because she was eighty-six years old and had become senile. Mother had someone in to take care of her until I got out of school, then I took over. She was a sweet, tiny little thing who wore a cameo on a little black velvet band around her neck, and said 'thee' and 'thy' and made quilts and crocheted bedspreads. She called me Mary—that was her mother's name. She had no idea who I was or where she was. I liked her, but I didn't like having to stay in the apartment with her every afternoon. I wanted to go to the drugstore and drink Cokes and sneak cigarettes with my friends, so you know what I did?"

Jock turned me around so that I was leaning against him in the car. "Tell me."

"Every afternoon I used to bundle her up in scarves and galoshes and walk her through the snow and rain almost a mile to the drugstore and sit her in the booth with all the teenagers. She'd drink her Coke and ask them if they would like her to make them a quilt, and then she'd say, 'Now repeat after me—"The Lord is my shepherd . . ." '—and go through the entire psalm. Everyone was nice to her and she had a wonderful time. I'd get her home just before my mother arrived, and do you know Mother never knew I ever took her out, and my grandmother never remembered. She lived to be ninety-four, probably all that exercise . . ."

"Amazing. How long did you live in that flat you rented?"

"Until I got married, but my mother lived there until she died—for thirty-seven years. And that same electric-shock feeling came over me again when she died. And just now, though nowhere near as strong, when you killed the impala . . ."

Jock hugged me to him and kissed the top of my head. "Oh, Betty, I'm so sorry. You know I think death is particularly hard for a ten-year-old—not young enough not to understand it, as I was when my father died, and yet not old enough to understand it . . ."

"Understand it! I still don't understand it, but I agree that at ten you don't even have any of the comforting beliefs or hopes or philosophies or whatever. I don't know . . ."

"But you do know, to let someone who is going to die anyway suffer a slow and ugly death is cruel and . . ."

"Of course, intellectually I know that, but emotionally I still get that horrid feeling."

"But I really want you to promise." His voice was very serious.

It was the only thing he had ever asked me to do for him. I looked into his eyes. "Jock, I know you did the right thing with the impala, and I'll do the same for you if ever you're suffering," I promised, never thinking that my words would come to haunt me more than anything in my life.

Jock kissed me, and then we just sat there in the Great Rift Valley and watched a herd of impala running and jumping about in the golden bush, some of them flying through the air in leaps much greater and more breathtaking than Baryshnikov's."

"Look at that!" Jock cried at a particularly spectacular leap.

"You know," I said, "I think that is why I don't like the ballet. After seeing that magnificent power and grace of the impala's leap, and watching a cheetah run at ninety miles an hour with such natural easy grace, the human dancer always looks unnatural—rather contrived and inept to me."

"I'll pay attention when we're at the theater in New York next month."

"I'm so glad we're going. I'm hungry for New York," I said and kissed him.

"And I'm ravenous for you." And right there, alone in the middle of Africa, we made love.

Before we were married I had taken a little flat in the center of Nairobi, and on their first school holiday I had promised the children to take them to Malindi for five days, but Rick had found some friends in Nairobi and didn't want to go: "Mother, I am fifteen years old, old enough to stay alone for five days." Jock had agreed with him and said he would stop in the flat to check that Rick was all right.

At the coast I had had a letter from Jock:

What it is to love you, to think of life ahead, to think of our journey in which we are going the same way. I am not too sure about this business of "You are you and

I am me, and we are travelling together." The truth is that without you I feel like a pretty wretched imitation of me. I am suspended in mid-nowhere until Wednesday. Then I live again. You are to know you are adored, worshipped, and loved by me every moment of every hour, together or apart, awake or asleep; and that without you there is nothing.

Rick I found drunk in bed with two girls, and he has sold most of the furniture to pay for the four remaining days of his freedom. I love you love you love you love you.

Jock

When we were married, since Rick had not sold the furniture, Jock moved in the flat with me. He had gone to a great deal of trouble to enroll the children in good boarding schools, and to my surprise all three of them loved it. A few weeks after we were back from our wedding safari to our house in the woods, we were excitedly packing up for our "big trip."

"I wish we were just going to continue our honeymoon and I didn't have to lecture," I told Jock. "But I've got to go. If I don't, I have to pay the lecture bureau thirty-five percent of every lecture I miss and we don't have any money. But thank God the children are well taken care of and you don't have a job and can come with me."

In December of 1963, when Kenya had become independent, Jock had given up his British citizenship and become a Kenyan. "After all," he explained, "I've lived in Kenya my entire life, and not to take out citizenship would be like an Irishman or a German living in the States always and not becoming an American. I'm going to be a Kenyan even though I know that behind our backs the Africans call all of us white citizens 'vanilla gorillas.' " Jock also believed the Africans should run their own country, so just at the time we were married he had left Parliament and now had no job.

But I did. Before we met I had signed up with the lecture

bureau to speak about East Africa throughout the States and had thirty-seven lectures to do; and now I was sorry.

"Why did you ever sign up to do this?" Jock asked, opening a suitcase and putting his shirts in.

"First of all I didn't know Prince Charming was going to come along at Malindi and swoop me up and carry me away from my life, and secondly I got hired—although it was by mistake."

"What do you mean 'by mistake'?"

"Well, after my first trip to Africa I used to bore people back in Baltimore with my slides all the time. One night I was showing them to my good friends John and Linell Smith and Linell's father, who is the poet Ogden Nash, was there. He loved the slides and said, 'Betty, you should lecture. The next time you're in New York, call Colston Leigh, my lecture bureau.' So I did. I told Mr. Leigh that I was a friend of Mr. Nash's daughter and I would like to see him about lecturing on Africa. He saw me, listened to me, and said enthusiastically he thought I'd sell. So we signed a contract then and there. Then he leaned back in his chair and said, 'Now tell me about your father.'

" 'My father?' I asked, puzzled. 'My father's been dead for over twenty years.'

" 'I thought you said you were Ogden Nash's daughter.'

" 'No,' I told him, 'I said I was a *friend* of Ogden Nash's daughter.'

"He stared at me a moment in amazement, then he burst out laughing. 'If I had known that I'd never have let you in here. But it's too late now, you've signed the contract.' Then he smiled and added, 'And I'm glad.' So that's what happened, and Jock, I've got to go. And I'm so glad you are coming with me."

"I couldn't stand being away from you two minutes, much less two months." He closed the lid of the suitcase and took me in his arms and kissed me.

Jock had briefed me and briefed me about East Africa. I knew all the history, all the politics, all the names of all the government officials, the mileage between one town and another and their populations, how crocodiles breed—and the only questions I was ever asked during the half-hour question-and-answer period were, "How old are you?" and "Are there any snakes?"

One of the many nice things about living in Kenya is that it is halfway around the world from America. If you go any farther you start coming around again, so we decided to go to Tulsa, my first lecture date, by way of Japan.

We oohed and aahed at the world as we rode mules in Ethiopia to see the remote Falasha, the black Ethiopians who are Jewish, display the Star of David, and speak recognizable Hebrew even though for thousands of years they have been totally cut off; as we rode elephants bareback in Ceylon; as we watched a Hindu open-pyre funeral in Bombay on what we thought was to be a romantic beach; as we went to a Chinese amusement park in Singapore; as we ate seaweed in our Japanese inn; and as we watched a Hawaiian called "the Waikiki Rabbit" surf standing on his head in Hawaii. And what amazed Jock most of all were the funeral parlors in the States. "They have no such wretched things in England, and nowhere else that I know. Why, I've never encountered such barbarism."

As we flew into Tulsa I told Jock, "I'm so scared. Maybe I'll be lucky and get run over by a truck so I won't have to lecture."

"You'll be super," he said, patting my hand. "I'll have to get you a stronger pair of rose-colored glasses . . ."

As the lecture hour grew closer, I grew petrified. I made Jock wait outside the auditorium so he wouldn't hear how awful I was; however, I seem to have been successful. Somehow I got through the next five lectures, always petrified before I was on stage, and never letting Jock hear me. Then I developed a ploy: I knew that he was so much more knowledgeable about East Africa than I, and would make such a smashing appearance and be so beguiling, that a few lectures later I faked being sick and Jock lectured in my place. Of course, the audience loved him and his British accent and his knowledge and charm—so it worked, the lecture bureau hired both of us, and for the next seventeen years we lectured together. (Laurel and Hardy, we called ourselves privately.) We lectured in every state but Alaska, going back to some cities as many as nine times.

Everyone always said, "You live in Africa. You must have had many harrowing adventures," and we did—we almost froze to death one night on the New Jersey Turnpike when our car broke down, and we were trapped on the top floor of a hotel fire in Tulsa, and once we almost went to jail in Texas. This is what happened in Texas:

"That'll be twenty-five cents please," said the American man in the uniform. We paid him, then drove the little Volkswagen slowly over the bridge toward the Mexican customs and immigration barrier.

A squat official poked his head in the window on my side. "Where were you born?"

"Baltimore."

"Driving license." I showed it to him. "And you?" he asked, peering over at Jock.

"Actually I was born in London, but only because my mother happened to be there at the time. I went to Kenya when I was two months . . ."

"Passport and visa."

Puzzled, Jock said, "But we were told we wouldn't need any documents—not just to come to the border town."

"For her, yes; for you not enough. You not American, you British."

"No," answered Jock, "actually I'm a Kenyan."

"You no. You go back."

With a flattering smile filled with supplication, I pleaded, "We've come all the way from East Africa just so we can spend this evening in Matamoros and see at least a little of your lovely country."

He was unimpressed. "You yes. He go back."

Two more men appeared and we went through it all again. They were adamant about Jock—no passport, no entry.

Filled with disappointment, we swung the car around, and at the U.S. Immigration Post on the other side of the bridge that official said, "Identification please." I showed him my driver's license. Then to Jock he said, "Where were you born?"

"London."

"Passport and entry visa please."

"I left them in Baltimore."

"Then you can't come in the United States."

"But," Jock said with relief, "I never left the United States because the Mexicans wouldn't let me in just now."

"You left the United States of America when you crossed this bridge, fella. And how do I know you crossed anyhow?"

I leaned across Jock and said, "Ask that man over there. We just gave him twenty-five cents . . ."

"I'm not talking to you, lady."

"Well, I'm talking to you . . ."

Jock poked me. "Officer, could you tell me where we are if we haven't been to Mexico and we're not in the United States?"

"You're in No Man's Land—and we've got a jail here." He glared at us. "Park over there, take this ticket, and report to the office."

"No Man's Land!" Jock and I said together and laughed weakly.

We started all over again. Yes, we were in the United States on a lecture tour. No, we hadn't intended to visit Mexico until that very afternoon when the ladies at the club in Corpus Christi told us about it. They said we didn't need passports, just as long as we were only going to a border town. Yes, of course we realized that the Women's Thursday Club in Corpus Christi is not the Department of Immigration of the United States of America.

"She can go. You have to stay."

Suddenly Jock exclaimed, "Aha! We just hired the Volks-wagen at the airport, not half an hour ago. Check with them." Relief flooded over us. Jock whispered proudly to me, "All one has to do is to keep one's wits in a tight situation."

"Your wife could have hired it, with an accomplice, driven over, picked you up . . ."

"Well," I interrupted, "why don't you ask the Mexicans if they haven't just turned us back?"

"Look, this is the Department of Immigration of the United States. We don't need the Mexicans to run it for us."

Suddenly there was a lot of commotion going on outside. The customs men were going all over our Volkswagen.

"What do they have?" I asked Jock.

Glancing out the window, he said, "Microscopes, tooth combs, Geiger counters, infra-red devices, lie detectors . . ."

A few minutes later they walked into the customs office, gleefully holding some white powder on a piece of paper. "Aha, look what we have here!" they crowed as they sort of sniffed it and disappeared to analyze it.

"Oh God," I said to Jock, "now we're dope smugglers."

"When I put the luggage in the boot I remember seeing what I thought was flour, which had spilled from a grocery bag," Jock said.

"It better be flour," I muttered nervously, reaching for a cigarette in my purse.

"I wonder if they will allow you to visit me from time to time here in No Man's Land? Do you think there may be any means by which I could receive much needed care packages out here on the bridge over the Rio Grande?"

"Maybe you can dig a tunnel out." As I rooted through my purse for matches, I came across a clipping the lecture ladies had given us from the Corpus Christi newspaper that day. It had a large picture of Jock and me and an article about our lecture, and that day's date on it.

The official came back. "Flour," he said, disappointed. We handed him the clipping, which he read, then said, "I guess you can't do much better than that." Happily we drove away to our next lecture.

Sometimes in one week we would have eight lectures, going from Tulsa to Pittsburgh to San Francisco, to Chicago, St. Louis, Portland, Boston, and San Diego, in that order, all in one week. The committees for the lectures always wanted us there the night before, so they'd meet us at the airport and take us to dinner. Then we'd collapse in bed for a little nap before we had to be up at the local TV station early in the morning. We'd have to read the matches in our hotel room when we'd wake up every morning to see what city we were in. We'd lecture for an hour, with questions and answers for a half-hour, then go on to the big luncheon with us at the speaker's table to answer some more questions. Sometimes some nice lady would invite us back to her house while we waited for the plane, so we could tell her aunt, who lived with her but was sick and couldn't get to the lecture, all the things we had said, which meant lecturing all over again. Finally we would fly to the next city and there that committee would meet us and take us to dinner and . . . the same thing all over again.

And so it went day after day on the chicken à la king circuit. It was as if our life was stuck in a record groove playing the same thing over and over again. Every day we said the same things, even wore the same clothes (our uniform, so we wouldn't have to lug a wardrobe with us). We were the total mechanical man and woman, being killed by the kindness of those we were lecturing to. They were overwhelmingly generous, but our schedule was grueling. Exhausted one evening after spending two hours with the committee members waiting for a plane, Jock said, "In order to circumvent all this lingering, what we need is a getaway car."

And I knew right away what I was going to give him for his birthday, but at the time I didn't know it would turn out to be William Holden's Rolls-Royce.

Chapter 4

WHEN Jock and I were flying to the States, I told him about my friend Paul, who has leprosy. "I always stay with him when I'm in New York. He is so lonely. Would you mind staying there from time to time, too? He has only one room in the Puerto Rican section of town, but his sofa pulls out and he puts a screen between it and his roll-away cot."

"Leprosy?"

"Yes, but it is not contagious." I paused. "Just infectious."

"Betty, I love you. But first you've asked me to stay in a convent with your nun friend sometime, and now I have to stay in New York with a leper . . . ?"

"But even though you're nervous about nuns and convents, you'll end up loving them. I promise you they won't try to convert you. You'll love Paul, too."

"Start from the beginning and tell me all about it." He adjusted his sling and put his seat in a comfortable position.

"Well, when I was asked by Westinghouse TV to be cameraman on a documentary in Tanganyika about leprosy—"

"Stop there. You've told me a little about that, but why did they ask you to do that?"

"I was doing some TV commercials at Westinghouse in Baltimore. I was the American Beer Indian girl. I wore a costume and a wig of long black pigtails and I danced on a drum—there was a huge billboard of me in the center of the city—it was ridiculous. Later I had my own interior-decorating show there, too. Anyway, the two heads of the station were fascinated with leprosy and were going to do a documentary on it—half-hour in Carville, Louisiana, our only leprosarium in the States, and the other half-hour on a leprosarium in Africa. Since I was the only one they knew who had ever been to Africa, they came out to the house one night to see my slides so they could get some idea of the terrain in Tanganyika. The next day they called and said they weren't going to send a cameraman after all, they were going to send me. 'But you saw my slides,' I told them. 'They're terrible.'

" 'They're awful,' they said, 'but you have an eye, so we are going to train you how to use a 16-mm camera, and when you're in Africa this summer, we'll pay you to film—okay?' Of course I agreed and learned how to work the camera, but I didn't know where a leprosarium was, so I went to the American Leprosy Mission in New York to find out. A man with a terribly deformed face and clawed hands answered the door. His name was Paul, and he told me about a Lutheran leprosarium in the Singida area of Tanganyika and arranged my going there to film.

"When I arrived at the leprosarium, I asked the missionaries if leprosy was contagious. I had heard the story of Father Damien in Hawaii, who had worked in a leprosarium for a long time, and how, one Sunday during his sermon, after he had been there many years, he merely said, ' . . . and we lepers . . .' But the missionaries said it wasn't very contagious. 'We aren't worried,' they told me. 'The good Lord sent us and He will take care of us.' Fine, I thought, but it was only the TV station who sent me . . ."

The cart came by and Jock and I got a soft drink and peanuts.

"Jock, the experience there was truly awesome. Of the five hundred patients, only about a hundred were Christians, but all of them went to church because they liked to sing. There was nothing in the church—no pews, no altar. Where the cross should have been, they had cut a cross-shaped aperture in the wall which the sun shone through. The congregation sat on the floor. The man who gave the sermon the Sunday I was there had the most positive case of leprosy in the entire leprosarium. Reading from the Bible, he said, 'And Christ came upon a group of men who were lepers. And they called unto Him "Have mercy unto us," ' and then he stopped reading and said to the congregation, 'And look at the mercy Christ has had on us. Look at what He has given us.' The only thing I could see that they had was leprosy. They had nothing else. Thirty-two patients were children, and they didn't have one doll, one crayon, one piece of paper—nothing. But they were so thankful for what they did have—which was medicine and people taking care of them—that one by one they crawled or shuffled to the altar where they placed a potato or an ear of corn in thanks for what they had. I never felt so ashamed in my life. All I have, and I'm not very thankful. Yet these were the happiest people. They laughed and sang and danced. They were filled with joy."

I took a sip of my drink and continued, "The only communication we had with the outside world was at 7 P.M., when the news came over the wireless, and the last night I was there it came over the air that Marilyn Monroe had committed suicide. She had 'everything'—beauty, money, fame—yet the people who had nothing but leprosy were filled with joy. I really started thinking about standards and values."

"Betty," Jock said, squeezing my hand, "you don't have to have leprosy to be happy and thankful, but go on about Paul."

"When I got back to the States it was just before Dan and I started Bruce Safari and Dan needed someone to work in his dog kennel. So I suggested we call the American Leprosy Mission in New York, because I had learned enough about leprosy to know the disease was arrested in those out of Carville, but they had a terrible time trying to find a job. Dan and I had a little house on our property and I thought giving someone a job and a home might be the answer for all of us. Someone could live there and take care of the dogs while we were taking people on safari. The part-time help he had had were all drunks and unreliable.

"So I called the American Leprosy Mission and Paul was interested, so the next time I was in New York I went to the mission to see him. 'Let's go get a cup of coffee and talk about this,' I suggested.

" 'You're not afraid of me?' he asked.

"I explained that I had learned a lot about the disease, for example not to call it 'leprosy' but 'Hansen's disease,' and that it wasn't contagious. I told him all about the job over coffee, and he really wanted it, but he told me upon considering it, he had realized his medical care and doctors, which he needed constantly, were free only in New York and he was afraid to leave the state. We talked a while more and then he told me he would have to leave soon because he had to go see Bishop Fulton J. Sheen. It was Thursday and Paul went to his house every Thursday for dinner. 'But I thought I read Bishop Sheen was in Rome,' I said.

" 'He is,' Paul answered, 'but I go anyway—he leaves a tape recording for me. His housekeeper gives me dinner and I listen to the Bishop on his machine.'

" 'How do you know Bishop Sheen?'

" 'Through my disease. I got it here in New York when I was eighteen.'

" 'New York!' I was amazed."

"Did he really get it in New York?" Jock asked, as surprised as I had been.

"Yes, there is quite a bit of leprosy in the States. Paul told me he was playing football and began dropping the ball. They couldn't diagnose it for a long time, but when they did he was sent to Carville. He was there for six years, then they discovered the sulphone drug which arrests it and he was the first one to get it. Astonishing story as to why: He told me he and his doctor there were good friends. The doctor was a young man, and one day he came into Paul's room and said he was tired, could he sneak a nap there while Paul was in the dining room? Paul said sure, and the doctor asked him to fill a prescription for him as he passed the pharmacy. Paul did—and this continued every other day or so. When the sulphone drug arrived, it was very limited in quantity, but Paul's doctor friend gave it to him first because Paul had been so nice to him. Of course, what Paul didn't know until later was that he had been filling morphine prescriptions for the doctor, who was addicted. The Feds picked him up and took him to Lexington, where he committed suicide."

"Good God," Jock said.

"Anyway, Paul's case was arrested first and he was released from Carville. He told me he was from a very poor family in Brooklyn, so he went home to his parents but they were ashamed of him and didn't want anyone to see him. He was pathetic to look at—he had no nose . . ."

"No nose?" Jock frowned.

"He has one now. The plastic surgeons went in through the roof of his mouth and gave him one. He looks much better with a nose, but his hands are still clawed. He's had sixteen operations on them—without anesthesia because he has no feeling whatsoever in his hands or feet; but the operations weren't successful. Anyway, his parents lived on the second floor of a little house—they rented the first floor out, and the only time Paul ever saw anyone was when the man downstairs came up the first of each month to pay the rent. Then one month his parents asked Paul if he would stay in the bedroom when the man downstairs came in. He did, and when he awakened in the morning his parents were gone—and he has never seen them since."

"This is a dreadful story," Jock exclaimed.

"Isn't it awful?"

"What did he do?"

"Well, he decided to commit suicide, and as he was walking the streets of New York trying to get up courage to do so, he passed St. Patrick's Cathedral, and having seen Bishop Sheen on television, he went inside and asked to speak to him. Paul wasn't a Catholic—did I tell you that? Well, the priest there told him not to be silly. He had to have an appointment to see Bishop Sheen, and he wasn't there in any case; but fortunately the priest saw Paul's desperation and took his name and address.

"Paul did not get up the courage to commit suicide that day but went back to his apartment. The very next day a huge black limousine drove up with Bishop Sheen in it. He told Paul to pack up his clothes, he was going home with him. Paul said he couldn't possibly do that, but the Bishop insisted and Paul went to his house on Thirty-ninth Street and stayed with him until the Bishop found him a place to stay on Houston Street, way down at the bottom of Manhattan . . ."

"Where you stay with Paul?"

"Yes. Bishop Sheen paid his rent and bought his food and sent him to air traffic school. Paul said he wanted to be an air traffic controller because it would be a job where he wouldn't have to face the public. He graduated first in his class, and when he called the airlines about getting a job, they all were interested in hiring him until he had his physical—then the doctors told him they knew his Hansen's disease was arrested, but they couldn't hire him because he would be 'bad for the morale of the other employees.' "

"This story gets worse by the minute. I'm going to get us some wine." He beckoned to the stewardess. "Go on, Betty. This is the worst story I've ever heard."

"Yes, it's so sad. Paul says the stigma of leprosy is worse than the disease. The Bible has done that—with lepers being 'unclean.' Also, 'leper' is now a totally unacceptable word. To them it's like 'nigger.' Only a 'Hansen's disease patient' is acceptable. And you know what? The missionaries told me a study was done and it was found out that the disease in the Bible is not leprosy after all. It's psoriasis."

"Really? I didn't know that," Jock said, paying the stewardess for the wine. "Go on, I'm spellbound."

"So Paul could get only a part-time job with the American Leprosy Mission. He told me he hated it, it depressed him so much dealing with nothing but leprosy in his life. So that first day when we were having coffee I said to him, 'Hey, Paul, I have to come to New York about once a week on safari business and I don't know many people here. Will you have dinner with me next Tuesday?' He was so pleased, but I told him the dinner had to be on me because he had to save his money to come on safari.

"The next Tuesday when we were having dinner, the peo-

ple sitting next to us got up and moved. I guess Paul's appearance upset them too much. At that time he still didn't
have a nose and because of his clawed hands he can't cut his
meat . . . so then I knew going out to restaurants would
never work. So I invited him down to Maryland for the following weekend, insisted he come, and sent him a train ticket.
He came and I had Jane and Colleen and a few other friends
out to meet him. It was the time of the Bossa Nova dance
and we taught him how to do it—he's a great dancer. He
asked me if my friends knew about 'his problem.' I told him,
of course, and tears came to his eyes. He said that whenever
he met anyone, they assumed he had been badly burned or
something, and when he told them what was really wrong
with him, he never saw them again. 'But your friends know
and aren't afraid of me either?' I told him no, I had told them
all about Hansen's disease and they knew his was arrested
. . . and they had seen the documentary."

"By the way, how was the film?" Jock asked, pouring my
wine.

"Fine. It won an award." I took a sip. "You know what
Paul told me later? I'll never forget it. He came down to
Baltimore almost every weekend from then on, and about a
year later he said, 'Betty, I was born that first weekend you
asked me down. You have made my life worth living.' So the
years went on and Paul and I became best friends. He does
volunteer work at Help Line."

"What's Help Line?"

"Oh, Jock." I smiled and leaned over and ran my fingers
down his cheeks and touched my favorite white spots on his
teeth. "I keep forgetting you're not American. It's where
desperate people call a number and get help for their problems. Paul won an award there: He's stopped more people
from committing suicide than anyone else. He says it's because he's been at the bottom and knows how despondent
and hopeless people can feel. He has such compassion. He
works there only two afternoons a week, at the mission two
afternoons, and the rest of the time he just sits in his apartment looking out the window, except on Thursdays when he

goes to see Bishop Sheen. So I began staying with him when I was working in New York. If I didn't get in until midnight, he'd be waiting up just to hear what was going on in the world."

Our meal was served to us, and as Jock and I ate the plastic food he said, "Bishop Sheen has just gone up in my estimation. Did you ever meet him?"

"Oh, yes. Paul was so grateful for all that he had done that he decided the only thing he could do for the Bishop was to become a Catholic. Paul invited me, along with Jane and Colleen, two friends I had worked with modeling, and who had always come to see Paul when he was in Baltimore, to come to his confirmation. Bishop Sheen had us all at his house for breakfast. He loves fudge, so we had fudge for dessert at breakfast.

"After the ceremony at St. Patrick's we all went back to Bishop Sheen's again and that is when I really liked him— because he lied. Paul was supposed to work that afternoon at the American Leprosy Mission. We told the Bishop how sorry we were because the three of us had planned to take Paul to the U.N. for lunch and then to a movie. Bishop Sheen picked up the telephone and said, 'American Leprosy Mission? This is Bishop Sheen. Paul is here with me and he is not feeling at all well. He won't be able to come in this afternoon.' So we took Paul with us and we all had a wonderful time."

Jock looked at me for a long minute. "Betty, do you have any normal friends?"

"Of course not. Look at you."

He laughed, then leaned over and kissed my cheek. "But seriously, why do you do this for Paul?"

"I *like* Paul—and I guess I expect to get some points in Heaven."

"Who's counting?" He paused a moment, looked into my eyes and said seriously, "You are filled with a tremendous amount of compassion, and you do bring joy to so many people. You really are a good person."

"I know. Bishop Sheen wrote an article about me and called

me a saint. Really. I'll give you a copy to carry with you at all times so you won't forget it, even when I'm swearing and throwing things at you."

He kissed my cheek again. "Of course I'll stay with you at Paul's."

So we stayed with Paul from time to time, and he and Jock became close friends, too. When we were lecturing on the East Coast, we would get Paul and just put him in the car and take him with us—to Philadelphia or Washington or wherever. Jane and Colleen still invite him for weekends, and my sister in Baltimore insists he come to Baltimore for every Thanksgiving and Christmas dinner, even when I'm not in the States. Paul is part of our family.

Jock got him a job with an airline in Nairobi, where they are more used to Hansen's disease, but Paul could not leave New York, where he still gets medical treatment. I cannot tell you how many times Jock and I rode the Staten Island ferry to go to the Veterans Hospital where Paul has spent so much time, sometimes for six months at a time. Because he has no feeling in his feet and his circulation is so terrible, he has a great deal of trouble with them and is often in the hospital having skin grafts that don't take, or do take, then burst open again. He never complains and is always cheerful.

Paul has brought much joy to our lives.

Chapter 5

J OCK and I were fond of nonsense and thought life should have quite a bit of foolishness in it, and one of my greater nonsenses was William Holden's Rolls-Royce. Holden had shipped it to Kenya from Switzerland to hunt from, and a few years later decided to sell it for $1,500. We didn't have $1,500, but I really wanted it as a surprise birthday present for Jock, so when we returned home I went to the Kenya bank manager and asked if I could borrow the money.

"What securities do you have?" he asked in his bank manager's voice.

"None," I told him, "but I'll give you the first ride in it." And sure enough he loaned me the money (and got the ride).

The Rolls was glorious—an old silver-and-black model with a window that went up and down between the driver's seat and the back, a bar made all of wood, and the smell of leather permeating the entire car. I drove it home, hoping Jock would be pleased but fearing he might be too British for such extravagance.

"Happy Birthday! Here's your getaway car. We can ship it to the States."

"Be still, my heart!" He beamed, delighted—"How marvelously unwise!"—and took me in his arms and kissed me.

I had to keep revising what I liked about Jock the most. He was handsome and charming and thoughtful and kind and intelligent and witty and romantic, and he adored me as much as I adored him. "My whole life is you, Betty," he would say over and over. "I don't even have another friend." We *were* friends, good friends, and that is what made our marriage so special. We were good friends because we had the same standards and values and interests. Neither of us liked sports, nor did we have any interest in owning horses or jewelry or yachts, so money never motivated us, and cocktail parties bored us and we weren't a bit interested in boredom.

We were together twenty-four hours a day; we loved our work and especially working together. We were the same tribe. We liked the same things: we loved New York—the noise and the rat race and going out every night to the theater or just walking the streets of plenty (there's no place to go for a walk at night in Africa). We'd look at the lights in the skyscrapers getting all mixed up with the stars, we'd laugh at the cab drivers hollering obscenities, and one night we saw a man going into the subway with a chimpanzee clinging to his neck wearing a pink tutu. "New York is so good for one's laugh life," Jock grinned and squeezed my shoulder. "New York's electrifying—it's not a city, it's a world, and everyone in it is so detribalized."

And we loved Africa—Kenya is a country just smaller than Texas, yet it is the world in microcosm. There are mountains—one over 17,000 feet—there is the Indian Ocean—and everything in between. Jock and I loved the bush, the animals, the ocean, staying home nights and reading books by the fire, the quiet. We loved doing nothing together. And although Nairobi is a cultural desert (someone described it as the most cosmopolitan hick town in the world), it is a fascinating place to live because many interesting people from the States and Europe come on safari, and every nationality lives there. At that time in Kenya we were less than one half of one percent white, but in that one-half percent there are Americans, British, Italians, Scandinavians, French, Germans, Greeks, and many other European nationalities; ten percent of the population was Asian and the rest were Africans.

Nairobi is seventy-six miles south of the Equator, 5,800 feet high, and a colorful city both intellectually and visually.

It is filled with lavender jacaranda, pink and red and purple bougainvillea, orange golden shower and yellow cassia trees; and as you walk around the streets still more colors assault you—Asian women in their iridescent saris of blues and greens and golds, and Sikh men in brilliant pink turbans, and Africans wrapped in many-colored kangas (brightly printed lengths of fabric worn by African women).

At first Jock and I were happy living in the center of this Technicolor city, but the word got around where we lived and soon everyone began coming to our flat for coffee instead of going to the Thorn Tree (the price was better), and we grew weary of being hosts and waiters and longed for our privacy again. So we found a lovely white house in Karen with gardens and rolling lawns and monkey-filled trees and bought it.

We also built a thatched-roof house at Malindi, almost in the Indian Ocean. Almost every weekend, we would drive with Shirley Brown the 378 miles east and one mile downhill to our fortress there against the twentieth century, glad that we had no telephone so no one could get at us. After our lecture tours, being so tired and over-peopled, we would go there for a week or two to divorce ourselves from civilization and fall apart in little pieces and renew ourselves. We would lie on the empty white beach in that world of living rainbow hues, eating mangoes and lobsters and listening to the light breeze tickle the palm trees into their familiar rustle; we would watch the twelve-foot tide flow in and out and the moon rise like a great orange ball out of the ocean. And before our lecture tours we would go there to store energy—like the wildebeests before their migration—for *our* two-thousand-mile trek through the U.S.

On school holidays we would spend weeks at a time there with the children and Shirley Brown, surfing and snorkeling and water skiing; and one day we were filled with awe as we all stood on a sand island in the Indian Ocean at midday and watched the total eclipse of the sun. In almost total darkness we watched the extraordinary effects, and saw the birds all fly back to their nests. Nights, since there is no TV, we would play games or just talk. During many of those nights we would be pole-fished. The Africans put razor blades on long mangrove poles, so you won't grab the pole, and while we were in the living room, they would put their poles in through the shuttered bedroom or kitchen windows and pole-fish everything out. Then the next day we would have to go to the marketplace and buy back our sheets and towels and clothes and cups and pans and so on. Although this was irritating and a nuisance, we'd finally laugh and wonder why they didn't steal more—we had so much and they had so little.

Quite a few days at Malindi our lunch ran away—we'd buy crabs from the fisherman who walked out of the ocean right in front of our house with them daily, but time and time again they'd escape from their basket in the kitchen, and we'd all have to crawl under the bougainvillea bushes and palm trees retrieving them, laughing and hollering as we wrestled with the angry things.

Our houses were filled with love and laughter.

Jock had become to the children a combination friend, big brother, and surrogate father. They gave each other nicknames. When McDonnell was tiny, many people, thinking my maiden name was too much for him, called him Donnell; then I began calling him "Donnellduk." Jock picked it up, then started calling Dancy "Dancyduk," and me "Bettyduk," and the children called him "Jockieduk"—and I am embarrassed to tell you it all stuck.

When McDonnell, aged eight, first went to school, the same one Jock had attended, Jock and I had driven the eighty miles north to see him. We peeped into his classroom, and wandering around the aisles was a dog, which the boys patted between carving their initials in the ancient battered desks and throwing wadded paper at their friends. The teacher, who approved of all of this, walked around with a gin and tonic after the lesson while the boys ate flying ants.

"The Africans eat them all the time," McDonnell explained to me. "They're really good—they taste like bacon." Perhaps they would have been more tasty than the lunch we were served, for the food was remarkably bad.

"Isn't this a swell school?" McDonnell was very enthusiastic. "We sleep outside on the verandah, and when there's a cricket match or a swimming meet in Nairobi, we take homing pigeons with us, then after each event we tie the results to a foot and it flies back here. And next term our whole form is going to climb Mount Kilimanjaro." (They did, and McDonnell was one of the youngest ever to reach the top.)

On our way back to Nairobi, I told Jock, "I hope Dancy's and Rick's schools aren't as unacceptable."

" 'Unacceptable'? Why, it's marvelous! They all love it, and scholastically it's excellent. I got into Eton from there. It's a school for boys, not parents." And he was right.

The strict British boarding schools allowed no smoking, no dating, and in my daughter Dancy's school not even makeup for the seventeen-year-olds. Drugs were unheard of. All three of them not only liked their schools but each of them became head of their various schools, and today say that they will send their children only to boarding schools.

A few times when their holidays coincided with our lecturing in the States, Jock's mother would collect them from school, put them on a plane, and we would meet them at the other end. The first time McDonnell was flying alone, Jock and I were at New York's JFK Airport, anxiously awaiting his plane to land. It did, but he was not on it.

Panicky, we telephoned Jock's mother in Nairobi, who said she had put him on the correct flight. "Don't worry," Jock tried to comfort me, "he's all right."

"He's eight years old and lost somewhere in the world. Is that all right?" I was shouting now. "Where can he be?"

"On a tiger shoot in India? Riding a rickshaw in Tokyo? Surfing in Hawa—"

"That's not funny."

"Look, he is on the passenger list . . ."

"So he's fallen out of the plane over the Atlantic!" I started to cry.

Jock put his arm around me and pretended confidence, but he was really just as much a Jewish mother as I. "Betty, I'll bet when the plane from Nairobi stopped in Greece or Rome he probably wandered around the airport and didn't get back on in time. He'll be on one of the next flights coming in." He kissed my forehead.

And sure enough, after two miserable hours, McDonnell came wandering into the customs hall, giving a nonchalant wave. The relief, not only for us but for the entire airline staff as well! I threw my arms around him. "McDonnell, where have you been?"

He looked at me in surprise. "Mother, I've been in school in Africa," as if I didn't know where he had been the last few months and just happened to bump into him at JFK. Not only was he unconcerned about being late, he was unaware of it.

"What airline did you come in on, Donnellduk?" Jock asked casually.

"The one that had that nice lady in a uniform who gave me Cokes—free." We kept interrogating him. "Well, once when the plane stopped I couldn't find it again and no one I asked spoke English but finally one lady did, the one who gave me the free Cokes." And we never did learn what airline he came in on.

The other two children arrived properly, and Christmas was nearly upon us. We all went to my sister's in Baltimore, and Jock fixed himself Gravy Train for breakfast. When my sister told him it was dog food, he was impressed. "It's quite good," he said.

Never having experienced an American Christmas before, he was astonished. "It approaches like the locusts," he said. "I've never seen so much commercialism, so many gifts for the overprivileged. Twelve days of Christmas! One is loathsome enough." And after the holidays were over, exhausted, he exclaimed, "Christmas is worse than Mau Mau."

It is impossible to describe what loving Jock and being loved by him was like. Let me give you an example of his love for me: We rented a little apartment in New York (our pit stop, we called it), because for both of us to say with Paul was too crowded for more than just a night now and then, and we were spending more time in New York between lectures. We got so tired of "eating out of suitcases" (as I called it) in hotels, and wanted a closet and a stove so we could unpack and stay home and eat scrambled eggs whenever we wanted to.

Every morning, Jock, an early riser, would creep quietly out of bed so he wouldn't disturb me, and go into the kitchen, eat his breakfast, and read the papers until I called him. Then he would bring me a tray of orange juice and coffee. "Jambo Memsaab," he would greet me with his lovely smile. Not only did he spoil me (I love to be spoiled), he thought it was a question of fairness.

He'd always had servants in Africa; and even at Eton he had put his shoes outside his door to be shined (if I had done that at my school they would have been stolen). And he was appalled at my having to do all the cooking and washing and cleaning, in addition to working with him, lecturing.

"What you need is a wife," he told me, "and I'll be it." So, happily, he ran the vacuum, went to the grocery store, and threw the clothes in the washing machine and dryer. He couldn't cook anything but orange juice and instant coffee, and even this presented a problem to him, because in the kitchen he could not hear me call when I awakened. Nevertheless, he bought me a police whistle so I could summon him and not have to get out of bed before my coffee. After a few days of blowing the whistle I couldn't do it anymore, it was just too gross—not for him but for me. Then he worked out a system whereby I called a friend from the telephone by our bed, who would then call Jock, who would answer on the kitchen phone and learn I was awake.

He tried so hard to please me in every way, and he succeeded beautifully. Never a Tuesday (the day of the week we were married) went by that he didn't give me a present. Sometimes something substantial, but usually a flower or a candy bar, always with a romantic card or note. Once he gave me Jackie Kennedy's hairbrush, on which she had written her name in nail polish. She had left it on her safari plane and the pilot gave it to Jock, who gave it to me.

"You keep the sun shining in my life," I told him one morning when he brought me my breakfast.

He sat on the bed next to me and kissed me. "Well, it's going to shine very brightly today for both of us because I just had a call—and we are going to the docks, because the Rolls has arrived!"

Chapter 6

☆

THE Rolls was lovely and we drove it across the United States for our lecture tour, but there were two problems. First, it had a right-hand drive and on the highway trucks would pass us and instead of seeing someone behind the steering wheel, they would see me sitting on the driver's side *typing*. (We had started to write our first book and I always typed in cars, where no one could get at us and we could discuss the text at length, uninterrupted.) This shock sometimes caused the trucks to swerve and we always feared being killed by a perplexed truck driver. The second problem was that it was extremely difficult to get spare parts. We even had to put truck tires on it, and soon it became a nuisance. As Jock said, "It's a nice car to visit your mother-in-law on Sundays but not to drive five hundred miles a day to work." So after a year or so we decided to sell it and get a dull but practical one.

We had a friend, a very elegant man, who collected Rolls-Royces. Of course he wanted to buy our Rolls, but currently he was broke, and could he pay us $2,000 of the $5,000 we asked (which was what we had invested in it by the time we got it in good running order and shipped) and pay us the rest later? We agreed and gave him the car. Just after that he became a Born Again Christian. Because he would holler "Praise be the Lord" in restaurants when he asked Jock or me to pass the salt and we did, Jock, being British, was embarrassed and preferred not to dine with him again, so we did not see our friend or the Rolls (or any money) for a year or two. Finally we called him and he said he was sorry about not paying but he was still broke, which was still all right with us.

Shortly after that, we were showing our New York apartment to a man interested in renting it while we were back in Africa, and he spotted a picture of the Rolls on our bulletin board in the kitchen. He grew very excited. "Where did you get this? Do you know it is a replica of a 1932 Silver Wraith with a Hooper body?!" (We didn't even know what that meant.) "There are only two of them in the States. It's a collector's item! I'll give you $80,000 for it right now."

Jock and I got dollar signs in our eyes and promptly called our Born Again friend. "Guess what? We have someone here who wants to buy the Rolls for $80,000. You still owe us $3,000, but we still have the title, so why don't we just split the $80,000 in half? Can we come and get it tomorrow?"

There was silence, then a cough, then, "Well, that won't be possible."

"Why not?"

"Because I gave it to Our Lord Jesus Christ."

"What do you mean?"

"Well, I took it apart, sold the parts, and gave the money to Our Lord."

So that was the end of our Rolls-Royce and any money. (And our friend.) And I told Jock, "When I get to those pearly gates, if I'm not picked up in that Rolls-Royce, I'm leaving."

Speaking of Lords, my sister Evelyn and her son Dick were coming to New York for a weekend and Jock and I wanted to take them somewhere fancy, so I called the Tavern on the Green. No tables; long waiting list; no. I happened to mention how disappointed I was to a friend who telephoned, and in a few minutes he called back and said, "It's fixed. Just ask for Lord Melville's table."

I was delighted we could get in, but Jock disapproved. "I cannot go around impersonating my relatives." However, I prevailed on his good nature to go through with the deception for the sake of Evelyn and Dick, who do not get to New York often.

As we were getting dressed, I noticed that Jock was putting on a turtleneck. "Aren't you going to put on a tie?" I asked.

"Lords never wear ties," he retorted. In the restaurant Jock asked the maître d' for his table in the Crystal Room. He didn't even have to refer to his long list. "Of course, Lord Melville," he said, giving Jock his card and washing his hands with invisible soap. "This way please . . ."

My sister was so nervous throughout the meal, she didn't enjoy it at all, but I told her she should be happy to spend an evening with the Lord.

On our way back to Kenya we decided to visit the real lord, Jock's cousin, in Scotland. On our trips back and forth we always made a point of stopping in Europe, if only for a few days to see old friends or new places. Also, breaking the trip made us feel almost human when we arrived in Kenya, instead of as if we were on instruments.

"Where shall we go on our way to Scotland?" Jock asked.

"My hair hates Paris, but I need blue eye drops, so let's go there."

"Good. We can have fun with our Swahili."

In Nairobi I had gone to the missionary language school from 8 A.M. to 4 P.M. every day for three months, and learned to speak Swahili—which is an exaggeration. Being incredibly stupid in languages and having no ear for them whatsoever, I learned to ask questions but I still can't understand all the answers. This was fine so long as I was with Jock or Helen, my nun friend (who had just been stationed in Nairobi), because she was just the opposite. She could understand but not speak, so I'd ask the question, then stand there looking dumb while the African answered me, then Helen would tell me what he'd said, and then I'd speak to him again in Swahili and so on.

I don't speak French at all, and Jock said his was just passable when he was drunk, but since he hardly drank we had a problem. However, we had discovered something very useful: In France we would speak to each other in loud voices only in Swahili, never a word of English. The salesperson, the waiter, the taxi driver would look perplexed, having immediately pegged us for a dumb American and Englishman, and would then try to work out what the hell language we were speaking and where we came from. Then Jock in his bad and halting French would ask for what he wanted, while they were still trying to figure us out, and they never had time to inflict that supercilious hostility on us. We liked it much better when they were the ones feeling stupid instead of us.

So we went to Paris and did all the things everyone does there, and it was, as it always is when you're in love, magical.

"By God, there's Hughy!" Jock exclaimed happily in the airport as we were about to leave Paris. I had heard a lot about Jock's old school friend and knew he was not only the Earl of Cawdor, but also the Thane of Cawdor. He still lives in the family castle, Cawdor Castle, the setting of Shakespeare's *Macbeth*. Hughy, a very colorful person, wore a black velvet suit with a white lace jabot at his neck, and a great cavalier's hat complete with white plume. The two school friends greeted each other with glee, then Jock introduced him to me. "This is Betty, who, as I wrote to you, is not only my wife but my life." Then he asked what Hughy was doing in Paris.

"I'm going to a costume ball tonight," Hughy answered with enthusiasm.

"You'll surely win," I told him, gesturing to his outfit.

"Oh, this isn't my costume. My costume's in my suitcase."

Jock promised Hughy we would come see him in Scotland, and we boarded our plane for London, where we went to have a maple nut sundae at Fortnum & Mason and tea with friends of Jock's who live on the Thames.

As we turned onto their road that runs along the river near Chiswick, I saw a familiar flag waving on a tall flagpole. "Look, Jock, the American flag!"

"And the Kenya one!" Jock exclaimed, "and that white one with the black Labrador on it is declaring their dog is in residence. I forgot they have a flag fetish." Later in the afternoon, someone from Argentina telephoned to say he was coming over, so our host nipped down into his flag cellar and got the Argentinian flag, which he ran up proudly next to the Kenyan and American ones.

In England we drove to Hampshire and Cotswold to see friends. Driving along, we tuned in the most interesting fifteen-minute radio show we had ever heard. There were no words, just sounds—not one spoken word. First there were sounds of footsteps of a person going up creaky stairs, whistling happily; then the brushing of teeth, the opening of a window, the closing of a door, the turning off a light; then snoring. Then came a muffled smash of glass from downstairs, quiet steps on the creaky stairs, the opening of the closed door; then the screams, the struggle, the dying gasps; finally, the sirens. I'm not going to tell you the outcome and ruin the story for you, but we knew exactly what was happening at every minute, without a word ever spoken.

When we boarded the train for Scotland and sat in our compartment, Jock told me, "If you're alone and want to remain alone in one of these public compartments, as I do now with you, you know what you do? You make sure you get on first and get into an empty one, then as the other people walk by and look in, contemplating sitting with you, you just crook your finger, leer at them, and beckon them to join you—as if you are luring them in. Boy, do they walk on! It never fails."

I laughed. "My favorite train story, I told Jock, which I am told is true, is that Albert Schweitzer came to London on his way from Africa for an award. He was to be honored and was met with great fanfare by the Prince of Wales, who had a band on the platform to greet him, and all that. Schweitzer's train pulled in but he did not get off. In a few minutes they saw him walking slowly toward them from the back of the train, carrying all his luggage himself. The Prince of Wales, realizing he hadn't come first class, rushed down the platform to him, asking 'Why did you come second class?'

"Schweitzer replied, 'Because there was no more space in third class.' "

Jock's cousin's (Lord Leven) proper name is Alexander Robert Leslie Melville, 14th Earl of Leven and 13th Earl of Melville, Viscount Kirkaldie, and Baron Balgonie. He and his wife, the Countess, were at Carr Bridge station to meet us. (Of course they use none of their names but merely introduce themselves to everyone as Sandy and Sue Leven.) They were the only ones there—the station is unmanned, a recorded voice merely announces the trains comings and goings. They drove us to Glenferness, the name of their 6,000-acre estate, to their house—the family's wonderful old hunting lodge.

The bathroom adjoining the guest bedroom where we stayed looked like the Algonquin Hotel lobby—it's bigger than our living room, with lovely Persian carpets and antique highboys. I thought a plumber had just left a loo and a bathtub there temporarily. Dinner looked like a Halloween party because the men were all in kilts, including Jock who kept his outfit, complete with his kilts, plaid and bonnet, the Leslie tartan and his sporran and caringorm, at Glenferness.

That night in our enormous bed with a much needed old fashioned bed warmer, we made lovely love and afterwards Jock asked, "Have you ever made love in Scotland before?"

"No, only in the lobby of the Algonquin."

He threw his pillow at me.

The famous Findhorn River flows through their property, and the next morning we walked along the high banks of the salmon-filled river and Sandy taught me how to shoot. High on the cliff, he threw bottles down into the river, and I pointed the .38 at them, pulled the trigger, and missed every one.

"You're right handed," Sandy said. "Are you right or left eyed?"

"I didn't even know there was such a thing."

"All right—let's find out. Pick a spot—any spot. See that nest on that tree over there? Well, with both eyes open point your index finger of your right hand to the center of it. That's right—now, leaving your finger lined up, close one eye, then open it and close the other eye—then . . ."

"Wow," I exclaimed, "my finger jumps a foot away when I look at it with my right eye, but it stays exactly centered with my left eye on it."

"That's why you can't hit anything—you're right handed and left eyed. That's quite unusual—you'll have to shoot from the hip."

So that's why I sound like Clint Eastwood when I say, "I shoot from the hip."

The next day we went on a grouse shoot with Sandy and Sandy's identical twin brother, who is just two minutes younger than Sandy but just plain old Jordy Leslie-Melville—no title, no estate, no nothing. I loved all Jock's relatives, as Jock loved mine—what a rare thing.

On our way to see Hughy, we spent a great deal of time in the village of Nairn, buying wool sweaters for us and the children (later, when we got back to Kenya and read the labels, we saw they were made in the U.S.A.). As we walked over Hughy's drawbridge and gazed out over the moat to the most beautiful gardens and up at the magnificent castle, I wondered what he would be wearing this time. Just in the entrance, old pewter crowns and medieval coronets and Shakespearean-type helmets were on wooden pegs, and right next to them hung Hughy's orange plastic motorcycle helmet.

When Jock told the lady at the desk who he was, she pushed a button on the telephone—"Lord Cawdor, Jock Leslie-Melville is here," and in a few seconds Hughy came running down the narrow stone circular stairway in blue jeans with a torn sweater and embraced us. "Come on up. I live upstairs in the daytime, when the tourists are here, but at 5 P.M., when it closes to the public, I come downstairs and live in all of it."

Upstairs was a mess. Just one large room with newspapers and magazines and empty beer bottles strewn all over the floor. "Sorry about this, but . . . ," and I thought he was going to say he had had a party the night before, ". . . but this is how I live." Hughy is delightful; he has done an excellent job of opening his castle to the public, and with touches of humor. For example, in the dungeon artifacts are displayed and the sign he has written about them reads, "The incredibly boring stone in the left-hand corner is . . ."

Hughy showed us all around and we had a glorious time, and the two good friends made enthusiastic plans to see each other soon again and departed with great merriment. How lucky it was that none of us had a crystal ball and knew then it would be the last time they would ever see each other. What a gift that we could not see into the future, so they could say their goodbye with joy.

Chapter 7

*L*ECTURING was fine but it was only a part-time job and we needed a full-time one. Having been the first American to organize non-hunting safaris to East Africa, and having taken so many people on safari before I turned it over to Dan Bruce, I suggested to Jock that perhaps he and I should go into the safari business. "But," he said, "I've never even been to Treetops. Living so near to it I never bothered—must be like a New Yorker never going to the Empire State Building."

When we first started lecturing, most people didn't know if Kenya was something to eat or step on. Jock said, "Most Americans must have been home with measles when they studied geography in school." Some said it was too far away for them to even imagine going there, but, little by little, Americans began to travel to Africa, and they often asked us if we would take them on safari. But we had always politely demurred, saying we weren't in the safari business.

Then at a lecture in Dallas a woman said she'd pay us anything to take her on safari, so Jock and I got into the safari business. We enjoyed taking her through East Africa very much, so I said to Jock, "Hey, we had fun, let's do it often. It's a better job then working in the gas station."

"You're right," Jock agreed.

"Let's send out invitations to people to join us on our private safari."

"What a good idea!" He gathered me in his arms. "You are such a life inventor. You make me feel so alive. I love you more and more each day." He kissed me, and no more invitations were written that afternoon.

But that evening, as we addressed envelopes, I asked, "Don't you think we're asking them to pay too much?"

Jock laughed. "That reminds me—when I was at Eton they raised the school fees, which were already extremely expensive. The mimeographed circular sent to the parents explained the reasons for the increase in fees, but contained a typing error so that it read, 'Regretfully, therefore, the fees must be raised from x to y per anum.' On receiving the letter, one parent cabled the school, UNDERSTAND REASONS FOR INCREASE BUT WOULD APPRECIATE BEING ALLOWED TO CONTINUE PAYING THROUGH THE NOSE AS USUAL."

We had a good response to our invitations and for the next three years we took our safariers on the "milk run"—to the usual, the best places on their camera safaris. Most places in the world look better in *National Geographic*, but not East Africa. The country is so lovely, it's like driving through a Rousseau painting—through profusions of wildlife—to the lodges, those oases of civilization amid thousands and thousands of miles of empty, undeveloped Africa.

Sometimes we would take those who wanted out of tourist-folder Africa to the real Africa, where we'd bump along on camel tracks with grass rising over our Land Rover's windscreen. We stayed in tents, or huts where elephants would put their trunks in the window and steal our shoes, or in "Dysentery Arms," as we called quite a few places, where the wine tasted like sheep dip and the garbage cans hung from trees so the hyenas couldn't overturn them. Although these places lacked the excellent food and swimming pools of the milk run's manicured lodges, everyone felt they were on safari when this was really Africa.

Taking people on safari was a happy job because it was the highlight of their lives. It may sound like a glamorous job, but I guess glamor is really something only an outsider perceives. The reality of being a tour leader is hard and tedious work. You're stuck with anywhere up to twenty-five strangers—the Methodist minister, the two gay men, the John Bircher and the left-wing radical, the smartass furrier from New York and the spinster from Des Moines—from dawn with the early risers till after midnight with the late-night drunks, answering the same questions and telling the same stories over and over again.

Mealtime for me was the worst. Just as I'd get the fork to my mouth, someone would ask how, when, and where elephants copulated, and because my mother told me I shouldn't talk with my mouth full, I was still starving when everyone else was finished and ready to go on a game run. So I developed a ploy and duped Jock. Just as we would sit down at the lunch table, I'd say, "Oh, Jock, tell everyone how you were charged by the buffalo," or attacked by a lion, or the history of Kenya—anything just so it lasted through the meal. Then I'd eat my food peacefully and spend the afternoon trying to remember other long stories for him to tell at dinner.

Jock and I survived being safari leaders so long because we were together and could cuddle up at night in bed in our tent and laugh at all the funny things that happened during the day and complain to each other about the irritating ones. Many of the people became and have remained good friends, and the animals are always superb, but after three years of eating sixty-six consecutive meals with people we might or might not like, I decided I'd rather sell eggs.

Also, we have more business than we could handle ourselves, so we joined Percival Tours, a large American worldwide travel company. Jock became Managing Director (because only the President of Kenya can use that title) and established a staff and couriers in Nairobi. We liked our new job of greeting the safariers and having them to the house for tea and a little lecture, but not taking them on safari anymore. We grew to handling 4,000 people a year, so it's a good thing we didn't have to take them ourselves.

Is going on safari dangerous? We've never lost anyone yet, because we made sure our safariers obeyed the "stay in your car" rule. But, alas, some tour operators don't. One time in Serengeti, four tourists and their African driver broke down in their safari bus (a mini-bus with a hatch); the driver said he would walk back to the lodge for help but the others must remain in the bus. Despite his protests, one couple insisted on going with him, and the other couple sat in the bus, idly watching the three of them through binoculars as they disappeared toward the horizon. Suddenly they saw a lot of commotion—the three of them had walked into a pride of sleeping lion—and the couple in the bus helplessly watched all of them being mauled to death by the surprised beasts.

Lion are the main danger of walking. During the day they sleep in the high yellow grasses and are impossible to see. But if you stay in your car you will be safe, because the animals have come to think of vehicles as merely another, if rather smelly and odd-looking, animal in the bush, and the fumes disguise our human scent; however, the minute you step out and they see a whole human form and smell it, it's trouble.

Another time a group of seven tourists in a mini-bus with their driver were looking at the hippo in the river which is the border between Kenya and Tanzania, when some Maasai *morani* (warriors) came loping across the water, hauled all the people out of the bus at spearpoint, stripped them, and took every stich of clothing and everything else—purses, wallets, passports. Not knowing how to drive, they just pushed the bus across the river and disappeared into the bush. Fortunately the driver knew the way back, so the group started walking, stark naked, in the hot sun two miles to the lodge. Other guests, game-viewing at the lodge, adjusted their binoculars as they sat on the terrace. What was this strange species coming toward them? The first of the naked group to arrive was an Englishman, who merely walked up to the reception desk and said in his understated British manner only, "May I have the key to room 7 please?"

But these are rare episodes. In twenty-five years of taking people on safari we have never had any disasters or international incidents. Thank God.

What is the most dangerous creature in Africa? The mosquito, because it kills more people than any other. What's the second most dangerous? The crocodile, because it takes the African women as they wash their clothes in the rivers. And the next most dangerous? The elephant, because it is the only animal big enough to smash your car, and you, to bits. (No guns are allowed in game parks.) So going on safari *is* dangerous? No, not at all, not if you take a malaria preventative, don't wash your clothes in a crocodile-filled river, and do what your driver tells you when elephant are about. (And if you come on safari with Percival Tours, I'll give you some more interesting tips.)

So Jock and I had the best of all possible worlds, spending most of each year in Africa bringing Americans on safari, and still having those two months twice a year back in the States lecturing. One evening in Africa, sitting on the sofa in front of a roaring fire, I said, "How lucky we are, Jock, to be able to live in both worlds."

"How lucky we are to be alive in this very short time on earth when the primitive world and the modern world overlap. It won't be long before they pave the bush and the primitive world disappears altogether." He kissed me. "But mainly how lucky we are to be together." We were not only deeply in love with each other, we were in love with our lives as well. Our life had such a vibrancy to it, and we were aware of it at the time too. Happiness is usually a remembered emotion—you're inclined to say, "Gee, that was fun," or "I was so happy then," but Jock and I realized how happy we were and, appreciating it, we always gave thinks to the gods that be.

Our first book, *Elephant Have Right of Way*, was published, and we came into quite some demand for media attention whenever we toured the United States, in newspaper interviews, magazine spreads—and on national television shows like "To Tell the Truth," "What's My Line?" and the "Today" show with Barbara Walters. At that time, Johnny Carson was on the panel of "To Tell the Truth" and when I came out he said, "I don't know what it is, but whatever it is, I want it." Jock never liked him thereafter.

Before I knew Jock, Jack Paar had picked me up in a hotel elevator in Nairobi, inviting me to get off on the mezzanine

and come to a party being given for him. I did and became
good friends with him and Miriam and Randy, as did Jock.
Jack wrote the introduction to our book, saying we were two
of his favorite people, and that we were "an endangered species—free, and decent, in love, and fun." He had become so
intrigued with Africa on his trip there that he now asked
Jock and me to help him produce a network special on East
Africa, which turned out so well we did a second together.
So for four years Jock and I worked with Jack, supplying him
with ideas and facts, arranging his filming safaris and traveling with him to remote parts, such as the Ituri forest in
Uganda to film the Pygmies, and Mount Kilimanjaro, where
he interviewed us on the first talks ever filmed on the 19,346-
foot mountain. No one seemed to know, or care, that it is
the largest lump of land in the world, or that it used to be
in Kenya but was given to Kaiser Wilhelm by Queen Victoria
as a birthday present, so the border was moved to include it
in Tanzania; but people *were* interested in the fact that sexual
desire stops at 16,000 feet.

Jack's shows recieved a lot of good press: "His humor is
still up to Paar," "Paar throws entertaining light on darkest
Africa," "See Africa from a unique point of view." Jack is
unique—an original, like no one else. His view of almost
everything is different from anyone else's; he notices the mi-
nutiae of everyday living and reminds all of us how odd we
really are. He is perceptive and spontaneously funny. Many
Africans pierce and stretch their earlobes, then put pretty
things through the loops to wear, like empty Kodak film boxes
or a can of peas, and the ones in the city carry messages from
office to office in their ears, which Jack christened "ear mail."
Noticing how the African takes everything literally, he said,
"If you want cologne, you better not ask for toilet water."
One night we were filming a scene at a black-tie dinner party
in Nairobi, when the host's donkey walked into the candlelit
dining room. Although the line was cut from the TV show,
what Jack really said was, "Get your ass out of the dining
room."

Jack is also wise. When Dancy and McDonnell joined Up

With People, an exuberant musical group of talented young people who travel around the world promoting peace and the joy of life, Jack filmed the group when they were in Kenya performing for the Maasai. The ocher-colored warriors, with their one pigtail hanging down in the center of their foreheads, stood there with their spears, naked except for a *shuka* (cloak) over their shoulder, fascinated with the music. Jack's wry comment was, "Music is almost as good as war in bringing people together."

When the Paars returned to the States from their last trip, Jock and I sent them a lion cub that was looking for a home. Jack loved that cub as much as it is possible to love anything. One day the lion ate the telephone cord in their living room, and Jack called the telephone company and asked for a new cord. "What happened to yours?" they asked.

"My lion ate it." And the telephone repair men were afraid to come to the house and face either a lunatic or a lion.

On our next trip to the States, the Paars gave us a dinner party at their house, and afterwards we were watching Jack's tapes of himself and Jock and me on "The Merv Griffin Show." "With so many talk shows on TV," Jack said, "our kids will grow up thinking the Last Supper was a panel show," followed immediately by the comment, "Why does Merv wear his hair like Captain Kangaroo?" We had driven up to New Caanan from New York that night with mutual friends who are Christian Scientists. "We'd better get going back," they said. "It's starting to snow."

Jack said, "I didn't think Christian Scientists believed in snow."

On the way back we said how we all agreed with Robert Morley, who commented to Jack one day when they were having lunch together, "Jack, my dear boy, the world was so much better when you were running it."

On this trip we had brought Shirley Brown with us. She had flown Pan Am in a cage, which humiliated her, but I had tacked a sign on it: "My name is Shirley Brown and I love you"; and everyone along the way coddled her, including the

Pan Am staff at JFK, who sent out for a McDonald's hamburger for her while she was waiting to go through customs. She loved New York and afterward tried to jump into every yellow car she saw, thinking they were taxis and she'd get a good ride. Central Park was Shirley Brown's favorite. She'd jump in the lake and swim with the ducks, and we'd throw her ball to her and romp around in the leaves with her until it snowed. The snow astonished her, so we'd throw snowballs at her and laugh as she raced down the bank to go into the iced-over lake and slipped around as she discovered there was no water—"Where did it go?" she seemed to say. We'd laugh at the ice skaters who fell down, and smile at the people in the horse-drawn hansoms and those riding bikes, and stop awhile and listen to the various groups playing music and watch the men playing chess with gloves on and wonder why they didn't play in the warmth of their own houses. Then we'd walk down Madison Avenue and marvel at the shops, but we couldn't go into any, because Shirley Brown was a shoplifter and took candy bars out of racks.

One day, when we were going to see Paul, we took her on the Staten Island ferry with us, and had a hard time keeping her from jumping in the water to chase the sea gulls. Jock and I waved to the Statue of Liberty, thrilled at the movie view of Manhattan, and bought Shirley Brown a hot dog and ordered two for ourselves. "Oh, Bettyduk, they have cider here—want some?"

"I never drink it."

"You don't like it?" Jock asked, reaching for his money.

"I love it, but when I worked at Johns Hopkins, we had to collect twenty-four-hour specimens from the patients for a seventeen-ketosteroid test, and one patient who was told to bring his specimen came in on the appointed day empty-handed. I asked him where it was, and he told me he had collected it in a cider jug, but on his way into town he stopped at a gas station and went into the office for a pack of cigarettes and when he returned to his car, someone had stolen the cider."

"Two root beers, please," Jock said to the man.

After seeing Paul, we went to a movie where we held hands and cried because Hayley Mills went blind and died, and her Seeing Eye dog cried and walked with the pallbearers at her funeral. And then we wanted a P. J. Clarke's hamburger for supper, but stopped on our way for a butterscotch sundae because we couldn't wait till after our hamburger; and walking home we stopped at a piano bar and listened quietly and talked easily; and walking on, arm in arm, I got sleepy so I put my head on Jock's shoulder and told him how wonderful he was and how beautiful he was, because he was, and how I loved him, not only with my heart and mind, but also with my eyes, and how I'd rather look at him than any sunset. I had told him all this before many times, but he liked to hear it. And then he told me how much he loved me and how beautiful I was and how he liked to work with me and talk with me and play with me because it all felt so right and so good. And then, right there on the street, he kissed me, softly; and when we got home he kissed me passionately and we made beautiful love; and I'd tell him, for the hundredth time, how all of me responded because sex is mainly between the ears. He understood, he always understood everything. Then, as every night, we'd have a bubble bath together and fall naked into bed, and wrapped around each other we'd cling all night long, until Shirley Brown woke us in the morning.

Did we ever fight? Sure. We had terrible fights about astronauts and how to cook scrambled eggs.

We had to go to Boston to lecture, and although my sister had baby-sat Shirley Brown in Baltimore while we did our big lecture tour, this last lecture was only for one night and Randy Paar volunteered to take her. When we got back we learned Randy had taken her to the Plaza with Jack, who was having lunch with Goldie Hawn, and Goldie had given Shirley Brown most of her steak. After that, Shirley Brown refused dog food, even hot dogs on the Staten Island Ferry— she wanted to dine only at the Plaza.

We met the Cronkites in New York, and when we returned to Africa, they came to our house in Karen for dinner, with their daughter Kathy and their son Chip, the night before they set off on their safari. On their second night out, they were camping about two hundred miles from Nairobi, and Chip, who was seventeen at the time, developed severe stomach pains, which Walter, who prides himself on being an amateur doctor, diagnosed as appendicitis. They piled Chip into the back of their Land Cruiser and drove through the night to the nearest lodge, about thirty miles away, for help. Among the forty or so people there, there was neither doctor nor telephone, so they drove another eighty miles through the blackness of the game park, dodging the animals that suddenly appeared and hoping no elephant would overturn their car.

Finally they reached Narok, euphemistically called a town, which consisted of one gas pump and a police station, where they telephoned the Flying Doctors. While a small aircraft can take off from Nairobi at night, there were no landing lights on the little grass strip at Narok, so they had to wait in their safari car, with Chip in agony, till dawn, for the plane to rescue them; and by 8:15 A.M. Chip's appendix was removed in Nairobi Hospital just before it burst.

So the Cronkites spent most of their safari in Nairobi visiting Chip. They had left everything in their tent two hundred miles away, so we lent them a car and some clothes, and they came to meals often. We all became lasting friends.

Since there was no TV in Nairobi, Jock and I never learned how to turn on a set. Later, when we were back in New York and Walter realized we had never seen him on CBS News, which he was then doing every night, he told us, "Listen, there's this wonderful magic box that has pictures that talk. Come on down with me while I do the news and I'll show it to you." So he showed us all around and we went in the control room while he gave the news, and afterward we all went to Chinatown and celebrated the Chinese New Year, and laughed so hard at Betsy and Walter's wonderful sense of humor.

(Just a few days ago, ten years later now, when I went to Chip's wedding alone in New York, I thought over and over how Jock would have enjoyed seeing him marry such a lovely girl. And how he would have loved talking to Meryl Streep, who was a bridesmaid and had just returned from Kenya, where she played Isak Dinesen in the film *Out of Africa*, and said she liked Kenya so much she cried all the way to the airport when she left. It seemed so unfair that Jock, who enjoyed life and people so much, was no longer here to do so. Because I didn't want to add a sad note to the joyful day I didn't tell Walter that the warthog we had named after him because he had been so intrigued with it when he had first seen it, had also died.)

Chapter 8

☆

THE sunrise over the Sudan desert looked like a Rothko painting. Looking out the plane's window on our way back to Nairobi, Jock said to me, "Africa's such a delight. It's sublime really, isn't it? But do you ever miss living in the States, do you miss Baltimore?"

"No. I love going back to see my sister and niece and nephew and my friends, but I wouldn't have left Baltimore if I had been content with my life there. Everyone always says, 'It must have taken you so much courage to move to Africa,' but the truth is it would have taken me a lot more courage to stay in Baltimore. There's nothing wrong with Baltimore, it's a good city, but I just had this curiosity about the world, especially Africa, and I didn't like leading a suburban life surrounded by so many incurably sane people. Auntie Mame said, 'Life's a banquet and most poor sons of bitches are starving to death.' My philosophy has always been you're only sorry for what you don't do, and so I always try everything on for size to see if it fits. If it doesn't, at least I don't have to sit around the rest of my life wondering what would have happened if. . . . I've made every major mistake there is to make, but then I try to correct them, or at least learn by them. But marrying you and living here wasn't one of them."

Jock picked up my hand and kissed it.

"Oh, I'd hate never going back to the States, especially Baltimore, but I guess I'm a nomad."

"You're a risk taker—and I like your philosophy."

"Kierkegaard said it more eloquently than I ever could. He

said, 'The greatest thing is the ability to step and prize the step above the fear of the dark. Not stepping is the supreme folly and cowardice, even if one steps into nothingness and falls, even if one stepped only to find one must step back.' "

"When did you memorize that?"

"Years ago . . . look!" I pointed out the window. "Below is Kenya."

About 4 A.M. the night we got home, when Jock and I were sound asleep, he nudged me gently and whispered in my ear, "Don't be alarmed, just be quiet, but there is someone about to come in our window." He said it just as if he were telling me someone was arriving for tea.

Alarmed, I opened my eyes and saw a leg coming in our second-floor bedroom window. Suddenly Jock leapt out of bed and ran toward the window yelling a war cry. It was the loudest, most furious noise I had ever heard from a human; it frightened me more than the leg, which immediately disappeared. There was a thud on the grass below and, peering out, Jock said calmly, "He ran off."

Coming back to bed, he said, "I heard the ladder being put against the window and knew it had to be a thief. Noise is a wonderful deterrent. I learned it at Sandhurst."

"Oh, Jockieduk, you're not only beautiful to look at, you're so brave." We hugged each other back to sleep.

The next night the telephone rang. It was a friend of ours, Earl Moorhouse, calling us in Nairobi from Frankfurt. He was very angry. "This wretched Lufthansa won't let us get off in Nairobi. They're making us go all the way to Johannesburg, then we must change planes and backtrack the 2,000 miles to Nairobi. Can you believe it?"

"Yes, easily," Jock said. "Can't you just walk off the plane in Nairobi and hide in the ladies' room or something? They won't delay the flight to search for you. Look, see if you can't work out getting off here tomorrow or getting on another airline—and if we don't see you at the airport, we'll just wait to hear from you."

Earl, a journalist, was moving to Nairobi from South Africa

with his wife and two children to open an office for a world-wide environmental organization, and first they all had gone to Rome for a conservation conference.

Early next morning Jock took Dancy to the airport, where she was to catch a flight to London to visit a school friend for her spring holiday. Half an hour later he telephoned me from the airport, very upset. "There's been a terrible crash. I was afraid you'd hear about it and worry about Dancy, so I'm calling to tell you not to. She's fine, standing right here with me. It's the most horrific mess—I've never seen anything so frightful."

I assumed he was talking about an automobile accident on the road to the airport. The road is hazardous and the standard of driving in Kenya is appalling. "There could be no one alive . . ." he went on.

"How many do you think were killed?" I asked.

"There's no way yet of knowing how many people were involved, but I can't believe there could be any survivors." The use of the word "survivors" seemed odd to me for a road accident.

"What was it?" I asked, puzzled. "A bus?"

Startled that I had not known what he was talking about, he said, "No, it's a 747 crash."

Dancy and Jock were among the closest eyewitnesses. They were driving along the airport road parallel to the runway as one of the first 747s to fly to Kenya was taling off. Dancy said, admiring it as it came toward them about 150 feet up, "It must be landing." In fact, the giant airliner was losing altitude.

"It can't be," Jock told her, "it's already beyond the runway!" The plane was sinking slowly, its nose getting higher and its tail lower. Dancy and Jock watched for a few agonizing seconds, hypnotized by the horror of realizing it was going to crash. Then there was an enormous red and black explosion shaped like an atomic mushroom, great plumes of flame as high as a skyscraper and dense black smoke with bits of airplane flung high in the air.

Jock and Dancy sat there white and shocked, unable really to believe what they had just seen. A minute later there came a second tremendous explosion as big as the first.

There was no access to the wreckage from where they had pulled up, so they drove on to the terminal. The scene there was chaotic. From the waving base people had watched as their relatives and friends took off—and crashed twenty seconds later. Now they were sobbing hysterically, clutching pillars for support, fainting. Jock found a telephone and called me.

"What's Dancy going to do?" I asked.

"She says she wants to go on her flight to London anyway," Jock replied. "The runway isn't affected. Her logic is that it's unlikely that there will be two crashes on the same day, and that if she doesn't get right back on the horse at once and all that . . . I agree with her. There just couldn't have been any survivors," he repeated. "Betty," he added in a different and sadder voice, "the Moorhouses could have been on that plane."

I felt myself go white. In the tension of the moment there hadn't been a thought about which airline it was, but now Jock told me it was Lufthansa.

"Well," Jock sighed, "They didn't disembark. If they were on board they never knew what got them—it must have been instant death. I've got to let other people use the telephone. I'll see Dancy off, then try to get a passenger list. Meet me in my office."

On my way downtown, the black cloud of smoke could still be seen rising over the airport and the sirens of police cars and ambulances wailed continuously, most unusual for a city that is generally placid. It was the first air crash ever at Nairobi's airport, and everyone in the city was affected by it. One could sense a communal awareness of tragedy. Usually tragedies are personal—while you are suffering, because someone close to you has died, the person next to you on the bus or in the elevator is reading a newspaper or laughing, but this day in Nairobi everybody was in the grip of the disaster.

Jock held me. "Dancy's plane left safely. I haven't managed to get a passenger list because Lufthansa rightly refused to release names until they know who's died and who's survived and next of kin have been informed. Miraculously, to my complete amazement, it seems there *were* some survivors."

Later in the day we were to learn that the 747, coming down as it did with its nose higher than its tail, had snapped in two just behind the wings as it hit a low bank upon touching the ground. The rear section exploded on impact and the giant column of flame and smoke had completely obscured the front half from Dancy's and Jock's view. Everyone in the rear had died, except a sailor who was flung clear and found himself sitting alone in the African bush still strapped in his seat.

Many in the forward part, including the flight crew, had survived.

Gloomily, we speculated that the Moorhouses, in all probability, had been aboard.

Jock's secretary came in. "The British High Commission is on the phone. They say you have some friends named Moorhouse who were on the Lufthansa flight . . ."

As a feeling of nausea rose in our throats, my knees weakened and I sank into a chair by the telephone. "Oh, God, they *were* on the plane . . ."

Jock grabbed the phone. "Yes, the Moorhouses are our friends . . . What! They're eating lunch in the Hilton Hotel right now!"

We couldn't believe it! We raced over to the hotel.

Earl Moorhouse greeted us in the lobby with a big smile. Yes, Lynn and the boys were fine. We went up to their room and there was much embracing and hugging; we found them in better shape than we were.

"Did you know you were crashing?" I asked.

"We certainly did!" Earl answered readily, lighting a cigarette and sitting on the other bed next to Jock. "We had plenty of time to realize *just* what was happening. As soon as we were off the ground, the whole plane started to shake—not just vibrating a bit, which you sometimes get on takeoff, but *violent* shuddering. We knew we were going down all right . . ."

"Did people scream or panic?" Jock asked.

"No, not at all. Everyone was very calm and completely quiet. The music was playing. Amazing—Lynn and I are really scared of flying, so much so that we had taken an overnight train all the way from Rome to Frankfurt in order to be able to go with Lufthansa—you know, German efficiency and all that. We . . ."

"But the poor Mickey Mouse lady didn't get out," interrupted Garrett, clutching his mother's hand, frightened eyes in a white seven-year-old face.

"Mickey Mouse lady?" I asked, perplexed.

"Yeah," explained Garrett. "She's the one who has the job of playing games with all the kids on the flight. We had the same Mickey Mouse lady when we flew from Jo' burg to Rome and she brought us books and games and cakes and she was really nice . . ." His little voice trailed off. "She was . . . she was killed . . . and so were all the children sitting with her when we took off."

"But this time when we took off from Nairobi," Lynn whispered shakily, "we insisted the boys stay with us and try to sleep . . ."

Earl interrupted. "Brendon was sitting near the window on the left, Garrett was in the middle, and I was in the aisle seat next to him; Lynn was sitting across the aisle from me. When the plane took off and began to shake and then started to sink, we crouched over, and then there was an enormous jolt, followed by another, and a terrific explosion. The ceiling fell in on us and the luggage racks were lying on top of the seat back . . ."

". . . And the seats came unhooked from the floor," interrupted Brendon, the six-year-old.

". . . And there was food and mess all over the place," added Garrett excitedly.

". . . And all the luggage and the coats were everywhere," said Lynn.

". . . And our row of seats had come loose," Earl went on,

"and of course we were still strapped in. I unbuckled Garrett and myself, but Brendon didn't move—I thought he was dead . . ."

"I was asleep!" yelled Brendon with glee.

"He was, he *slept* right through it!" Earl exclaimed. "But thinking he was dead I grabbed Garrett and started fighting my way through the rubble, lifting the hunks of ceiling out of the way . . ."

Lynn cut in, "I shook Brendon and he woke up. We followed Earl and Garrett. That old man, remember him?" she asked her family. "He was in the seat behind us with blood all over his face . . . and then that other man whose son was in the rear, he kept going to look for him but there was nothing there, not even a part of that section of the plane, just a hole."

Earl began to pace the floor. "We could see lots of flames coming up right outside the windows on the left and I knew we must get out fast. I was picking up pieces of debris to make way up the aisle so that we could get out . . ." He showed us a cut on his hand, which was apparently the only injury sustained by any of them.

"Yeah," interrupted Garrett, "and the food from the little kitchen—you know—it was *all over* the floor, what a mess!"

"Brendon and I followed Earl and Garrett," cut in Lynn, "and somehow we got to the exit and flung ourselves down the chute and . . ."

"Flames were coming from all around us!" Garrett remembered.

They were all interrupting each other, recalling things they hadn't yet had time to think of or to put into words, but the prevalent emotion among them was a manic excitement.

"We slid down the chute and ran from the wreckage and then twenty seconds later a huge explosion demolished what remained of the 747," Earl told us.

Brendon said, "Me and Mommy were barefoot. We had taken our shoes off before takeoff . . ."

"Yes," added Lynn. "We stumbled and tripped over that rough ground."

Earl interrupted. "We didn't know where we were heading, but we all just kept running—into the African bush. Then we saw twenty or thirty Africans running toward us . . ."

"The group working on that new road," Jock commented.

"When we met," Earl continued, "the Africans picked up the children and hugged them, and embraced the adults . . ."

"Then two of them saw that Brendon and I were barefoot, and do you know what they did?" Lynn asked. "They took off their shoes and gave them to us."

"Look!" squealed Brendon, holding out his feet with "truck skins" (shoes the Africans make from strips of old tires), sizes too large for him. Lynn's were identical.

"The Africans had no cars to take us to safety, so they stayed with us and tried to comfort us. But soon a Land Rover arrived," Earl said, lighting another cigarette before resuming his pacing in the tiny room. "An Italian was driving it. I think he said he was supervising the work on the road. Anyway, a lot of us piled into the Land Rover and he drove us to the airport building . . . and someone finally brought us here."

After more excited talk—they obviously had a need to spill out and repeat what had happened—Lynn and the boys decided to bathe, so Jock and I went with Earl to the Lufthansa office to try to call his and Lynn's parents to reassure them.

The scene in the reception area was heartrending. Anxious, desperate people kept coming in. A young man gave the girl at the desk a name—his fiancée, he said anxiously. She glanced down her list. "All we have is a list of the people who are alive in the hospital," then she looked up with sad eyes, and shook her head no. The silence was terrible. "Maybe she's in one of the hotels . . ."

He slumped, hope diminished, saying, "No, I checked with the hotels before coming here," and he left with a blurred thank you.

Then a Japanese man asked about his brother. Again the list, again the silence, the shattered hope.

The station manager came in and made an official statement. There were fifty-nine dead, he said. They had been
able to identify only one; the others were charred beyond
recognition. There were ninety-eight survivors, some in hospital, of whom only two were critical; and the balance were
in the hotel, except for one who could not be accounted for.
The cause of the accident was not yet known.

Within an hour of the accident an appeal had gone out for
blood donors—Nairobi's blood bank was simply not up to
meeting the sudden need—and within two or three hours
over a hundred people, the big majority Africans, had made
donations for the injured. And who were many of the recip-
ients whose lives were saved by black African blood? Mostly
white South Africans whose apartheid policies at home are
to oppress blacks.

The Lufthansa man continued at the press conference. "A
team of experts has already left Germany and will open their
inquiry at once. The black box has been recovered. It records
all relevant technical information about possible causes of a
crash. The captain and the engineer—indeed all the flight
crew—are alive and unhurt, so we expect to know the reason
before long."

There were numerous questions from the press. How much
freight was being carried? What did it consist of? Was the
plane full of fuel and was that why it burned so fiercely? The
answers revealed that it had been carrying less than half the
number of passengers it could, only a fairly small freight
consignment of normal goods, and adequate fuel for the 2,000
miles to Johannesburg. It was by no means overloaded. It had
been carrying perhaps fifty percent of its possible payload,
but thirty-two seconds after leaving the runway the plane hit
the ground in a nose-up attitude, causing the tail section to
be torn off, and caught fire.

As the technical questions were being answered, I wondered how Earl could keep from saying to Lufthansa, "I told
you I was going to get off in Nairobi."

Then Earl went back to the hotel, and Jock and I went to
buy clothes, combs, and toothbrushes—everything for them.

82   BETTY LESLIE-MELVILLE

The Moorhouses had nothing—no luggage, no money, no passports—everything was gone.

It was evening when we got back to the hotel room. Earl told us that some survivors had already boarded other flights back to Europe, where they could recover in the peace of their own familiar surroundings. They were exhausted, so we said goodnight, and as Jock and I lay in our bed holding each other, I told him, "I'm glad Dancy called to say she arrived safely. Oh, Jockieduk, this crash is so terrible . . . but it's so poignant, too. Imagine the Africans giving them their only shoes—you know they can't afford another pair, and their giving blood . . ." I started to cry, and Jock patted me to sleep.

The next morning we called them—they were fine, and yes, they would love to come to our house for lunch. It was a very cheerful meal and afterwards we went to Nairobi Game Park, where the boys were thrilled with the lions and zebras and hippos, then back to the hotel. It was then we learned that one German lady, who had escaped from the wreckage unscathed, decided to rest on the beach under the palm trees by the Indian Ocean in Mombasa. She hired a car and driver to take her there, and had been killed in a road accident on the way.

And we also discovered what had happened to the missing person. He had fled blindly from the wreckage, somehow missing the helping hands, and had kept going until he reached the road, where he was picked up by some kind souls who took him home as their guest.

The following day we took the Moorhouses apartment hunting—remember, they were moving to Nairobi. We found a suitable apartment, which the owner had half promised to somebody else. "But these people were in the 747 crash," Jock told the African landlord.

"In that case they need it more. I'll have it repainted tomorrow, and they can move in right afterwards." They stayed for dinner and seemed fine.

But the following day I picked them up to take them to the apartment, and halfway there Lynn started to scream hysterically. My first thought was that perhaps a snake had slithered into the back seat, where she and Garrett sat, but it was the movement of the car along the straight road that had evoked a similar sensation to roaring along the runway.

Thus, four days after the accident the shock hit Lynn. She went to pieces, and that night Earl and the boys began to have terrible nightmares. It was the beginning of a period when Brendon and Garrett couldn't sleep, except in the same bed with their parents; and as well as the bad dreams, Garrett started weeks of sleepwalking and clambering over the furniture looking for a door and his way out. For many of the other survivors it was the same—a delayed shock that only surfaced four or five days later.

So, suddenly and quite understandably, everything closed in on the Moorhouses. They didn't want to move into the apartment and they didn't want to say in Nairobi. They wanted to go home to family and friends and places they knew. They could not bring themselves to fly, so Lufthansa paid for their sea trip from Kenya to South Africa.

We've had many good letters from them, and nearly a year later Lynn wrote in one of them: "Garrett has had nightmares for months. He seems a little better now, but is still anxious about traveling (he doesn't trust anyone). Brendon would happily travel in anything. He is now convinced of his power to escape from all danger . . . Perhaps when he grows up he will be the new Houdini."

And so the tale has a happy ending for the Moorhouses, and for the other survivors too.

Sometime later, Earl flew to Nairobi for another environmental conference. It was the first time since the accident that he had been in an aircraft. He arrived on a Lufthansa 747.

Jock asked him, "Aren't you afraid of flying?" to which he replied, "No, of crashing."

"Things always happen in threes," my mother always used to say. And so they did. The second drama after the air crash had a sadder ending for us. Jock's eight-year-old nephew went fishing on Lake Naivasha one Saturday afternoon with his little friend and his friend's father. They didn't call or come home for dinner, or all night, nor the next day. When there was no sign of them anywhere, Jock got a little plane and began to fly over the lake to search for them. As the heart-stricken days passed, other planes joined in the search, and it wasn't until five days later that all three of their bodies appeared on the shore. A hippo had bitten the boat in two, and all three of them had drowned.

It was unbearably tragic and so sad, and watching Jock's suffering made it even more painful for me—I loved him so.

Most people think of hippos as funny birthday card animals, but they are extremely dangerous when they are out of the water. And can they run! Jock and I have had an angry hippo chasing our car at thirty-two miles an hour—that fast. In the water they are nasty as well. On the Kasinga Channel in Uganda, an average of 200 fishermen get killed by hippos each year.

The third shock came at Christmas. A friend of ours, a very pretty young Irishwoman, her husband, and their two daughters were trimming the tree Christmas Eve at Malindi. As she plugged in the lights on the tree, she was electrocuted. One daughter ran to her and got stuck to her by the electricity. Her other daughter, who had on rubber thong sandals, pried them apart, but the mother was dead. Her husband, who had just had an operation and was in a wheelchair, watched the entire horrendous episode. Jock, the children, and I were at Malindi, too, and we spent a sad Christmas morning at the funeral.

When we returned to the house for our celebration, I read a poem of Sean O'Casey to everyone: " 'I have found life an enjoyable, enchanting, active and sometimes terrifying experience, and I've enjoyed it. A lament in one ear maybe, but always a song in the other. ' " I told the children, "Life is sadness *and* it is joy. We've had our sadness, now it is time for our joy."

Tragic as it was, the good that came out of it was a realization of what we did have—happy, healthy children and each other. Tragedy brings you up to getting your priorities in order and appreciating the really important things that we so often take for granted. When we all gave thanks that day at dinner, it wasn't for the turkey or the bicycle or the new camera, it was for the wonderful gift of life and love.

Chapter 9

THE next year, 1973, Jock's mother died, and Jock inherited all the seventeenth- and eighteenth-century furniture his father had shipped from his estate in Scotland to Kenya in 1919. His family's grand piano, for example, was taken 300 miles to their farm from the port of Mombasa by ox cart on a dirt track, and their possessions had such sentimental value for Jock that he didn't want to sell any of them. We also now had all the furniture Karen Blixen had given to Jock's mother, and we needed a larger house to accommodate it all.

Even before this we had halfheartedly been thinking of looking for a larger house, so we'd have enough room for all our friends and all our children's friends who were constantly arriving from various spots on the globe to stay with us. So we looked and looked and finally fell in love with a lovely old dilapidated mess with grass growing over the windows and bought it. "But you can't *live* in there," friends advised us. However, it was solidly built from hand-carved stone and needed nothing structural done, and Jock and I could see that with some cleaning up and decorating it would be our dream house. And it was.

Isolated, it stood on 200 acres, yet it was only eleven miles from the center of Nairobi. We could afford only fifteen acres, but the rest of the land remained completely wild. Our quarter-mile dirt driveway was through the forest, and the road leading to our property had no name. We lived on "No Thru Road," the nearest sign read.

The twenty-two-room house had tall sunny windows, five fireplaces, and a history. Sir David Duncan, the MacIntosh toffee king, had built the house in 1932 for his wife to play bridge in when she came to Nairobi from their home up-country. Their only neighbor was Karen Blixen, who lived two miles away. When the Duncans moved to South Africa, the house was then used by British Intelligence as a head-quarters during the Mau Mau emergency. Later it was rented to an American couple with the CIA, who kept their horse in the two-story entrance hall, as well as their cheetah, which ran up and down the massive double stairway for its exercise all day, living inside, too. They also had a chimpanzee which swung from the minstrel gallery and took a bath every night in the Italian black-painted glass-walled bathroom.

Jock and I shoveled out the mess, moved in, and loved it (that is everyone but Shirley Brown who refused to get out of the car for three days). It became even more than our dream house, because there was a surprise that added another dimension and unwittingly started the most extraordinary chapter of our lives. Wandering about our property were three huge Maasai giraffe, whom we named Tom, Dick, and Harry. They'd nibble our trees and flowers, then just stand on our front lawn and stare at us, silhouetted against snowcapped Mount Kilimanjaro, 130 miles away, which on a clear day loomed into view. Jock and I sat in our sunroom, looking at the tallest animals in the world standing in front of the tallest mountain in Africa, and as the sun went down and turned the snow pink, he hugged me to him. "Betty, what more could we possibly ask for in this world? We have all this and each other—how presumptuous it would be to ask for any-thing more."

Yet we got even more.

A few months after we had moved in, a friend called to ask a favor. He had an 18,000-acre ranch on which lived the last remaining Rothschild giraffe. (The Rothschilds are dif-ferent from the other two non-endangered species in that they are the only ones that have five horns—the others having three. They also have white legs.) Our friend said he had sold his ranch to Africans, who had split the land into ten-acre plots and now the giraffe were knocking down their fences and destroying their crops, so, understandably, the Africans were poaching the giraffe. Knowing our property supported giraffe with the right food and climate, he asked if we would take a Rothschild so that there would be at least one left. "After all," he pleaded, "you'll be helping save an endangered species. There are only 130 of them left in the world. There used to be some in Uganda, but with the Idi Amin situation they've all been destroyed, You could really help . . ."

"But we don't know anything about giraffe," Jock told him. "I'll talk to Betty and call you right back."

Of course I was all for it, and although Jock was intrigued he was skeptical, but to please me he said yes, and once again we decided to get involved in something we didn't know anything about. He picked up the phone. "How do we get one?"

"There's only one way," our friend answered, pleased. "Jock Rutherfurd. He . . ."

"I know him," Jock interrupted. "We went to boarding school here together . . . Go on."

"He managed my farm for years and foresaw what would happen to the giraffe when I sold it, so he experimented capturing some in order to move them to a safe place. He's the only man in the world who's crazy enough to catch a giraffe from a horse, but it's the only way you can do it on this land. It's pocketed with aardvark holes three feet deep and two feet wide, which are hidden in the grass. You can't possibly drive a car across it and to gallop a horse is lethal, but he's got a horse as crazy as he is—they'll do it."

"They'll tranquilize one?" Jock asked.

"No, baby giraffe and sea lions are the only two animals that can't take tranquilizers. He'll catch it himself from horse-back."

"He'll lasso it, you mean?"

"No, he doesn't know how to lasso, he just grabs it. Listen, don't worry, he's done it before." (He didn't tell us his chances of being killed about equaled his chances of staying alive.)

"How can we reach him?" Jock asked.

"When I sold my place he pushed off. I don't know where, but if you leave a message in every bar in the country for him to contact you about saving these giraffe, he will."

We did, and six weeks later Rutherfurd arrived at our house carrying a warm Tusker beer. Shaking Jock's hand, he said with a winning smile, "So you committed matrimony, eh?" I guess I expected a Clint Eastwood type, but he was short and blond and had an interesting way of crinkling up his nose when he laughed, which was often. He was so anxious to save the giraffe that he quickly agreed to capture one for us. "After we get it we'll put it in a stable up there for a few days, then we'll bring it down here to Nairobi."

"How?" Jock and I asked in unison.

"In a mini-bus." His nose crinkled up and he reached for another beer.

So the following week we took the seats out of the back of a Percival mini-bus, and Rick, Shirley Brown, Jock, and I drove merrily off to the ranch at Soy, 225 miles to the north, and met Rutherfurd for the capture. The other member of the suicide mission was an African named Kiborr, whose one-eyed horse was gay. Thank goodness, because if he had not been in love with Rutherfurd's mentally ill horse, Douglas, he would never have followed him over the hazardous course, and we would not have been able to get a giraffe.

We wished Rutherfurd and Kiborr luck as they rode off, with all the zeal of Kamikaze pilots on speed, over the terrain booby-trapped by aardvarks right into the middle of a herd of giraffe. They were all traveling at about thirty-two miles an hour, and the men looked like tiny ants amidst the mass of giant animals, which kicked wildly at them and occasionally did somersaults when their feet went into one of the aardvark holes.

Our hearts pounded as we watched this mad scene through binoculars. Rutherfurd was following the technique he had told us he would: Giraffe put their babies out front to protect them, so he was boring through the center of the herd, with flying hooves just missing him, to the front where he cut a baby away from the others. Then after he and Kiborr chased it away from the herd, Rutherfurd rode alongside the racing baby and, still at a full gallop, threw his arm around its neck, then jumped off Douglas and fell to the ground, wrestling with it. If Rutherfurd won, we'd have a giraffe; if the giraffe won, we'd have a funeral.

When we saw Kiborr galloping up to Rutherfurd and the giraffe with a rope, we leapt into the bus and, with Rick walking in front and directing us to dodge the holes, arrived where Rutherfurd was holding his prize. Panting, he grinned, "It's a girl!"

Kiborr beamed. *"Twiga ni mzuri sana."* (Giraffe is very good.)

She lay uncomfortable and undignified in the grass, her huge brown eyes glaring at us through the longest lashes I'd ever seen. I touched her, she was like velvet; her soft mane was golden brown and shaped as perfectly as if it had been cut by Sassoon—she was unbearably beautiful. I fell in love. I kissed her nose, I patted her on her head, I talked to her in baby talk, telling her her name was Daisy and how much we loved her. She hated us.

"Let's get her into the bus," said Rutherfurd, wiping the sweat from his brow.

Have you ever tried to get an eight-foot, four hundred–pound giraffe who was mad as hell into a mini-bus? But somehow, dodging kicks that came sideways and backwards and forwards, and a lot of pulling and tugging and pushing, Rutherfurd, Kiborr, Jock, and Rick got her into the bus. I helped a lot—I stood there wringing my hands, wincing, and fretting. Rutherfurd took the horses back, and Rick and Kiborr held Daisy in the back of the bus while Jock drove and Shirley Brown looked at her, perplexed, and I patted her and spoke softly to her. Then with great difficulty we got her into the stable, which had been padded with bales of hay.

It was painful to see her so frightened and I wanted to open the door and set her free to join the herd once more: Yet I knew that she, along with all her relations, would be poached.

"Leave her now," Rutherfurd instructed, swilling down his warm Tusker, "let her calm down till morning. We'll try her with some milk then. She's got to drink it within forty-eight hours."

"She is so lovely," I said as we walked away.

"Hey," Rutherfurd smiled, "do you know the word for giraffe in Arabic is *zarafa*, and it means 'lovely one'?"

"I didn't know that," Jock said, "but I know they used to be called 'camelopard' because they thought they were a combination of a camel and a leopard."

That night we lay in our tent, in one camp bed, too excited to sleep, and talked about Daisy and the capture.

When Jock moved over to kiss me, the uneven weight caused the camp bed to topple over and we fell on the floor, in a puddle of water—the fall had knocked over our water carafe! We had to hold our noses to keep from laughing and awakening Rick and Rutherfurd, who were in tents on either side of us.

The next day we tried all day, but the lovely camelopard would not drink; nor the next. As the hours went by, we loved her more and more and she hated us more and more. Forty-nine hours later, Daisy still hadn't taken a drink, and as Jock and I stood at the stable door coaxing her, unsuccessfully, to do so, we felt hopeless and so terribly sad. Then suddenly, for no apparent reason, she walked to Jock, who was holding the pan of milk, put her face into it, and drank and drank and drank! Then she looked at Jock and bent down and kissed him. And from that minute on Jock was her mother.

On the way back to Nairobi, Rick and I sat with Daisy, who was sitting folded in the back of the Percival bus, and Shirley Brown sat next to Jock. He drove into a petrol station and said, "*Saba juu* ("Fill it up"), and you can imagine the attendants when, instead of the usual tourists inside, they saw a giraffe. We were nervous all the way, and although Daisy didn't complain, she certainly was not happy.

In Nairobi we got her into a *boma* (pen) we had had built for her, and because it was colder than we had thought it would be, we hung a torn and smelly tarpaulin from the back of the bus in her corner to block some of the cold. Well, like Linus and his blanket, she fell in love with it, and for the next year or so she rubbed against it, hid behind it, peeped out from under it and over it, and was totally besotted with the awful thing.

That first night she drank her milk when Jock gave it to her, kissed him good night, and exhausted, sat down in her padded pen and went to sleep immediately.

Rick, Jock, and I, also exhausted, sat down to a bowl of soup. It was not until then I remembered. "It's Thanksgiving!"

"Soup on Thanksgiving?" Rick frowned.

"Never mind," Jock told us, "we may not have a turkey, but do you know anyone else who got a *twiga* for Thanksgiving?"

The next morning she was delighted to see us, or at least she was delighted to see her mother Jock, who, after feeding her milk, gave her some slices of carrot, trying to buy her affection. And did it work! She loved them; and suddenly our life was filled with carrots. They were everywhere—in our pockets, in my purse, on the window sills in the house, on the bedside tables, on the bathroom floor. Daisy was a carrot addict; and Jock and I were giraffe junkies.

Obsessed with her, we did everything we could think of to please her. We snapped off branches of the thorn tree in the garden for her to eat, and she was delighted. After a few weeks the tree was disappearing, so we sent our gardener sneaking around to a neighbor's to filch some, and then we sent Rick's *syce* (an Indian word, used also in Kenya, for someone who looks after horses) out on one of his horses to places farther away every morning to steal some more. One day, when Jock was giving Daisy her noonday milk, she nudged his thumb. He held it up and she took it into her mouth and began to suck it. She'd suck for about thirty seconds, then drink a few sips, then nudge his thumb and suck some more. She would suck only his thumb, and eventually mine, but no one else's. I kissed her constantly—her breath smelled divine. Usually one says someone has indescribably bad breath, but hers was indescribably good. I'd never smelled anything so sweet before, probably because I don't kiss too many people who eat only leaves.

It did not take her long to develop a definite personality, often acting like Sarah Bernhardt. She laughed, sulked, pouted, played, had moments of ecstasy, confidence, insecurity, and showed many other facets of personality that would make a psychiatrist reel.

Before we got her we had decided we would never keep her captive, nor would we ever have any fences; after keeping her in the *boma* for six weeks until she got used to us, we decided it was time to release her. Everyone was nervous, afraid she might run away and we might never see her again—that is, everyone but me, and I was hysterical. Tensely we opened the gate of her *boma* and sang "Born Free." She wouldn't come out. "Come on," we coaxed and pleaded and finally bribed her with carrots to take a step, then another out into the big world, but she would not leave Jock's side.

Full of wonder, she followed Jock everywhere, tasting all the leaves he pointed out to her (he knew which ones Tom, Dick, and Harry liked). The thorn tree was, of course, her favorite, so after a few hours we left her at one to nibble contentedly and started to the house to get some coffee; she left her meal immediately and came running right up to the gravel driveway which she sort of tiptoed across, then right up the steps to the house to go inside with us. "Betty, we cannot let her inside," Jock insisted. "She'll slip on the waxed floors." So we had coffee outside with her. Finally she folded herself down on the lawn for a little rest, keeping an eye on Jock to make sure we didn't leave her sight. When we got up to go into the house again for lunch, she quickly got to her feet and came running up the steps again, so we had lunch outside with her too; and for the rest of the afternoon we all just hung around together until it was time to put her to bed in her *boma*.

The next days were carbon copies of the first—the thorn tree diminished, the blue flowers disappeared altogether, the orange and pink bougainvillea bush looked naked. She even ate the bamboo and cactus. Everyone else has trees and shrubs that grow, but ours got smaller each day. Eventually she let us go in the house, but she would peep through the library window if Jock was making a telephone call and put her head through the window over the lunch table, just to make sure he knew she was there. She had imprinted (bonded) on Jock totally. I was a herd member—she liked me fine, but she loved her mother Jock. Soon she grew used to our being inside part of the time, but because she would not go to the forest to eat without Jock, every evening the two of them would go off to the edge of the woods and Jock would stand there with Daisy (bored) while she ate. Then he would give her her bottle and his thumb, and only then would she go to bed with her tarpaulin.

Soon Daisy developed a wretched habit of going on walks in the woods with Jock, Shirley Brown, and me. She was delighted to have us in her restaurant. Too delighted—she wanted to play with us. She'd charge at us playfully, so that if we didn't get behind a tree we'd be mown down. Each charge culminated about ten yards beyond us, and she would stand there stripping leaves off branches until we had gone another fifty paces, and the whole rotten business would start all over again. "Jock, this really frightens me. I thought you said giraffe didn't go on walks," I complained. "She's just too big to play with us like this."

"She wouldn't want to play with you if she didn't like you so much."

"I wish she hated me. I'm not going on any more walks."

So do you know what Jock did? He made me a sandwich board out of burlap sacking stuffed with kapok, and presented it to me. "Now you can go with us. It's to go over your shoulder and will go down below your knees." He was very pleased with his creation.

I wasn't. "What am I supposed to do? Wear it with rubber knee boots and a motorcycle helmet? I wouldn't even go in a suit of armor." I reneged on the walks.

After a few weeks devoted to adjusting Daisy to her freedom, Jock had to go back to work. Unbelieving, she'd watch him drive off in the morning, then stand in the same spot in the hot sun all day, as if she were planted and growing there. Not even carrots would entice her to move. When he returned she'd run up to the car, put her head in the window, kiss him, then run around in circles. "We've got to do something about this, Jock. It's so sad, she's miserable when you're gone. But today I thought of the solution. We have to get another giraffe to keep her company."

"Oh, God," was all he said.

And so we went back to Soy with Rutherfurd and Kiborr, and it was the same movie all over again. And I fell in love again. Only this time it was a boy. Where Daisy was three months old when we captured her, he was only three weeks old, and because he was smaller and I was now used to giraffe, I was not gun-shy of him as I was of Daisy; and he imprinted on me. He was so adorable and such a good actor we named him Marlon. (Yes, after my favorite movie star.)

Daisy, for whom we had gone to all this trouble, hated him. We spent a lot of time paying attention to her and finally erased her jealousy, and soon, like all children everywhere with new babies, she just ignored the kid, then tolerated him, and finally, when we released him from the *boma*, became his friend. And they became friends of the warthogs which also live on our property.

One day when the Cronkites were there and we were all watching the giraffe, Betsy said, "It's enchanting just watching them walk across the lawn."

"Karen Blixen called them 'giant speckled flowers floating over the plains,' " I told her.

"They walk like the sea," Jock added. "But watch, they'll come running to us when we call." And they did. Betsy and Walter were giving them some carrots when a warthog we knew appeared with a tiny new baby. It was then that Walter became intrigued with the little thing, and we named it Walter Warthog (and never told him later on when we found out that it was a girl).

When the Cronkites left, Jock said, as we strolled back to the house at dusk after feeding Daisy and Marlon, "Our life is flawless. It gets better and better. We've been married nine years now and I'm more in love with you now than when we were first married. Imagine my not falling in love until I was thirty."

"I fell in love the first time when I was three. I made my father take me to see him every Sunday. I would stare at him and he would stare back at me with those black eyes of his, and I would melt. I wasn't fickle, my love never wavered . . ."

"I'm jealous. What's his name?"

"Robert."

"Do you still love him?"

"Oh yes. But he died, when he was just twelve years old."

"What from?" Jock asked, growing kind now.

"From lung cancer. He smoked too much."

"At twelve?"

"Yes. Robert was a gorilla in the Baltimore Zoo. I love gorillas."

He hugged me. "Would you like to go to the Congo and see his wild relatives?"

I threw my arms around his neck and kissed him. "Oh yes!"

Chapter 10

FOR two years, in somewhat desultory fashion, Jock had been trying to get landing rights to fly to Bukavu in Zaire (formerly the Belgian Congo) to see the gorillas. Being used to living in Africa, we were not unduly disheartened never to receive a reply to our standard cable, "Request permission fly Bukavu to film gorillas." So you can imagine our surprise, after two years, to get an official response. The telegram read: "Impossible film gorillas from airplane."

What are ya gonna do?

Jock had telephoned Jack Block, our good friend with whom we planned on going, and he renewed efforts to get in touch with Adrian Deschriver, the gorilla man who knew officials in Bukavu; and by taking advantage of a shortwave radio link used by Belgian missionaries, instead of the moribund Zaire network, we were finally granted proper landing rights. Jack had just telephoned Jock and told him.

"Hurray! Does that mean we can fly in without fear of being shot down?" I asked Jock.

"Yes, of course." He paused. "Except over Uganda and Tanzania." (The only two countries we were flying over.)

The following night we invited the group going to see the gorillas, and Eric Risley, to our house for dinner. Eric was the only person we knew in Nairobi who had made the same expedition.

"A big male—a silverback who leads a group—can weigh up to five hundred pounds," he told us, "and is sixteen times as strong as a man." The "think bubble" over my head had sixteen Arnold Schwarzeneggers being done in by one gorilla.

"They are very gentle," Eric's voice continued to the rapt candidates for the trip, "but you mustn't run from them. If they charge, you must stand perfectly still or they could wring your head right off your neck." He sipped his wine.

"How can you not run?" Doria Block wondered aloud.

"Can someone tie me to a tree?" I asked.

"Once," Eric continued, "Mushamuka, the lead silverback, grabbed Mshenzi, the African game warden, by the ankle and threw him over his shoulder like a pinch of salt. Luckily he landed in a bush and wasn't hurt."

Gentle? I must have looked anxious because Eric smiled at me. "Don't worry, Betty, they've never been known to charge or harm a female." I could imagine all the men in our party going up the mountain in drag.

Eric lit a cigarette and looked at it. "I always give this up two months before I go to visit the gorillas. All that climbing in the high-altitude rain forest. Must be fit, you know. Very tough climb, very tough."

That was too much for Doria. She decided not to go, but out of sheer gorilla love, I was still determined. To hell with my head being wrung off and/or perishing from a heart attack in the 10,000-foot-high rain forest. I would fulfill my dream of seeing gorillas in the wild.

The next morning I called a friend to say goodbye. "We're off to see the gorillas in Zaire."

"That's very dangerous," she said.

"I know," I answered, not without a tinge of pride.

"Friends of ours were just there, and they blew up the car right in front of them."

"Blew up the car?"

"Yes. Blew up the car," she repeated slowly as if to a child, "with dynamite."

Long silence. "Betty . . . are you there?"

Finally I laughed. "We're going to see the *gorillas*, not guerrillas."

We got a giraffe sitter for Daisy and Marlon, and as Jock

and I said a misty-eyed farewell to them and Shirley Brown, I told Jock I felt a tinge of disloyalty at deserting them, even temporarily, to switch attention to a hairy primate that could wring my neck.

Half an hour later we were taking off in Jack's Cessna—Jack, Jock, and I, Dr. Esmond Bradley Martin, an authority on wildlife and a good friend, Dave the pilot, and Rick, who was in a high state of glee having received the trip as his Christmas present from us (in July) when Doria dropped out at the last minute.

I don't like planes, have never believed in the law that keeps any of them aloft, and, gazing out at a large herd of zebra below, I tried to force myself into imagining that they were a school of zebra fish swimming in the Indian Ocean and that I was viewing them from a glass-bottom boat instead of from the air. Also, I fretted over Eric's words, echoing now from the night before: "You must never fly around Bukavu after noon. It's the worst weather in the world—terribly tricky winds and sudden, violent electric storms, mountains everywhere. No, it's definitely not advisable to fly except in the morning. Three of the six regular Bukavu pilots have died this year," he continued happily, "and not one plane has been found. The forest is far too dense to see through, and the canopy of trees just closes over a crashed aircraft."

I was beginning to think it had been a mistake to invite him to dinner. Well, it's early in the morning, I comforted myself, we'll be there before noon; and for the next hour I found something else to worry about! Although everyone assured me that a flight plan had been filed and permission granted to overfly this area, as we did, I envisioned Tanzania mistaking us for an attacking Ugandan plane, or the trigger-happy Ugandan air force picking us up as the spearhead of an invasion from Tanzania, about which Amin was paranoid at the time. Dave was well aware of the warring situation and flew very high all the way, altering course to conform exactly with the border, so that either side would be confused. Dave pointed downward and said, "We've just crossed over into Zaire." Glancing down, I saw the mountain slopes rise to meet us. Roads snaked through the forested slopes, but not one vehicle—only miles of empty snakes through really spooky country, just a mass of jungle. The search party will never find us, I thought.

Peering down, Jack Block said cheerfully, "Remember when those thirteen United Nation soldiers had an emergency landing down there in the days when this was still the Congo?"

"Yes," Jock answered. "They survived the crash, miraculously."

"Only to be eaten by cannibals," Esmond reminded everyone matter-of-factly.

Eaten by cannibals! You can see I was having a nice time. Soon we began our descent, however, and through the haze ahead we could see Lake Kivu. The pilot talked mystical aviator's lingo into his radio and static answered. Then I worried how Dave could ever understand the response—it sounded to me as if he were communicating with a deranged robot—but Dave looked confident and told us with a grin that the control tower had given us clearance to land. "Is there radar?" I asked stupidly, and everyone just laughed. The "control tower" turned out to be a tin shack with no windows, just a man sitting inside with his back to the airstrip.

The "airport" was a euphemism as well. There were no permanent buildings, except for one tightly locked prefab called the "Salon d'Honneur," which was for the sole and private use of President Mobutu Sese Seko, which loosely translated means, "The rooster that leaves no hen intact."

"Betty, you must be relieved that he's not here today." Jack laughed.

The Africans working at the airport spoke no English and we spoke no French, but everyone was happy in Swahili. Dave pointed to the Cessna and addressed a man wearing oil company overalls, "Fill it up for our return trip please."

"There is no petrol," he answered pleasantly.

"No petrol?" we all said in unison.

"Oh, no." He smiled. "We haven't had any petrol for two years."

"No petrol for two years," we all repreated, as if we were a Greek chorus.

"Well, we'll have to get it in the next city," Rick suggested.

Dave fiddled with the filler cap on the wing. "The next city to the west is Kinshasa, twelve hundred miles away, Nairobi is only six hundred miles, but I don't have enough petrol to get back. I suppose I could make it to Rwanda and refuel there, then come back for all of you . . ."

The man in overalls interrupted, still smiling, "But there is no fuel in Rwanda either. There is no fuel in *all* of Kivu Province or Rwanda."

That was for openers.

"Let's go meet Adrian," said Jack. "He'll sort this out. First, where's the men's room?"

"There are no toilets," the African said, his grin widening. "No water either," he added happily.

Everyone had his hopes set on Adrian Deschriver as we climbed into a clapped-out mini-bus, but I had a sinking feeling as I remembered Eric Risley saying that he had once come to Zaire, having sent a dozen messages to Adrian, only to find that he had received none of them and was away on safari himself.

With no gas how were we going to get out of Zaire? Cable for another plane to bring us petrol? It had only taken two years to get a response to the first cable.

"If I were those guys at the airport and hadn't had any gas for two years," offered Rick as we bounced along, "I know what I'd be doing now—syphoning the gas that's left out of *our* plane."

"How many kilometers to town?" Jock asked, ignoring Rick, which meant he agreed with him.

"Two times ten," the driver answered. That's how they say twenty in Zaire.

As we approached Bukavu, Jack and Esmond, both of whom had been there before, peered out of the mini-bus window, alas-ing and alack-ing about how it had changed. Pointing along the lake's edge to boarded-up and falling-down buildings, Esmond said, "Those were elegant restaurants, and those dilapidated wrecks up there in the hills with tall weeds growing in their roofs were beautiful chalets."

"It used to be known as the Switzerland of Africa, and now it's just rotting away. It looks like the result of World War II," cried Jack.

Gone, too, were the surrounding coffee, tea, and pyrethrum plantations, as well as most of the topsoil. Since the steep slopes had been cultivated without the benefit of terracing, the lake was brown from the many little streams gushing into it from the hills like muddy soup, and the fish floated dead, killed by the surfeit of soil particles. The roads had craterlike potholes, and, worse, the manhole covers in the streets were gone. The driver told us they had been stolen. (What can you do with a manhole cover?) He drove as if in a Dodgem car at an amusement park, trying to avoid them. Not one traffic light worked but there were so few cars about it made no difference—the formerly elegant and alive town had disintegrated. Tattered Africans with sunken, defeated eyes stared at us as we alighted from the rusting mini-bus and climbed the steps into the magnificent Hotel Residence, which had once had a menu boasting delicacies imported from Paris. The floors were marble, but the elevator, an ornate cage in gold leaf, didn't work. We checked in and walked up three floors to our huge suites with high ceilings, torn rugs, and an elaborate French telephone in each room, which of course didn't work either, and no hot water. But there was a fantastic view of the lake and the mountains in the distance, and of garbage and dead rats on the streets below. Jack Block, fastidious owner of the famous Norfolk Hotel, the world-renowned Treetops hotel and the best lodges in Kenya, was numbed.

The minute Jock and I were alone in our room, Jock beat his chest and said, "Me King Kong. You Queen Kong," and, imitating a gorilla, walked toward me with his knuckles almost dragging on the floor.

But just as he was about to throw me onto the bed, Rick

knocked on the door. "Adrian Deschriver's downstairs in the dining room. Join us there."

"Damn," said Jock.

I patted his face. "Come on, I can't wait to meet him."

Going downstairs, I said, "The intrepid gorilla man—I bet he's a tanned Tarzan type, rough and grizzled, probably sweaty, and gruff in speech . . ."

As we stepped into the dining room, the first person I saw was a mild and pallid man of middle age and medium build in a pale blue shirt and neatly pressed pants. He looked like the local bank manager. I was about to walk past him when he approached with a self-effacing manner and in a soft voice said, "How do you do, I'm Adrian Deschriver. We're about to take the lunch, come to the table please."

Looking around the dining room, I could see the remains of the splendor that had once been. There were heavy wooden beams and chandeliers in the beautifully proportioned room, as well as bits and pieces of leftover antiques. Two African businessmen were having lunch, but otherwise it was empty except for our party of seven.

To soothe our anxiety about getting petrol, Adrian explained right away that he could acquire some smuggled gas for the plane—so let them syphon out what little remained in the tanks. Reassured, we picked up menus and Adrian laughed, "No sense looking at those—we take whatever we get. I haven't been able to buy the meat, the milk, the coffee . . . *rien du tout* for two years." He spread his hands and shrugged. "There isn't a Coca-Cola or a soft drink because the factory ran out of diesel fuel—and nothing is imported anymore. The government ran out of money and could pay no bills for things from abroad. You can see the roads are terrible, no autos . . ."

There was not even Evian water, which Eric had insisted we buy in bottles, having warned us against drinking the water.

As we waited for our surprise meal, I asked Adrian how long he had been in Bukavu. "I was born in Brussels," he replied, "and my parents brought me here to the Congo Belge when I was eight years old." Then he stopped as if he had said too much. We egged him on and he continued shyly in heavily accented and occasionally hesitant English. "My dream as a child was to be the hunter of elephants and I was lucky to see the commencement at the age of nine when I shot my first elephant. When I was old enough I became a—how you say—a hunter professional, and although I spent most of my time in the forest it wasn't for years that I discovered there were gorillas in there too. Then I made over three hundred trips in five years before I was able to get close enough to photograph even one."

Esmond asked Adrian if he knew Diane Fossey, who at that time was doing a study on gorillas in Rwanda. "Yes, but there are only forty gorillas there, and"—he smiled, making a joke—"in all of Uganda I understand there are only four . . ."

"Five," Dave cut in, referring to Idi Amin, "five."

"How many are there here?" I asked, expecting the answer to be perhaps fifty or a hundred.

"Between five and six hundred."

Rick asked him about poaching.

"Ah, poaching is not so much a problem," he explained, "because the government is tough and poachers are shot on sight, but the gorillas will become extinct anyway, just from natural devolution," He gave the word the French pronunciation. "They have only one baby every four years and the population is gradually shrinking. Gorillas are just meant to disappear, I think, but we'll probably never know," he went on sadly, "because man will wipe them out somehow before they reach their death naturally."

"Man, the greatest predator of all," commented Jock.

The waiter arrived with "lunch." The meat was inedible.

"Goat?" Rick asked.

"Probably rat," Adrian answered calmly.

No one could swallow it, so we had potatoes for lunch. Happily for the others, the last remaining industry in Bukavu (though it closed soon after we were there) was a brewery, which produced a passable beer called Primus at $4 a bottle; but not being a beer drinker I asked about the availability of wine, and was told, yes, indeed, they had wine. Prudently I asked how much? $40 a glass. Champagne, $80 a glass, so I didn't drink anything. And this was before inflation. Lunch, so to speak, was $25 each, which even by New York standards is rather expensive for six boiled potatoes.

Adrian told us that in 1959, before independence, there were 5,000 Belgians in the Bukavu area, and that by 1961 there were only a hundred left, and he was one of only four now remaining.

"Do they resent you?" asked Esmond, knowing the anti-white and certainly anti-Belgian feelings that still remain in Zaire.

"No." He shrugged and sipped his beer. "There was fighting in much of the country until 1967, when a hundred fifty white mercenaries were pushed back as far as Bukavu." Adrian looked at us in his quiet way and explained, "In one final day of bloodletting the mercenaries massacred two thousand Africans before running out of ammunition and crossing the border into the safety of Rwanda. I fought against them with the Congolese here. They have not forgotten it."

During the next hour we learned how the government in 1973 had taken over all the Belgian businesses and plantations without paying any compensation. What remained on the farms and in shops was soon stolen or fell apart, and the town had not functioned since. Thus ended Bukavu. In 1960, he told us, there had been 80,000 Africans enjoying proper jobs and a reasonable standard of living. Now there were 200,000 in and around the city—jobless, hungry, desperate people—all needlessly so, since the high rainfall and fertile soil is perfect for growing food and profitable cash crops. But the soil had mostly gone, washed away, because people were too indolent to terrace and conserve this God-given region.

Later Adrian drove us around in his car, running on smuggled gas, and we saw more of the ruins of what had once been a truly beautiful vacation and residential spot. Palm Beach turned Bowery.

I asked Adrian if we could go to the marketplace, because Eric Risley had told us that the Zairean *khangas* were particularly beautiful and had asked if we would buy two or three for his wife.

"A lot has happened since Eric was last here," Adrian told us. "The marketplace is out of bounds now. Even the police and the army keep away—it's too dangerous, too many starving people about. Dead bodies lie in the streets—you don't want to go there."

We didn't.

"Last week President Mobutu announced that the Belgians are welcome to return and claim their houses and plantations and businesses once more. But they won't come." He gave his shrug. "What's to keep them from being sent home all over again once they've rebuilt the region and made it again profitable?"

That evening Adrian took us to a restaurant where the decor was early formica but the meal, surprisingly, was excellent. Hiding in the kitchen, because she had no official work permit, was a Belgian chef. Groups of Africans, all men (the Zairean custom in Kivu is not to take your wife when you go out), sat at the other tables—probably government employees on fixed salaries from Kinshasa who could afford such living.

During dinner we mulled over the eternal question: Will the Africans ever succeed in lifting their own countries from Third World poverty? And sitting in this dead city of Bukavu, Jock and I were finding it hard to maintain our belief that it could in the end be done. As white people with our lives rooted in Kenya, we realized how lucky we were that we lived in practically the only independent African country which functions reasonably well. Having spent the afternoon seeing what had happened to Kivu Province in just a decade and a half, it would have been absurd if doubts about the future of much of Africa had not assailed us. Certainly the people were free of Belgian colonial rule and of much that was wrong with it, but it seemed they had used that freedom only to destroy an Eden and to bring themselves to the very edge of starvation and despair.

Our brief visit, however, concerned more pleasant things and soon we were talking about *the* subject. "The gorilla group I've built the good rapport with is led by Kasimir, a huge silverback," Adrian explained, "but they've moved too deep into the forest to reach in the short time you've got. Instead we're going to look for Mushamuka's group of about twenty-seven. Mshenzi, the Zairean warden, has established his links with them."

"Twenty-seven!" exclaimed Rick. "How many are usually in a family?"

"The largest I've seen was thirty-two," Adrian answered.

"Suppose we were to approach them without you or Mshenzi—what would happen?" Jock wanted to know.

"You wouldn't see them at all. They'd just fade into the forest when they heard you coming. We'd better get some sleep now. It's going to be a hard day tomorrow."

Back in our room Jock said, "Sleep? No! Love!" and we climbed into one of the hammocky beds and made beautiful love, then slept. We always slept together in one bed, even one berth on a train—we simply could not stand sleeping apart.

The following morning we were picked up by Adrian and Mshenzi—remember the warden who had been grabbed by the ankle and thrown over the silverback's shoulder like salt? Our car dodged its way around the potholes and turned up into the forested hills of the Kahusi Biega National Park. The painted sign at the entrance was a crudely executed head and shoulders of King Kong, like an advertisement billboard for the film, and the reality of what we were about to undertake hit me! *This* time I was not going to the movies or the zoo.

Adrian had founded the park in 1960, with the full support of President Mobutu, who despite obvious shortcomings nevertheless did believe in looking after the wildlife heritage in his country. But one of Mobutu's conditions, much to Adrian's disapproval, had been that tourists should be allowed in to see the gorillas. This explained my feelings that Adrian, although polite and friendly, was taking us under duress— that he disapproved of disturbing the gorillas with such invasions. I was inclined to agree with him, but not to the extent that I would forgo the experience.

There was a collection of buildings and huts at the park gate and we paused there. "I must pick up Patrice, my faithful gun bearer," Adrian explained. "First I hunted elephant with him and now we track gorilla together."

"Is he Belgian too?" Jack asked.

"He's a Pygmy."

And here in the rain forest of the mountain gorillas and the Pygmies, what did we see first? Seven Japanese men with cameras round their necks. I had regarded ourselves until now as intrepid adventurers in remote and inaccessible central Africa, and was only partially mollified to learn that they were a group of high-powered scientists who had been there for months making a film on the gorillas and were leaving. We would be alone.

The Japanese are not renowned for their towering stature, buy they were as giants alongside Patrice and six other Pygmies who stood waiting for Adrian. At a signal from Adrian, Patrice and the other Pygmies scurried over to our mini-bus and scrambled into it, bringing with them a distinctive odor, not unpleasant, but odd.

We set out on a surprisingly good tarmac road that climbed steadily into the 9,000-foot hills. The potholes in this road looked as if they had been mended, but Adrian pointed out that the work had been done just prior to a visit by the President, and lacking tar or proper road-repairing materials the holes had been filled up with earth, which was tamped flat and painted black to look like tar.

The dark green forest, thick with hanging vines and broad-leaved plants, crowded the road, and, after several miles of twisting up even higher, we parked. Then we milled around by the side of the road, slinging cameras and binoculars over our shoulders and tucking light waterproof jackets through our belts in order to leave our hands free for pulling ourselves up the densely forested slopes that lay ahead. Most of us wore tennis shoes, on the good advice of Eric, and the jackets were to prevent our getting soaked by sudden violent downpours that he had also told us to expect. Either we'd be cold from the showers, or else we would be unbearably hot through a combination of exertion and the high-altitude sun at midday.

Or dead?

We were a much bigger party than I had anticipated: I counted sixteen men and me, or rather nine men, seven Pygmies, and me. In Belgian days the Pygmies used not to be classified as human beings. (They were not classified as subhumans or animals either—their existence was simply not acknowledged by demographers.)

There was one Pygmy who looked much older than the others, and I was distressed to see that he was allocated by Patrice to carry a coolbox almost as big as himself, filled with Primus and a few soft drinks that Adrian had rustled up from God knows where. The tiny wrinkled fellow went to a nearby tree and quickly stripped it of long lengths of supple bark, which he used to make a strap around the box, arranging to carry it on his back with a loop of bark around his forehead taking most of the weight. I feared he would not get very far.

With a final glance at the car, and even the road—those symbols of civilization that I might never see again—I fell into line near the back of the column and took my first step into the dense green habitat of the mountain gorillas.

Squeezing Jock's hand, I whispered to hin, "It's—beautiful. It's unreal." There was an eerie enchantment of tall trees with lichen draped on their branches, forming a green canopy over our heads, through which the sun streamed in beautiful shafts of light. Vines hung down everywhere, better than the best film set that one could conceive for a Tarzan movie. There were little webbed paths made by antelope and forest hog, and one of the Pygmies led us along these with the assurance of a taxi driver threading his way across Manhattan. From time to time the paths would disappear and the little men would hack with *pangas* (machete) at the vines and bamboos until we intersected another path. For the first hour or so, we were very jolly, cracking jokes and laughing at each other as our feet got tangled in vines and we slipped and fell.

Three hours later nothing was beautiful or funny: it was the roughest terrain imaginable and, at that altitude, extremely hard work. On and on we went, with branches slapping us in the face and the stinging nettles reaching out to taunt us as we climbed over fallen logs, under bushes, around clumps of impenetrable bamboo, and through a large swamp with elephant grass as high as a gorilla's eye. My tennis shoes kept slurping off in the cold, ankle-deep muddy water of the swamp, and I would have to reach down through the mire to retrieve them before putting them on again.

On the far side of the swamp, the ground rose more steeply than ever, and as we began to climb it I found myself on all fours, the only possible way I could pull myself up the slippery incline. My heart banged in my chest, in my head, and through my whole body, and I started to giggle nervously, because I knew I was going to die—and it would be very inconvenient dying out here. What would they do with my body in the middle of the rain forest in the middle of Africa? Would the old Pygmy with the picnic box put that down and strap me on his back with the bark thongs instead? I took one last deep breath to announce to Adrian, who was four places ahead of me, that I was going to perish, but at that moment he turned and raised a hand for us to stop, then whispered something to Jack, who passed the message down the line. "The Pygmies up front have reported that they've just found a freshly made nest. We can rest now for a few minutes." I collapsed and lay prone, gasping for breath to bring me back to life.

What a gift this pause was, because now with a bit of luck no one need ever know what an unfit weakling I was, and as the only woman in the party, I hated to be the first to quit.

Other then Adrian, and Jock, who was raised at 10,000 feet and was also a mountain goat, everyone confessed to being just as exhausted, and not wanting to be the first to give up either. Jack Block threw himself on the ground and with a sign of fatigue lay back—right in a moist, fresh, generous dollop of gorilla poop. It was all over the back and sleeve of his shirt, and added to the exertion of climbing we now had to fight for extra breath to laugh. The smell was indescribable, and there and then, deep in the jungle, we drew straws as to who would have to sit next to him in the car.

Like Stanleys and Livingstones, we sat around in the dense jungle drinking water out of canvas canteens, while we tried to recuperate sufficiently to appreciate the sight and sound of the particularly magical spot in which we found ourselves. Adrian said, "Well, phase number one has been successful— we've made contact." Though there was nothing to be seen or heard, we had evidence in the shape of the nest and Jack's smelly shirt that we were in the gorillas' immediate vicinity. "Every day," Adrian explained, "each gorilla makes himself a new round nest of leaves on the ground, carefully arranging it with a hollow center—like a bird's nest for a giant—then lowers himself into it for the snooze. When they have had enough rest, they search for bamboo shoots, their favorite food.

"I was about to lose heart," he now confessed, adjusting his cap. "We've walked so far into the forest already; unless we'd come across them when we did, I would have had to make the decision to turn back so that we could reach the road and the car again before the night."

Glancing at his watch, he went on, "Their rest time is probably over, so they'll be somewhere ahead of us collecting food. Patrice says this nest is from last night, and, since they seldom move more than a mile or so from where they've slept, we should be close."

"Do Patrice and the gorillas get along well?" I asked, just able to sit up.

"They hate each other." Adrian grinned. "Gorillas hate Pygmies because they've been hunting them over thousands of years. And Patrice particularly hates them, because once he and his brother decided to kill Kasimir, my big silverback. But Kasimir killed Patrice's brother instead, with a single karate chop. So in revenge—the Pygmies are very big on revenge—Patrice went after Kasimir's father, who was even bigger than Kasimir, and this time Patrice succeeded in killing him with a poisoned arrow. Then he ate him. Raw."

Silence from our group.

Adrian continued nonchalantly, "For two weeks, Patrice returned to the rotting carcass every day for lunch, and the smell got so terrible I finally complained and asked him how he stood it. 'Stand what?' he asked. 'The smell,' I told him. And do you know what he replied? 'Oh, that,' he said, offended. 'We don't eat the smell; we eat the meat.' "

Just then the bushes parted, and Patrice and the other Pygmy who had gone scouting with him returned. Jack Block grabbed Patrice by the arm. "Why didn't you tell me you ate Kasimir's father before I came up here with you?" Jack teased in Swahili. "How do I know you won't eat *me*?"

Patrice actually fell down laughing.

"Was Kasimir's father tasty?" Jock asked him.

"Ummmmm, very!" Patrice answered with a great smile.

He and Adrian and Mshenzi went into a huddle to discuss the tactics of how to approach Mushamuka and his family. Then Adrian gathered us around. "From now on walk as quietly as you can, and please no talking. The gorillas are very near and we must not make any noise." Falling into line again, we made our way cautiously forward, stepping over little bamboo shoots, which the gorillas had picked and dropped. Excitement was high. We had been going about fifteen minutes when Adrian stopped and whispered to us in a worried voice, "I fear we are going to have a charge today. When we're not welcome, the lead gorilla gives a special odor—do you smell it?"

Sniffing, we certainly did smell something, but none of us gorilla neophytes could tell if it was the regular gorilla smell or the special warning-signal smell. Adrian assured us it was the latter and told us that whenever he smelled it he always stopped. We stopped.

I whispered to Adrian, "Why aren't we welcome?" and he said Mushamuka just didn't want visitors that day. I hate feeling unwelcome in any situation, but not feeling wanted by a band of wild gorillas on their own home ground made me extremely uncomfortable, so I suggested to the group we turn back. "After all," I pointed out, "it's not polite to intrude, and we've had a nice walk." No one paid any attention to me.

I noticed a couple of the Pygmies delving in a little pouch and then lighting a primitive pipe made out of bamboo, and in a second I got a whiff of something a little more familiar—*bhangi* (marijuana). Enraged gorillas ahead and stoned Pygmies behind—what's a nice girl from Baltimore doing in a place like this?

I also noticed that those in our party who had been eager to be at the front when we started out were now a little less pushy; in fact, there was a certain amount of unexpectedly polite after-you-ing, but Adrian beckoned us impatiently, and timidly we all followed. Once more he stopped and we waited tensely. There were sounds ahead of footsteps, followed by the noise of breaking bamboo and occasional fragments of gorilla chatter. Soon we could hear them plainly, but still we couldn't see a thing. It was very spooky. After a minute we heard the gorillas making their way down the hill toward the swamp from which we had just come, and we made our way back to the swamp, too. Adrian held up his hand. Urgently he put a finger to his lips as he cautioned us to be extra-quiet. The Pygmies now crept silently to the rear of the line, their job done—great gorilla trackers, but not great gorilla lovers. Adrian and Mshenzi were at the head of our line, the rest of us frozen, not moving. Quietly Jack Block leaned down and picked up a stick and touched the back of Rick's ear. Thinking he had been gorillaed, Rick jumped three feet straight up in the air, spinning like a ballet dancer and landing in a Kung Fu stance facing Jack. We had to hold our noses to keep from laughing out loud.

Adrian signaled to us that we were surrounded on three sides by the great apes. Very softly he whispered, "If Mushamuka charges, which I think is likely, you must not run. You must not even move. The only thing to do is to stand

absolutely still and look him in the eyes—even if he comes
to within a meter of you. You can take pictures, but not until
later, and when you do, raise your cameras very slowly—no
sudden movements or he might become violent. Remember
if he does, there's nothing Mshenzi or I can do for you, since
we cannot carry guns in the park."

I listened to these instructions as if my life depended on
them, which it did; but at the same time I knew I could not
simply stand there when a 500-pound silverback male lead
gorilla sixteen times stronger than Arnold S., came yelling
and charging at me and beating his goddamn chest. What if
he didn't notice I was a girl? Tension was building up more
than ever, and I sidled into the midddle of the men, and Jock
put his arm around me and held me close to him—perhaps
they'd all hold me if instinctively I started to run when the
great primate came to get me. Would my headless body run
around like a chicken's after my head had been wrung off?

Very gingerly we made our way along the side of the swamp,
about ten paces from the forest's edge. Once more Adrian
stopped us and pointed to a little cluster of bush about fifteen
yards ahead and gestured that Mushamuka was behind it. I
could neither see nor hear anything resembling a gorilla, but
from Adrian's and Mshenzi's stances just ahead of us I could
see how very tense they were. Although they knew he was
there, they had no way of knowing which way he would break.

Everywhere was silent and golden. The reeds in the swamp
were golden, the golden sun shone overhead, golden flowers
were all around us, and we stood in a clump like a bunch of
golden bananas.

No one moved. No one made a sound. Then very quietly
Mshenzi spoke to the bush. "Jambo Mushamuka," he said
softly.

"EEEEEKKKKK!" A chilling scream, a black FLASH, and
a huge hairy monster came bounding out of the bush toward
us. I felt a terrible stab of pain, then another, and again and
again all over.

We were standing on a nest of *siafu*, the marching "safari
ants" of Africa, and they were marching right up our legs

and fiendishly biting every one of us. From the corner of his eye Adrian saw us jumping and jerking and grabbing our legs and frantically reaching inside our clothes to pull them off—I even had ants in my bra—and he shouted in an angry whisper, "Keep still. They're only ants, this is a *gorilla*—he can kill you."

In fact, Mushamuka hadn't come directly at us but had veered in a mock charge across the front of us and stopped about five yards away and was now standing there glaring at us. Just at the moment when we should have been raising our cameras—very slowly—to record this highlight of our lives, we were having the bejesus bitten out of us by a mass of ants and were unable to control our spastic jerks from each bite. It was a Laurel-and-Hardy-see-the-gorillas scene.

Astounded, the great silverback stood and watched us; then on all fours he bounded off into the forest to join his family. He didn't charge again, but Adrian Deschriver almost did he was so angry, and I don't blame him. As the warden responsible for our safety, he was the one who would have been answerable for the incident, and we had invited just such a disaster by failing to keep still at the critical moment. Sheepishly, like scolded kindergarten kids, we took a few steps forward away from the ants and rolled up the legs of our pants to pick off the little bastards.

Then all of a sudden we could see Mushamuka again a little way up the bank to our left. Just above him a great hairy black arm poked out of the top of a small tree, reaching for berries at the end of a long branch, and at the right of Mushamuka we could see a female with a baby scampering off from behind a bush into the forest. Mushamuka eyed us for a bit longer. It was incredible to be so close and to see him so clearly—no more than a dozen paces away. He looked like King Kong's twin brother. He stared at us a while, more perplexed than angry, then shambled off into the forest.

By nature, gorillas are gentle, pacific creatures who would far rather move out of the way than have any kind of confrontation. Indeed, that is exactly what they had tried to do as we approached—they kept moving farther away—but for some reason that they could not understand, we had persisted and pushed Mushamuka to the brink of thinking it was time to scare us. He succeeded.

Adrian relaxed now, knowing that the charge was over and that it would not be repeated, and suggested that we, too, go into the forest and have lunch with the gorillas. They often joined him. But quietly, he reminded us, and if the gorillas did join us when we were eating, we should not move, we were to remain seated—above all we should not stand up.

We followed the gorillas up the slope a little way to a glade, and then flopped down around the aged Pygmy who had carried the heavy coolbox all the way, without a murmur of complaint or even the slightest sigh of fatigue. (I had noticed, though, that he was one of those who had taken repeated drags at the pipe). We could hear the gorillas all around us, moving about tantalizingly close but just out of sight, and the sound of their eating bamboo shoots was just like giants biting king-sized celery—"the woods are alive with the sound of munching," sang Rick. Then we heard a new sound—the beating of chests. It was not the hollow booming or thudding kind of noise I had expected, but instead was more like the rapid slapping of bare buttocks with a cupped hand. Adrian whispered that they beat their chests not out of anger, as early explorers had reported, but more as a tension-releasing action. So the gorillas beat their chests and the Pygmies smoked their marijuana . . . but what about *our* tension? I was tempted to reach for the pipe.

As we waited for the gorillas to join us, Adrian quietly unpacked the lunch and I have to admit the hard-boiled egg I ate didn't go down as easily as it usually does. I thought how, within the space of an hour, the gorillas had introduced us to a brand-new smell, a brand-new sight, and a brand-new sound. I didn't want any more new experiences. Rick, nervously tossing a boiled egg to Patrice, missed his aim by mistake, and hit Esmond on the head from behind, which understandably alarmed him considerably.

But Mushamuka must have warned his family that a bunch

of jumping-around crazies had arrived on the scene and that they had better stay away from us. And that was what they did; we never saw another gorilla. Our own fault.

After lunch we were faced with about a five-mile trek back to the tarmac road, but luckily a major game trail, heading in approximately the direction we wanted, made it easier.

When we reached the tarmac, a mile north of where we had left the car, Adrian smiled and congratulated me on how well I had done. "I'm actually surprised you made it. Most women, especially American women from cities, only manage a mile or two of this before saying, 'I can't go on.' "

"What happens then?" I asked.

"A Pygmy has to carry them back."

"Well," I said aside to Jock, "I'd rather drop dead of a heart attack than have the humiliation of being carried Pygmyback."

Since Bukavu had not been such a delight the night before, we planned to fly directly to Virunga National Park (formerly Albert Park), on the southeastern shore of Lake Idi Amin (formerly Lake Edward), to spend the night there at the lodge. We thanked Mshenzi and Patrice and the others and bade them goodbye, then headed for the airport.

Adrian was to follow us in his own little plane, which looked as if his mother made it. Hailstones the size of golf balls had put enormous holes through the stretched fabric wings of this quaint craft the day before we arrived, but he had Scotch-taped them and would fly along behind us. Alone, needless to say. Later on he flew this same sick airplane all the way to Nairobi, with a big drum of petrol (smuggled) inside, and hand-pumped it into his tank, which only held enough fuel for four hours—the Nairobi trip being six hours.

Exhausted, covered in mud, and appalled at the way Jack Block still smelled, the rest of us flopped into the seats of the Cessna for the half-hour flight. We had just enough fuel to get there. It was late evening and there were clouds everywhere, we had no radar, and on top of that everyone wanted to fly over 14,000-foot Nyiragongo, the only volcano in the world which is in a constant state of eruption. Everyone, of course, but me. The volcano was not my idea of fun but the others seemed to enjoy it. They oohed and aahed and said the scenery in this part of Africa was spectacular beyond belief and all those things. Jack told us that Adrian had once climbed to the lip of the volcano with his best friend to look down upon the vast, bubbling red lava lake below, and his friend had slipped and fallen into it, never to be seen again.

Jock held my hand tightly and whispered we'd be fine, not to fret.

Two elephant were on the grass airstrip to meet us. (You will note that I say "two elephant," but "several gorillas." I also say, "I caught seventeen fish," not fishes, and I never say, "I have four dog." Domestic animals and gorillas are plural, and the rest are singular.)

The lodge was splendid, even with, or perhaps because of, the two elephant which walked among the buildings and looked in the dining room windows. Though apparently placid, one of them had a tumor that was causing it such pain that it had killed a man the week before, and one of Adrian's tasks on the following day was to shoot it.

Eric Risley had told us about these elephant at the lodge, and also about another called Joseph, which would walk among houses in Vitshumbi, a nearby fishing village where the streets were so narrow that the huge animal could only just fit between the buildings and everyone had to scrinch up the doorways to let him pass. He was old and friendly, and children would actually swing from his tusks—a totally wild elephant that had reached a proper accommodation with man. "Just a natural city boy," Rick commented.

After lingering in a delicious hot bath, we met for drinks and dinner and a postmortem—happily not in the literal sense—of Our Gorilla Trip.

Jock, who has lived in Africa all his life and has had many extraordinary adventures, including being charged by buffalo and scared by a lion (the long stories), declared it an epic day—the best expedition he had ever taken. Rick said it was the finest Christmas present he could remember, and the rest of us raved correspondingly.

To paraphrase Shakespeare, "Appetite increases by what it feeds on," and now that I had seen gorillas in the wild for myself, my curiosity was not satisfied but heightened, and I couldn't get enough of Adrian's stories.

"When I'm by myself I don't simply go up to spend a few hours with them, as we've just done," he explained. "I spend days and nights with Kasimir's family. My particular friend is Broken Arm—she has a crooked arm from a fracture. Let me tell you what she does: The best bamboo shoots are the tender ones that have not yet come up out of the ground, and gorillas can detect these in some way and dig for them. I have no idea where to find them but Broken Arm does, and she also knows that I have a knife. She shuffles around, looks for the hidden shoots, and when she finds them she comes back to me and taps me on the arm, which is the signal that I must follow. Then she leads me to the spot and points to where I'm to dig then up for her, and I do. This goes on many times a day."

"She actually taps you on the arm?" I asked, amazed.

He nodded. "But I won't give her the knife."

We were all silent thinking about this for a moment then I asked, "Do you ever talk to them?"

"No. That would make me un-gorilla-like. They don't communicate much out loud. But I touch them and they touch me."

Jock and I said we talked to Daisy and Marlon all the time. Adrian just shrugged. Then Jock asked about the excellent documentary that was done on Adrian and the gorillas—we had seen it in the States on television—and were particularly intrigued by the part involving the baby.

Adrian told us, "I had heard of a baby gorilla being sold in a marketplace, probably taken there by poachers who killed the parents just to have the baby to sell. Pretending to be a buyer, I met the poacher and 'got' him." He sipped his wine. (I was afraid to ask exactly what he meant by that.) "Then

I took the baby, which was sick, to my house, and nursed it for a while. When it was well, I used to take it up to the forest to get it familiar with its natural surroundings, especially the cold and the damp, since I would let it go when it was big enough. They were making the film at the time, and on the last day of shooting we bumped into Kasimir, who was enraged to see me with a baby and, much to my surprise, came after me. He charged me and snatched it from me and carried it back to the other gorillas."

"We saw that in the film," said Jock. "It must have been terrifying."

Adrian smiled and continued: "What was *not* shown on television was that ten days later, when I went up again, the foster mother who had adopted it held it out for me to see. It was dead. It had probably died of pneumonia, and she seemed to want me to know."

I felt myself breaking out in goose pimples at the thought of this near-human act by a gorilla. There was a pause while we digested this, then Esmond asked, "You've been dealing with five hundred–pound gorillas for years now. Have you ever been hurt?"

"Only once—just recently, as a matter of fact. I was bitten in my own kitchen." He paused and I knew that this naturally reticent man was afraid that he was talking too much. We urged him on.

"I had heard about two babies that had been taken from a poached mother. They were for sale, and sick. I made a night flight and rescued them. One lay unconscious on the seat beside me the entire trip back, and the other was desperately ill as well. I took them home and nursed them back to health; it was during that time that one of them bit me on my leg. But now they love me—and everyone else. Except each other." He laughed. "They seem to say, 'I just can't stand that ugly thing—that hairy one with the pushed-in face.' "

"What'll become of them?" Jack asked.

"I can see they're going to be a real problem. My wife one day was trying to paint the living room, so she locked them out. They didn't like that. They wanted to come in, so they just yanked the door frame and hinges off and sauntered in."

Can't you imagine in the future someone being invited to Adrian's and walking into the living to find a 500-pound gorilla sitting on the piano stool, beating his chest?

We moved out onto the veranda and, over coffee, the conversation turned to flying. We had heard that Adrian had taught himself to fly from a book. He explained it quite logically: "The roads were destroyed after the fighting, and the only way to get around was by air. World Wildlife Fund had just bought a little plane for me, but there are no instructors here. What was I to do? I got a book, read it, and taxied the plane fast along the runway many times. Then one day I just took off. That was easy—getting down was not. The only thing that bothers me now are the terrible storms in this region. One day I did a mistake and lost control fo the plane *complètement*—I could see nothing, and the book said in that kind of a predicament to turn off the engine and put the wheels down, I did so, but I was still going up. Then I realized I was upside down." He laughed and shrugged.

"I hope you're going to write a book about all this," said Jock.

"I have the rough manuscript. But they want me to go to Europe to work on it. If I do I will come crazy back." He looked at his watch and stood up. "Because of the shortage of fuel to run the generator they turn the lights off at ten P.M." So we all made our way to bed and to our assorted gorilla dreams.

At dawn we met again for an early morning game run in the park. There was a moment of crisis while we waited for the only driver, who had been arrested the night before for smuggling, but the police finally told Adrian, okay, he could go to jail *after* he had driven us around all day, for which we were very thankful. We hoped it was petrol he had been smuggling and that he could give us a few tips, but discovered it was homemade booze. Perhaps we could fly the plane on that . . .?

Rick asked the driver if he thought we would see any hippos and he answered, "twenty-six thousand of them," and by the time we returned to the lodge for lunch, after following the river and driving along the western edge of the lake, we had a feeling he had underestimated.

We witnessed two more extraordinary things that morning. As we drove into Vitshumbi, the fishing village, we saw a crowd gathered on the shore near the dugout canoes, which were surrounded by hundreds of pelicans. We parked the car and as we walked up we could see everyone was intently watching something. We pushed our way through, and there lay six Africans on a cement slab on their backs, wearing only shorts, each holding a raw fish in his hands and eating it, eyes, head, guts, skin, everything. Revolted, I turned away thinking it was some kind of oathing ceremony, but we learned that it was village justice. The men had been caught stealing fish, and this was part of their punishment. "One thing for sure," Jock commented. "I'll never snitch any fish in Vitshumbi."

Then on the way out of the village we passed the open marketplace, where lots of people were milling around, and milling right among them were dozens of marabou storks. The people didn't shoo them away, and the undertakerlike birds seemed at home with everybody, just as if they did their marketing there, too. It was such an incongruous scene that we stopped a few minutes and photographed it. When we got back to the lodge I mentioned it to Adrian, who had been out shooting the elephant with the tumor.

"How long were you at the marketplace?" he asked.

"Five minutes," I estimated. "Why?"

"Too bad you didn't stay longer—then you would have discovered the reason the storks are there."

"Why?" Jock asked.

"Well," he answered, "there are no toilets in Vitshumbi, and as the people squat to defecate, the storks run up behind them and catch the feces—to eat—even before it falls to the ground.

No one said anything. Jack Block was the first to recover. "Marvelous," he exclaimed. "I'm going to take every loo out of all my hotels and lodges and put marabou storks in instead—it'll put an end to all plumbing problems."

Next Adrian quietly announced that he had eighty-eight gallons of smuggled fuel for us. How? we asked. "Well," he explained, "to get fuel, people mine gold in the Bukavu area and sell it to the banks. . . . Diamonds are also smuggled into Burundi from Zaire, so in fact Burundi is a diamond capital, although there were no diamonds in the country . . ." It was a long story and I still don't understand how we got our gasoline, but there it was, liquid gold. We paid triple the cost—happily—and spent the next four hours pouring it from four-gallon cans through a chamois to clean it, then into our fuel tank.

Soon we were aloft, skimming the rim of Nyiragongo again with its seething red lake. It was lucky that we passed when we did, for a week later, in an awesome eruption, the massive volcano hurled lava and ash and poison gases tens of thousands of feet into the air, killing some villagers on its slopes and burying part of the town of Goma, fifteen miles away. Eerily, the graveyard for Belgian whites was not touched. But we had no hint of this as we headed home.

We flew away filled with awe for Adrian Deschriver. And we knew we'd never forget his gorillas, either.

Not ever.

Chapter 11

As we drove into our driveway, Shirley Brown came running up to the car and gave us enthusiastic kisses as we let her in. I asked Jock if he thought Daisy and Marlon would remember us, and he said of course. The sun was just going down and on the lawn, right in front of the house, lay Daisy and Marlon with Tom, Dick, and Harry, the three wild giraffe, just beyond them. What a lovely reception committee. We stopped the car and walked toward Daisy and Marlon, calling their names, and they rose to their feet and came loping up to us, kissed us, then ran around in circles with glee. There was no question that they remembered us.

"We love them so much," I said to Jock later on over supper in the library before a roaring fire. "What is it that makes us care so much? Do you think it's their beauty? . . . their innocence? . . . their vulnerability? Anyway, aren't we lucky to have succeeded not only in saving their lives but also in making them so happy? But I worry so about the others up there, getting poached. . . . I wish we could save them too . . ."

"Now we're going to have the entire herd here?" he asked, taking a spoonful of the wild raspberries just picked from our property.

"I know that's impossible, but I know what *is* possible. In the States people organize charity balls and raise money. What if we had one here and then gave the money to the government to translocate them to a safe place? You know the government has had that plan for a long time and would do it now if they had the money. Look, they say it will cost five hundred dollars to move each Rothschild giraffe. If we could raise even five thousand, that would move ten of them, a breeding nucleus."

"But Betty, Nairobi isn't geared to charity balls and . . ."

"Let's gear it, then."

So with the help of the children and many friends, we got free food from the hotels, free liquor, free tables and chairs, a free band, free auction prizes, and we sent out invitations inviting people to come help save the endangered Rothschild giraffe. I was afraid no one would show up, but that night car after car arrived. And what a smorgasbord of people—there were British and Americans and Africans and Indians and Italians and Spaniards and Greeks and Swedes and Swiss and Brazilians and Germans, even diplomats from Turkey and Iran—over three hundred people in all.

Dancy and McDonnell and Rick and their friends volunteered, and they took tickets at the door and were bartenders and car parkers and raffle-ticket sellers for the night. We ate, drank, danced, and were merry until 4 A.M. Lecherous professional hunters were eyeing other than their wives, their boldness increasing as the level of the Scotch in the bottles sank. A turbaned Sikh danced with Lady Lindsay; Kim, now the Duke of Manchester, danced with a Greek lady; an African was jitterbugging with a pretty Indian girl in a sari.

When we had been organizing the gala, I told Jock, "I think we should have one special thing at the party, and I've an idea—remember I told you how I danced in those musicals in Baltimore? Well, my friend, Betty Harrison, who also danced, is arriving to stay with us the day before the giraffe ball. Now you have a hint, but my idea is still going to be a surprise for you."

"Oh, God," Jock muttered, smiling.

When I met Betty the following day at the airport, I said, "Guess what you're going to be tomorrow night? A giraffe's ass!" Secretly we rehearsed, and right after the auction on the big night there was a roll of drums, a dimming of lights, and a twelve-foot cloth giraffe, with eyes that lit up red, appeared at the top of the wide double staircase, and to the strains of "Sweet Georgia Brown" made its way to the center of the dance floor. Four suspiciously feminine-looking legs then involved themselves in a very professional tap dance routine, which brought prolonged applause and cheering from the enthusiastic crowd. After a few encores, both ends of the giraffe shed their disguise and revealed me and my friend, Betty, who used to dance professionally. As no one in Nairobi knew I was a dancer, they were very surprised, and as Jock and I lay in each other's arms in bed, having a postmortem of the entire evening, talking until after dawn, Jock told me, "You were the highlight of the whole evening." (However, I kept hoping something would come of my performance and was secretly disappointed not to have received any offers. But for one night, I comforted myself, I was a star and wallowed in fame as a tap dancer.)

The next day we waded through the debris and sat down like Scrooges to count our take. Over $6,000—enough to save twelve of the endanged species. Everyone in Nairobi had joined together to help rescue the Rothschild giraffe and had a wonderful time doing it.

The following week I said, "Jock . . . if we founded a wildlife organization in the States, so people could get their tax deduction when they gave money for the giraffe, we could probably raise enough money there to save all the *twiga*."

"How could we raise money?"

"Well, we could start by having a Giraffe Gala in the States."

So when we returned for our next lecture tour, we founded the African Fund for Endangered Wildlife, the acronym being A FEW, meaning there are only a few left. Our first gala was at the Explorer's Club in New York, and everyone came in black tie or in safari dress (and some with a black tie and bush jacket), except Sigourney Weaver, who arrived in a stunning leopard costume complete with tail. The big auction prize was a Percival safari for two; George Plimpton and Peggy Cass, both of whom had been to our house to see the giraffe,

volunteered to be auctioneers, and extracted outrageous prices
for all the auction items, because they made everyone laugh
and lose their heads—especially Jock and me, who donated
ourselves as "Maid and Butler Service for a night."

The man who bid the highest for us ($700) said he would
like us at his apartment the following week by six o'clock for
an eight o'clock dinner party he was giving for thirty-two
people. That morning I called him to confirm we would be
there and asked, "What are you having to eat?"

"A loin of lamb."

Jock and I arrived, were given appropriate uniforms, then
the host showed us the most enormous piece of uncooked
meat I have ever seen. "What's that?" Jock asked. "I thought
Betty said you were having lamb."

"No, I told her we were having lion."

"Lion!" Jock and I exclaimed in unison.

"Yes," he replied, beaming with enthusiam.

"You can't eat lion, it's inedible," Jock told him rather
rudely. "No one eats lion. Humans don't eat meat, which
eats meat."

"But I paid $180 for it and that's all I have to give them,
other than noodles."

"Where'd you get it?" Jock asked, thinking someone must
have shot it in the Bronx Zoo.

"New Jersey."

"*New Jersey?*" we said again in unison.

"Yes, in the safari park there."

"Did it die?" I asked.

"No, no. Lion overbreed so much there that they cull them
and sell the meat."

"But that doesn't make it edible," Jock said. However, that
was all there was, so since it was too big to go in the oven
we got a saw and sawed it in half, and boiled one part and
roasted the other. All the guests arrived, and as we were
serving and they'd ask what it was, we'd say "Lion," and
they'd laugh, thinking we were kidding, and they enjoyed it
hugely. Jock and I had noodles for dinner.

Some of the guests were incredibly condescending. They

tossed their coats at Jock, the "butler," without looking at him, and when I was helping at the bar and commented to one lady that I liked her bag, she was horrified that the "hired help" would talk to her. It was an interesting experience— afterwards we were both far more aware of how we acted toward waiters and coat-check girls. When we left, the host said he would give us good references any time we wanted.

We had raised $30,000 at the New York Gala, and now we had enough to give to the Kenya government's wildlife department to translocate many of the endangered giraffe to safety. We also started a "Save a Wild Child" campaign, and anyone who "adopted" a giraffe by sending $500 could have a giraffe named for him. So our giraffe have funny names: A Catholic lady adopted one and named him John Paul after the Pope; we have another named Intercontinental Hotel, and another Pan Am, and another Richard Chamberlain. We had had lunch with the real Richard Chamberlain in New York, and he arranged to come to Kenya and go on the translocation with us.

Now right here, I want to deal with something. I hate criticism (especially "constructive criticism"), and I don't want to be accused by you of name-dropping. Because we live in Nairobi and everyone in the whole world eventually comes there, and because we had written a book about Daisy and Marlon (*Raising Daisy Rothschild*) which was published in the United States, England, and Japan, and *Reader's Digest* condensed it in their world-wide edition; and because *National Geographic* and *The New York Times*, and *WWD* and *Town and Country* and *Life* and *People* (twice) did articles on us and the giraffe; and because we did the "Today" show again and Carson's "Tonight" show, people knew about the giraffe and wanted to come to see them. So we met lots of well-known people whom we'd never be likely to encounter were we living in the States. This was compounded by the fact that the news was passed along, "If you're going to Nairobi, I know some crazy people there who have these giraffe that put their heads through the dining room window at lunch." And next thing you know, Margaret Mead is having her thumb sucked by

Daisy, and Brooke Shields is feeding Marlon carrots from her own mouth.

Not to write about these things, just for the fear of being called a name-dropper, seems ridiculous when our spending the day with an Ethiopian prince or William Holden is more interesting than writing about someone no one has ever heard of. We never approached a single celebrity in our whole lives—they simply arrived in Nairobi, and I'm just trying to share our good fortune with you.

We were not jet-setters. We worked hard and flew coach on planes. So now can I tell you about the night we had dinner in New York with Frank Sinatra, and the night Marlon Brando came to dinner at our apartment in New York?

The Sinatras, the Cronkites, and Jock and I were having dinner at our mutual good friend Milton Gordon's, and Sinatra wanted to know what made the Rothschilds different from other giraffe. As we were telling him how only the Rothschilds have five horns, Walter said, "How can such horny giraffe be an endangered species?" Frank and his wife Barbara were charming, concerned people (their special concern is child abuse). When they offered us a ride home, Frank casually jumped into the front seat of his limo, and I was really disappointed that no one, not even our doorman, saw that we were riding home with Frank Sinatra.

Another night the Cronkites were coming to dinner at our apartment to see Walter's old CBS friend Jack Beck, a long-time friend of ours. We had earlier met Brando at Jack's house in California, and Jack called us that day and said Marlon was in town, too, could he bring him? I'm going to say no? To my idol since *Streetcar Named Desire*? Although in California he had arrived in a beat-up old station wagon and was very relaxed and friendly, he still made me nervous. Jack had warned us that he did not like making films and refused to discuss them, that the only reason he made them was for money, which he then gave for conservation in Tahiti or to American Indian efforts. That lunch lasted for five hours and I, who talked all the time, could think of nothing to say. Perhaps tonight I'd shine.

I was worse. We have only six forks in New York so I had to ask Marlon and the Cronkites and Jack Beck to lick theirs and hang onto them between courses, which I didn't mind doing, but that was about all I said all evening. I was remarkably dull and tongue-tied—just plain vanilla. Jock was amused by my feeble behavior; he was getting a big kick out of it.

Marlon is highly intelligent and fun. He was teasing Walter about how the newscasters were getting so Mickey Mouse that soon the news would be sung to snappy tunes. To demonstrate, Marlon stood up and started singing, so Walter jumped up and tap-danced along with Marlon singing the news that World War III had broken out.

They wanted to see our slides of the giraffe, but we didn't have a screen and living room walls were red, so we went into the only other room, the bedroom, to project them on the white wall there. Betsy sat in the only chair, Jock sat on the desk working the projector, and Marlon and Walter sat on either side of me on the bed. Boy, Betty, I thought, you've come a long way from selling eggs in Baltimore.

"What is the name of that giraffe?" Marlon asked me, pointing to Marlon.

"Marlon," I admitted, embarrassed that he was finding out I had been mad for him since I was fourteen. "We named him after Marlin Perkins," I lied.

When they left I went up to Jock and hugged him. "Wasn't it a fun evening?"

"Yes, but I'm not going to make love to you tonight—and maybe never again."

"Why not?" I asked, puzzled.

"Because you'll pretend it's Marlon."

I laughed and pulled him down on the sofa and sat on his lap. "Not only do I like you more than I like Marlon, I think you are *much* sexier. I love you, only you."

The next day, Valentine's Day, flowers arrived from Marlon with a lovely thank-you note, and he telephoned as well. George Plimpton also telephoned to tell us the *Village Voice* newspaper had just called him and asked him what was the most exciting kiss he had ever had, and he told them "Kissing Daisy Rothschild." Jock brought me almost a room full of daisies, my favorite flowers, and a big box of my favorite chocolates—Hershey Bars with almonds, but best of all was our romantic dinner in a lovely restaurant, just Jock and me— and our love.

We arranged another Giraffe Gala in San Francisco, and Anne and Gordon Getty, whom we had never met but who were on the committee, very kindly invited all sixteen committee people to dinner at their house, with us as the guests of honor. We arrived for the party, but the Gettys did not. The butler showed us into their elegant house and told us Mrs. Getty had just come home from the hospital and was unable to leave her bed, but would we come up to her bedroom and meet her? We did, and she was lovely and friendly and sorry she could not join us downstairs. The other guests, who were mostly friends of theirs, arrived and were properly attended to by servants—but no sign of Gordon Getty until about an hour later when he put his head into the living room. "Hi, everyone," he called happily. "Sorry I can't join you tonight, but you all know my passion for opera and it's Tuesday night. . . . Have a good time, see you later," and he disappeared, until we were all drinking brandy after a gourmet meal beautifully served by many servants. It was about midnight when he strolled in. "Everything all right?" Everyone enthused—we had all had a wonderful time. "Well, I'm going to bed—stay as long as you like. Good night," and we all stayed talking and laughing until way after midnight.

I told Jock later that I wouldn't mind having dinner parties at our house all the time if he and I could go to the movies.

When we finished our lecture tour it was time to fly back to Nairobi to meet Richard Chamberlain for the translocation of the first twenty-three giraffe to safety.

Chapter 12

RICHARD arrived and stayed at our Nairobi house for a few days, and our Malindi house for a week, then he, Jock, and I drove up to translocate the giraffe to Lake Nakuru National Park, where there were no other giraffe. Twenty-three of the ones old enough to be tranquilized had been captured, put in a *boma,* and were now ready to move. As we walked toward their *boma,* Jock asked what was wrong with me.

"I'm miserable. I'm looking forward to the idea of saving them but not the physical aspects of the translocation."

He put his arm on my shoulder. "Betty, in dealing with wild animals it is inevitable that things will go wrong, that some will lose their lives. It's your fear of death, isn't it?"

"Oh, I'm fine—really." But really I was dreading it.

We were met by Rutherfurd, Dr. Chawdry, the head of the capture unit, and his brother who was out from England and along for the ride. Rutherfurd told us that during the accumulation of the twenty-three giraffe only one had died from the tranquilizer and the others were fine. They had been together in the *boma* for two weeks, getting psychologically prepared to be a herd, so that when they were released they would not simply scatter all over the park but stay together and eventually breed. "We'll take them to Nakuru in the morning," he said, taking a sip of his warm Tusker beer.

"What about the remaining ones up here?" Jock asked Rutherfurd. "How are they?"

"Two were poached and eaten, and five were shot, probably

by the police to feed themselves and their dogs. Come on, let's go get another beer."

At the pub we went over and over the plans for the big event in the morning. Richard was so interested in every detail and asked many intelligent questions. All this time Dr. Chawdry's brother had been eyeing Richard, and suddenly he asked, "Are you Dr. Kildare?"

"No," answered Richard nonchalantly and quickly changed the subject. "I can't wait to get another look at these giraffe. I've adopted one, and I want to pick out my namesake."

Chawdry looked at his brother as if he were demented. "Kildare? No, his name is Richard . . . Chamberman, didn't you say?" Of course, Chawdry had never heard of Richard, but the Dr. Kildare series was rerunning in England, and his brother had obviously watched it.

Richard is not only handsome and intelligent, he is gentle, pleasant, sensitive, and very witty; he has no star ego. In our kitchen, for the trip, he had made a marvelous snack of cashew nuts, peanuts, dried apples, apricots, and raisins, which he had put in a big plastic bag and passed around the car. Now, on our way back to the *boma*, he complained, "All the apricots and cashew nuts have been poached; only the peanuts and raisins are left." Then he made up a very funny song and sang it all the way.

The giraffe in the *boma* stood happily and just stared at us, as is their custom, as Richard picked out his stepchild. And my heart went out to each one. Please don't die any of you, please get to your new home safely.

The next morning Rutherfurd and Chawdry climbed into the *boma* and waved small branches to make the giraffe move into the crates where delicious leaves had been tied, and into which the giraffe had been going for two weeks quite voluntarily to eat. We could see that the giraffe regarded them as happy places; and when, for the first time, men suddenly trapped them inside by sliding strong poles behind them, they looked a mite bewildered at first, then merely started to nibble the leaves.

Soon each giraffe was in its padded crate with the door

closed. Because the crates were already standing on round logs, they were easily pushed onto the backs of trucks that had been backed into holes dug to make them level with the crates. And soon the first eight giraffe to be translocated were ready for their hundred-mile journey.

We followed behind the trucks and laughed at the giraffe's heads sticking out above the cabs and their looking around amazed. I felt sorry for one because she wasn't tall enough to see out and missed the scenery the others seemed to be so much enjoying along the way. We crossed the Equator at nearly 9,000 feet in a chilling mist. "I bet this is the first time a giraffe has crossed the Equator," I remarked excitedly.

But Jock blew it by saying, "At least thirty million giraffe must have crossed just in the course of their wanderings." He patted my knee.

"But they've never been to Nakuru," I said, not to be outdone, as we came to the town. These giraffe had never seen buildings or cars or heard such noise and, although they were calm, they did look astounded. No less astounded were the people of Nakuru, most of whom had never seen a giraffe. African children began running behind the strange procession in true Pied Piper fashion, shouting and laughing. And then it was down a long hill, which afforded a panoramic view of the park. "What is that?" Richard asked in surprise, for amidst the tranquil colors of nature was an enormous mass of brightest pink and crimson.

"You mean that Pepto-Bismol pink?" I asked, pointing to it.

"Lake Nakuru has three million flamingos on it," Jock explained. "That's what you're looking at." Richard could not believe it until magically the colors flew away and there was a lake after all.

As the trucks drew up, the uniformed Game Scout on duty at the entrance to the park came sharply to attention. Peering in disbelief at the lanky, speckled cargo, he pointed at a sign prohibiting people from bringing animals into the park. (We'd always assumed it meant dogs and cats.) "You can't come in here with those," he shouted at the lead driver.

Now he tells us—after two years of fund raising, ecological surveys to make sure Nakuru is a suitable habitat for giraffe, endless meetings with government officials, files, approvals, licenses, red tape . . . *now* they aren't allowed in the park? But it turned out it was his first day on duty, and no one had told him about the translocation. What had he thought? That some people were taking their giraffe for an afternoon tour to see the flamingos?

Fortunately the unloading of the giraffe into their holding *boma* there was simple. The first two merely walked out of their crates and cantered into the *boma* for ten paces, looked around, then sauntered over to guzzle a thorn tree. As the others came out of their crates, they ran over to their friends to share in the feast and to compare notes about their trip and their new home. "See, Bettyduk," Jock whispered to me, "it wasn't so bad after all, was it? They're all fine."

As we departed, Rutherfurd and Chawdry and Richard and Jock and I all congratulated ourselves and each other, and Rutherfurd went and found some beer.

They brought the remaining giraffe down on successive days, and when they were all accumulated and had stayed in the *boma* for a couple of weeks, there was to be a ceremonial release by the Minister of Tourism and Wildlife. Richard had gone back to the States, but the rest of us met again and stood around under the towering yellowy green–barked acacia trees, watching the fifteen Game Scouts in crisp khaki uniforms form the guard of honor in front of the platform that had been erected and swathed in the colors of the Kenya flag. The twenty-three giraffe were milling around in their *boma* behind the dais, consumed with curiosity.

The wire mesh across the opening had been unfastened and was now held in place by a fancy green ribbon tied between the gateposts. Following the speeches, the ribbon was to be cut and the giraffe would bound into the setting African sun to freedom. The Minister of Wildlife was already an hour late, but who cared? Certainly not the giraffe.

Soon a shiny white Citroën CX 1000 swept down the grass track and the beautifully dressed official climbed out. Then, from a neatly buntinged dais in the middle of the African wilds, with the guard of honor at attention to one side, the impeccable Cabinet Minister read a formal speech with great dignity in which Rutherfurd, Chawdry, Jock, and I were congratulated.

The twenty-three giraffe composed the biggest segment of his audience. One of them, very rudely growing bored with the speech, decided to investigate the shining green ribbon and strolled over to the gate, bent down, seized it in its mouth, and gave a great tug, undoing it completely.

Another nervous official tiptoed over and tied it in place once more, just in time, for the Minister finished his speech, stepped down from the platform, and moved into position. Kenya newsreel cameras rolled, the Minister smiled into them, then cut the ribbon, stepping back quickly to avoid being trampled in the stampede as the giraffe bounded into freedom.

Nothing happened.

The nearest giraffe peered at the open gap before turning to nibble at a branch. The others ignored it completely. After a minute of embarrassed silence, half a dozen of the park staff went and tried to drive the giraffe toward the thirty-foot gap. Although they would go right up to the threshold, they would not go out but kept wheeling around and loping to the far end of the *boma*. They liked it fine right where they were.

So the Game Warden, the Minister, and Jock entered the *vlei* (glade) in an open Land Rover and roared around the *boma* trying to push out the reluctant giraffe. Finally they forced one to leave its prison, the others followed, and soon they were all at liberty in their new fifty-five-square-mile safe home, and the ceremony was over.

The Minister shook the necessary hands and everyone drove away, except Jock and me. We lingered for a few minutes, watching the happy culmination of much effort. Jock put his arm around me.

"Do you realize, Betty, that we have succeeded in getting a breeding nucleus of these rare Rothschild giraffe free at last in a safe place where they and their descendants can live forever?" He squeezed me closer to him. "We have saved an endangered species."

We kissed, then just stood and looked at twenty-three of these lovely creatures standing serenely not fifty paces from us in this beautiful place. Realizing they would not die, they would live and breed, I turned to Jock to say something, but the beauty of it choked me up, so Jock kissed away the tear on my cheek.

And as we left, the giraffe were sneaking furtively back into their secure *boma* again.

Chapter 13

"WHY are you saving animals when there are starving people?" we are frequently asked. It is a very good question, but there is also a very good answer. Aside from being an animal lover; aside from the fact that—like a van Gogh or Michelangelo—once destroyed, a giraffe, an elephant, or a rhino can *never* be re-created; aside from the esthetic value of animals—saving the animals *is* saving the people. Tourism is Kenya's largest foreign-exchange earner, and without the game literally hundreds of thousands of Africans would be without jobs: the game wardens, the safari drivers, the waiters in the lodges, the people who build the lodges, those who build the roads to the lodges, the farmers who grow the vegetables for the lodges, and so forth. The game must be saved to save the people by providing jobs for them. Kenya has an eighty per cent unemployment rate. Our slogan is, "Help the Africans help themselves"—based on the excellent axiom, "Give a man a fish and you feed him for a day, teach him how to fish and you feed him for a lifetime."

"Why doesn't the African save his own game?" is another question we hear often. Kenya is a poor country, with an average per capita income of about $300 a year; the government has other priorities, such as education and health, and there is no social security, no free medical facilities, no free education. Conservation is a luxury one can afford only if he has enough food to feed himself and his family, and is not plagued by malaria, bilharzia, and malnutrition.

Eighty-five per cent of the Africans never see the game.

On their wages (if they have any at all), they can't afford game park fees, much less a car, and you're not allowed in game parks without one. So they do not know the beauty of the game, or its economic value for them—only its threat, for, as the Rothschild giraffe did, the animals destroy the Africans' crops, their only livelihood, and so they become enemies. This is utterly understandable and utterly appalling. But what to do about it? How do we teach the African that the game is valuable to them? We had an idea and, like others, it came about by chance.

One day, not long after Jock and I had bought our house, we were taking a walk farther from home than usual, and we found ourselves in a most splendid forest. Trees taller than I had ever seen in Africa formed a canopy of lacy leaves through which the sun streamed, over the rolling hills and down to a twisting, sparkling stream that bounced and spilled on its rocky course into small waterfalls. We found small still pools where spoor of bushbuck and hyenas and a leopard had recently come to drink. Wild Maasai giraffe loped away in this secret wonderland as we approached, warthogs and antelope scurried here and there, birds filled the woods with music, and after some rain wonderful patches of open rocky outcrop sprung thousands of tiny wildflowers out of little pockets of soil trapped between the stone. We walked there every evening.

It was particularly astonishing because it was still within Nairobi's city limits. Inquiring, we learned that this land had been the boundary between the warring Maasai and Kikuyu tribes, which they had never crossed but left completely alone. We invited botanists out, who documented the forest as primeval, while ornithologists documented 164 species of birds in this small strip of about fifteen acres.

Whom did the land belong to? Jock came home one evening, depressed. "Betty, it belongs to an African who is going to bulldoze it down Tuesday to build a housing development. Can you believe it?"

"Oh, no."

We were very depressed, but Shirley Brown wasn't; she,

as always, was overly enthusiastic about her walk and tugging at our clothes to hurry us. Jock took my hand. "Come on, let's go. You know, if Shirley Brown were a person she'd be a real pain in the ass."

We paused in our walk to sit on a large rock in the stream, and sadly Jock said, "So this beautiful piece of untouched Africa, which has provided a home for animals and birds and insects for a million years, will be lost forever." He tossed a pebble into the water for Shirley Brown to retrieve. "I would like the poorest of the poor, those children who live in cardboard boxes in the city, to come here to see the animals and the trees and the stream—they've never seen such things. My dream would be to put some of the endangered Rothschild as well as a few Grevi zebra and other endangered species in here, then let the African schoolchildren come out and walk around, not only to see this beauty but to learn. We could make this forest a nature sanctuary—there isn't one in independent Africa—build an educational center and show films on conservation, so they'd know why they have to save the game. . . . I'd love to do that. Then I'd really feel as if I'd done something worthwhile."

"And it would sort of be a way to say thank you to Africa for all it's given us," I added.

"I asked the owner what he would take not to bulldoze the land and he said $80,000, but we don't have $80,000. Oh, Betty," Jock said, pulling me up from the rock and holding my hand as we continued our walk, "I wish I had some money, I guess this is the first time I've ever wished I weren't poor."

"We may be poor as far as money goes," I told him, "but we're the richest people I know—we live a very rich life. We have each other, and happy healthy children, and Shirley Brown and the giraffe, and a beautiful house and jobs we love, and we travel and we have our enchanted forest . . . for a while, at any rate." But I could see Jock was so distressed about the housing project that I tried to change the subject. "Look at these lovely wild orchids hanging from this tree."

"They are going to split this into two-and-a-half-acre plots."

"Isn't it nice these holes the aardvarks have dug serve as inverted apartment complexes for the hyenas? If I were a hyena, I would like to live here."

"We've never seen another person in here," he said, ignoring me.

So we mortgaged our house and acquired the property; and every evening, as we walked in our enchanted forest, we planned how to make Jock's dream of an educational nature sanctuary come true.

A few weeks later an old Arab friend of Jock's telephoned to say he had a hot prospect for buying our forest: This Arab friend of his would leave it untouched and put only one house on it, which he would use only about two weeks a year. His prospect is so well known that I shall call him the Sheikh of Araby. His emissaries kept showing up in Nairobi, usually to do other business but with a possible deal of buying our land, which they looked at time and time again.

We asked them to lunch one day and four of them arrived, wearing *kaffeyahs* and pink *dish-dashes* (long hats and pink robes), were very polite and courteous, and ate with their fingers. Yes, they had spoken to the Sheikh and he was very interested in buying our land. "Please ask him to come and stay with us and see for himself," Jock told them.

He would be in touch with us soon, we were assured. The weeks rolled by and we heard nothing from the Sheikh.

"Those damn Arabs . . . ," I complained. I was in a bad mood, so I took it out on Jock. "Everyone needs his own culture and after nine months here of nature and beauty and empty spaces and quiet and lots of British people and good taste, I am hungry for New York and neon signs and hot dogs and pollution and noise and dog poop and bad taste and our American friends."

"But Betty, last week you said New York is filthy, noisy, and dangerous."

"That's right, and isn't it wonderful? And that's what I want now. I'd rather go on safari in Henri Bendel's than here."

"Then let's go a few weeks before our first lecture, so you and I can just play in New York."

I threw my arms around him. "Jock, you are the most wonderful person in the whole wide world. You are so good to me always—what would I ever do without you?"

"You'll never have to do without me. You have made my life so joyous, so much fun, so . . . crazy, so good."

Thus we rented the house the next week, preparing to travel, and as always I was reluctant to leave the giraffe and Shirley Brown and had a tearful farewell. "If only I could explain to them we're coming back; if I could tell them I'd bring them a present and send them postcards every day . . ."

"Betty, the children are excellent giraffe sitters, they'll be fine," Jock comforted me. "We're going to fly to the moon together right now."

I ran my finger over the white spots on his teeth. "You're right—you're *always* right. I love you."

It was a dark and stormy night as we approached the airport. Our hand luggage, as usual, outweighed what we checked in. So we had to drag that to the departure lounge, walking up the only escalator in Nairobi, which has never moved. After an interminable wait on uncomfortable blue plastic seats, which seem even more uncomfortable at 1 A.M., we boarded and took our seats on the plane.

After a few minutes the plane started lumbering down the runway, then just as it took off and we were about 300 feet in the air there were three loud explosions accompanied by terrifying red flames outside. A hush began; nobody spoke a word. We were not climbing. I looked at Jock, whose face was grim. The flight crew began running to compartments labeled "Emergency" and getting things out like torches and knives and whistles. I knew we were going to crash. I didn't want us to die. As the passengers remained silent, I turned and looked at an Englishman behind me. He was reading a newspaper. How could he calmly read a newspaper as he was about to die? We had been scared out of our minds for fifteen minutes now, which seemed like an hour to me. "Why doesn't the pilot say something?" Jock asked.

As if he had heard him, the pilot finally broke his silence. "As you know, we had a little bit of trouble on takeoff," he said in his irritatingly calm British voice. "We are now going to jettison the fuel for forty-five minutes, then land again in Nairobi. Everyone have a drink on us."

"They're going to dump this fuel all over Daisy and Marlon?"

A grisly hour finally passed and the pilot said, "All right, folks, the fuel is gone, but now the tower informs me that they have no I.L.S.—that's Independent Landing System, and it's too foggy to land without it. Maybe we'll go to Mombasa . . ." He clicked off for a few minutes.

"How are we going to go to Mombasa with no fuel?" I asked Jock. "This is so misera—"

The intercom interrupted, "No, Mombasa's no good. The weather there is worse than here," he said matter-of-factly. He obviously was not going to panic. "We'll make the approach on radio beacons, same as we always used to." He permitted himself a little chuckle. "But I must warn you that if I really can't see you'll feel a sudden thrust of power to climb out of it and we'll try again." He was telling me more about his problems than I wanted to know.

The undercarriage came down, the flaps came down, then we waited and waited, slowly descending through dense cloud . . . and there came a moment we knew by instinct was shared by every passenger's deep intake of breath—we were down. Wild cheering broke out among the passengers, which means a few Brits said, "Jolly good," or "Good show," and everyone started filing off the plane.

The stewardess looked annoyed at us. "What do you mean you want to go home? You heard what the captain said, only just over an hour to fix the engine. We should be taking off about 4 A.M."

"Look," Jock said, "obviously we know Nairobi better than he does. Or is it just that you don't want to have to pay to put all these passengers up in a hotel, so you'll tell then every hour it'll be just an hour more? We are going home."

As we walked through the deserted airport, Jock said to me, "Lucky our tenant isn't moving in until tomorrow."

"Where have you come from?" the sleepy Immigration man asked.

"Nairobi," we told him.

"But this is Nairobi, you can't come from here." So we explained (and explained) to him, and then to the customs man, and then to the luggage people that we didn't care if our bags had to stay on the plane. They'd catch up with us someplace in the world. And we went home to the comfort of our own bed.

When we awakened at 10 A.M., we called the airport and learned the plane would take off about noon. Everyone from the night before looked terrible. They had sat up all night on the blue plastic chairs, and only some were given a proper breakfast because they ran out of eggs. The poor souls collapsed exhausted on the plane, but Jock and I enjoyed our daylight flight, admiring Mount Kenya, the Nile, Khartoum, Cairo, the Alps, and finally France and England, then on to the good old U.S. of A.

The minute we got to our New York apartment we found a message saying that the Sheikh of Araby accepted our invitation with pleasure and would be arriving in Nairobi in his own 727 in two days' time to stay in our house. With sixteen bodyguards.

We could not return because of our lecture commitments, but after many telephone calls we succeeded in conning Rick to be in charge of Operation Sheikh. "But you don't want his cooks and flunkies in the house," Rick shouted over the phone from Nairobi. "They'll push the furniture against the walls and do their cooking in the center of the parquet floors on an open charcoal fire."

"We can have new floors put in. We need him to buy the land, so we can put up an educational center and get our house back." I told him.

Rick sighed. "The people you've already rented it to might not like sharing the bathroom with the Sheikh and his harem."

"Look, Rick, the Sheikh won't stay long. Tell the people in there we'll pay for them to stay in a hotel for a few days."

"Mother, that is why they rented your house—to get out of the hotel."

"Work it out."

The next day Rick called us back and said he'd succeeded in a not too amicable agreement for the temporary eviction of our tenants and, as we didn't have enough rooms to accommodate all the bodyguards, he would have to pitch tents for them on the lawn.

As I walked through Bendel's, I bet I was the only person in the store worrying about the giraffe on their lawn running into tents and terrifying the armed Arab bodyguards inside.

All was made ready for the Sheikh. He never showed. Never cabled or called, and after a few days, our disgruntled tenants reinstated themselves. Though we assumed that was the end of the Sheikh chapter, to our surprise there was to be more, but we did not know it at the time.

We did our lectures, had a Giraffe Gala in Dallas and one in Philadelphia, and in New York we played in Central Park and ate hot dogs in a telephone booth one day when it was raining, and pushed our way through the Christmas crowds to Rockefeller Center to watch Santa Claus ice skating under all the twinkling lights, and as we walked by F.A.O. Schwarz, two life-sized stuffed baby giraffe peered at us from the window.

"I'm so homesick for Daisy and Marlon."

Jock put his arm around me, and we sang "Rudolph the Red-Nosed Giraffe" as we continued our walk on the streets of plenty. We passed a hotel for dogs (at $15 per night) and wished there were one for giraffes; we passed a young girl on a corner playing an excellent violin to help pay her tuition at Juilliard, and a man playing a trumpet on another corner, and I told Jock, "I wonder how much I could collect for the Rothschild giraffe by tap dancing on the corner of Fifth Avenue and 60th?"

The next afternoon, when Jock came in from the store, I was very excited. "Guess what? Daisy's going to be a movie star! We've just sold the movie rights for *Raising Daisy Rothschild*!" I told him all about it.

"You mean we might have enough money to build the nature center?" Jock was ecstatic. "Oh, Bettyduk, isn't this good news? We did such a good job writing that book together." He gathered me in his arms. "I think we do everything well together, and I have something in mind right now . . ." His blue blue eyes sparkled as he took off his sling.

People always asked us how we wrote together. Well, I was in charge of construction. I wrote all of the book, then handed it to Jock, who told me it was "incoherent, inarticulate, and ungrammatical." But at least I had his attention. Then he corrected it, added paragraphs and chapters of his own, and we worked together on the corrections until finally we had a book. It was a perfect working relationship because he never would have started and I never would have finished.

We loved writing and especially writing together. Did we ever fight about it? Sure—especially me. Jock was extremely easygoing, and I have a wonderful disposition as long as I have my own way. I have a temper and occasionally I would throw the manuscript across the room and tell him to write the goddamn book himself—all that; but he would merely smile and pick it up, and we'd start again.

And now we had sold *Raising Daisy Rothschild* for a film. (We got just about enough money to pay for our telephone calls to Nairobi, for the period we had been in the States, to find out how the giraffe were, not enough for even a start of the education center.) The producer had a reassuringly non-plush office on Madison Avenue. No Hollywood mogul but Mr. Nice Guy. Did we want to write the script? No—we didn't know how. (Mistake number 1.) Did we want to play ourselves? No—we didn't know how to act. (Mistake number 2—since when did that matter?) That night at dinner, Sidney Carol, who wrote *The Hustler* among many other successful movies, told us emphatically, "Take your money and walk away. What they'll do to it will break you heart." (Mistake number 3—we didn't listen to him.)

We thought the movie would be a *Born Tall* and that it would be a fun experience to have a movie made about us. It turned out to be the worst experience of our lives.

Chapter 14

THERE was a lion asleep in our driveway.

Now you may not thing that is odd, since we live in Africa, but the truth is that here in Nairobi we see more Kentucky Fried Chicken shops than we do lions. What made this particular lion really odd was that it was asleep in a cage in a truck in our driveway—and had come from Hollywood. A visiting lion, a tourist lion? No, a working lion flown in to act a part in our movie. At the end of the filming the lion would collect its money and go home, an eminently sensible way of going about the business because the alternative would be to capture and train a wild lion and then have to worry about what to do with the poor thing afterward. Lion rehabilitation is costly and time-consuming and a doubtful process in any case; a tame lion from Hollywood sidesteps all these problems.

However, this one did create a problem for Rick. We had forgotten to tell him about the lion in the driveway the day it arrived, and coming home late, he heard a noise from the parked truck and called "Jambo" (the Swahili greeting), assuming it was the driver. No reply, of course. He called again, louder, but still there was no response, so he pulled back the canvas cover and found his face six inches from the gaping mouth of a snarling lion.

The producer, animal trainer, and film crew had arrived that day, too. The trainer said that because Daisy was too big to play herself, and also because the stars might easily be injured by the kick of a larger giraffe, which insurance wouldn't cover, he wanted to capture three more to play her. Jock and I were busy trying to get all the endangered giraffe out of Soy by translocating them to safety, so it was not as if giraffe who were minding their own business in the wild were dragged in for the sake of a movie; therefore we agreed to keep the three new ones after the film crew left. Thus, as with Daisy and Marlon, the first giraffe captured for the film was provided by Rutherfurd and Kiborr on their horses.

He was such a happy little giraffe right from the start. Not shy or afraid of people, he was stocky and cocky and loved carrots, which he ate with great enthusiasm and sucked his bottle down with glee, then gave everyone a kiss and ran around in circles. We named him Milton Gordon, after our friend who had just agreed to "adopt" him.

I had Gordon to myself because the animal trainer, who was staying at our house, was busy for a week with his California lion (which he put in a cage under our bedroom window) and his dog, which he also had flown in to play Shirley Brown in one scene. Shirley Brown hated the dog, but not so much as the wardrobe woman they hired in Nairobi, because the American dog was making twice as much money as she was.

When a scientist told us the most important ingredient in raising a wild animal is love, we thought he was demented. But in dealing with Daisy and Marlon we had learned he was absolutely right. Giraffe are especially delicate, sensitive, high-strung creatures, so I was very busy giving Gordon lots of love, something as vital as food itself.

The trainer, however, was used to animals born in captivity, an entirely different thing. When he took over the little giraffe, be began jumping into its stall, which startled Gordon, and putting a rope around him frightened him, and pulling him around the lawn terrified him. The trainer neither sought nor listened to our advice, but of course we gave it anyway, reasoning that since we had been hired as consultants for the giraffe, and particularly since we were the only two people in the world who had spent the last three and a half years successfully capturing and raising two wild baby giraffe, it gave us valid views on the subject. But the trainer was having none of our advice and soon told us to stay away from Gordon.

Although the little giraffe had adjusted surprisingly easily to his new conditions, now that I, the one special person to love and to love him back, was taken away, he grew timid and afraid.

We told everyone again and again how important the love factor is and how if he were affection-trained we could lead him with a carrot just like a donkey, and no ropes would be needed; but the trainer said it was his job to have tractable giraffe and he'd do it his way, and the director said he had hired, at top price, the most professional animal trainer in Hollywood and had a contract with him. So Gordon was hauled around with a rope every day.

The actors arrived—Susan Anspach played me; Simon Ward, who starred in *Young Winston* and was wonderful, played Jock; and Gordon Jackson, who was Hudson the butler in "Upstairs, Downstairs" and also wonderful, played the bad guy in what Jock referred to as the regrettable script.

The next morning at 6:30 A.M. Jock awakened me. "Get up, it's re-valley time."

"Re-valley? What's re-valley?" I asked sleepily as he kissed me.

" 'What's re-valley?' You know what re-valley is."

"I don't know what re-valley is." I kissed him back and yawned.

"Re-valley is the sounding of the bugle early in the morning to awaken the . . ."

"Oh, you mean *reveille*. Stupid foreigner," I said, ruffling his hair.

" 'Re-valley' is the proper pronunciation," his said stuffily, but he didn't kiss me stuffily. "Oh, God, I wish they didn't need the bed downstairs right now."

"They need the bed now? That's okay, I couldn't make love to anyone who says 're-valley' anyway." I threw my pillow at him.

The bed was dismantled and hauled downstairs and reassembled for a scene where Daisy kisses the movie Jock and Betty good morning through the window. (Gordon couldn't reach the second floor yet, though the real Daisy could.) The trainer led the trembling little giraffe, who was not yet used to people, much less lights and cameras, down to the house and while the lights glared on him and people shouted and ran around him, they filmed him kissing Simon and Susan good morning in their bed over and over again. The actors as well as the entire crew all fell in love with him.

On his way back Gordon pulled so hard at the rope to get to the safety of his own *boma* that it was all four men could do to hold the little thing, and his breathing was so hard I feared he would die right then.

Again and again Jock and I begged the director and the trainer to let us handle him. We pointed out his terribly nervous reaction and warned that he would go into shock. "Stay away from Gordon," was the reply.

The poor little little thing grew thinner and thinner, and finally he became sick. We called Paul Sayer, our vet, who examined him and said he was far too frail to be trained anymore, the best hope for him was rest, and he told the trainer to let me be with him alone. So I went in and stayed with him, stroked him, and spoke to him softly. Though he still took the carrots I offered him, his little mouth, which was once strong and enthusiastic, was now listless and pathetic, and he sucked his bottle of milk weakly. But soon he knew I loved him because he began to nuzzle me and suck my thumb again. He looked at me through his long beautiful lashes, as if to beg me not to leave again, and to tell me he was trying very hard to live. He didn't want to die.

He did try very hard not to die, but it was too late. Three nights later, while he was standing up in his *boma* trying to nibble the thorn leaves I had left for him, he just dropped dead.

He was eight weeks old.

Forgive us all.

Jock took me in his arms and held me close, as I cried and cried about the unnecessary, disgraceful death of that little baby giraffe. Jock's eyes were filled with tears, too, as we clung and tried to comfort each other.

When we told Rick, who was working on the film, that Gordon had died, his grief manifested itself in anger. Enraged, he complained bitterly. They fired him.

Later that day my sadness turned to anger as well when the trainer and the director said we were conservationists, they weren't—they were film makers.

"Everyone hates animal trainers," he said, "but then they all fall in love with the cute little animals in the film—which they wouldn't have been aware of in the first place if the film hadn't been made," The director agreed.

Now we were really angry.

Jock in his coldest and most cutting British voice said, "It is possible to have adorable animals in movies and happy healthy animals at the end of the film."

And my temper erupted and I pointed my finger at them and hollered, "Get out of our house—all of you. Now!" So they packed up and left.

And were back the following morning. They asked Rick to come back to work. He told them, "Are you kidding?" They told Jock and me that since there were two more captured baby giraffe about to arrive from Soy, a boy and a girl, they had now decided to act on our suggestion and pay attention to the love ingredient and assign one person to each giraffe. The trainer said the male was unusable because he was so ill-tempered and kicked too much, so he assigned him to me. After four or five days of my sitting with him and sweet-talking him, and bribing him with carrots and milk—and being kicked at and hated by him—he finally came to trust me and soon started sucking my thumb and kissing me, so they used him in the film and I wished I hadn't made him usable. But because he had me and knew I cared and was there with him when he came back from his "takes" to comfort him, he survived. (And today, five years and 3,000 pounds later, he still sucks my thumb and kisses me and still thinks I'm his mother.) He is John Paul, the one a Catholic woman adopted and named after the Pope.

The little female giraffe, named June Murphy after the woman who adopted her, was assigned to one of the animal trainer's assistants, but she seemingly became so stressed she just collapsed. Paul Sayer came at once—her temperature had dropped right off the thermometer and her heart had stopped. Quickly he pulled a syringe out of his bag and jammed Dorpan (a heart stimulant) into her heart and got it pumping again. For two days and nights he and I stayed with her constantly, until finally she came out of her coma. If it had not been for Paul, I am certain she too would have died.

I then took her over completely, and because she couldn't work in the film anymore, she soon was happy, playful, and healthy. (She recently produced a beautiful baby girl.)

The animal trainer went to Soy, and Rutherfurd captured another giraffe (getting a concussion this time). But this one died soon after the capture, probably succumbing to the shock brought on by the chase and capture. Anyone who has dealt with young domestic animals, to say nothing of wild animals, knows that these things can happen. The second baby giraffe Rutherfurd got died the day she was brought to Nairobi, and the third one named Howard Gilman lived. (And today he is the proud father of June's new baby.) Of course I am convinced that if Jock and I had been at the capture both those giraffe would have lived, but perhaps I am wrong. We couldn't be there and in Nairobi at the same time, making sure the ones there were kept alive, which wasn't easy; but finally the filming was finished, the film people left, and the three film giraffe lived with us happily ever after.

There was no way to negate the giraffe's death, but the only way to keep animals from dying in films in the future was to try to prevent such things from happening again. Jock and I felt a responsibility to do this.

Animals have rights, too, but there is no one to speak out for them; so we decided we had to, and began our losing battle about Rights for Animals in Films. But that is another book.

We feared our film, *The Last Giraffe*, would be the biggest bomb since Nagasaki; we feared we would be betrayed, not portrayed, in it; but the giraffe were excellent, and the film

Jock and Betty (in necklace of giraffe you-know-what) at a Giraffe
Gala in Baltimore. (Fred Kraft, *Baltimore News-American*)

My children (*left to right*) Shirley Brown, Dancy, Rick, McDonnell (1978). (*Betty Leslie-Melville*)

The entrance hall to our house, the Giraffe Manor, in Nairobi. (*Betty Leslie-Melville*)

Jack and Miriam Paar, Jock and I on our way to see the Pygmies in the Ituri Forest. (*Randy Paar*)

Jock and I with William Holden's Rolls-Royce.

Daisy drops in for breakfast with Dancy, Rick, and me.
(*Jock Leslie-Melville*)

Our friend and visitor Richard Chamberlain loves to feed Daisy. (*Betty Leslie-Melville*)

Daisy and I training Shirley Brown. (*Jock Leslie-Melville*)

With Marlon and me, it was always "love conquers all."
(*Jock Leslie-Melville*)

Our giraffes sunning themselves on the lawn. (*Jock Leslie- Melville*)

An attentive Daisy moments after
giving birth to baby "Jean Coburn."
(*Jock Leslie-Melville*)

Jock, Betty, and the two born
freeloaders—Daisy and Marlon.
(*Marion Gordon*)

Jock. (*Betty Leslie-Melville*)

Jock on one of his
walks with Shirley
Brown. (*Betty Leslie-
Melville*)

was a big plus for conservation. And we now had three more giraffe, which enchanted us and filled our lives with constant joy.

When Daisy and Marlon had first seen the new babies arrive, they stared at them transfixed, and Marlon was so upset he had to suck my thumb for twenty minutes for reassurance. Then every day they passed right through their many acres of forest with its readily available trees in order to deliberately filch and devour the babies' leaves that we cut and tied on the *boma* for them. Pure jealousy, but soon they no longer felt threatened and grew bored with them. And now they are intimate inseparable friends (and I do mean intimate—Daisy just produced John Paul's offspring, another adorable female.)

Chapter 15

AT least Jock and I learned enough never to get involved with another movie again. But the children
didn't. They had finished school in Kenya, and Rick
had attended Georgetown University, gotten a degree in political science, then decided to return to Kenya to work in
films, Dancy and McD had gone to an elgant ski resort that
posed as a finishing school in Switzerland (which they claim
almost finished them). Then after going to "college" with the
musical group Up With People, they returned to Kenya, which
they loved and regarded as home, and Dancy got a job as the
stand-in to the lead in the "Born Free" TV series, and
McDonnell got a job in film production. So they were all
involved one way or another in movie making, which of course
also involved Jock and me, but only peripherally.

While Rick was location manager for *The Rise and Fall of
Idi Amin*, our library was used as the French Embassy and
the front lawn for the war. To film the scene where Idi Amin
built a hut so low that the British Ambassador would have
to stoop before him to enter, the film crew re-created this
hut on our lawn. The giraffe were fascinated and stood all
day watching the enormous thatched-roof thing go up. When
the crew finally left at dusk, they said they would be back at
6:30 A.M. to start filming.

To their distress, when they arrived at dawn in their generator truck, they saw that the giraffe had eaten the entire
set. Most of the roof was gone, and what was left was being

nibbled away by all the giraffe but Daisy, who had her head bent way down in the doorway auditioning for the part.

In the movie Rick also played the part of the American journalist who was killed by Amin's men, not because he was an actor but because he was the only American around. He had two lines and thought of himself as a soon-to-be star.

"Will you be at our dinner party tomorrow?" I asked him.

"Mother, I have to study my lines, I can't come to a party. And by the way, what agent should I get? Do you think my right or left profile is better?"

The rushes came back—his big discovery time was here! He walked out two minutes after he first saw himself—he thought he was dreadful. Poor baby. (Even though he was twenty-six at the time.)

Jock and I went to the premiere of the film in Nairobi, and as we walked into the theater's lobby we saw Abdullah, an African who had worked on the film as props person and whom we liked very much. We shook hands with him and asked if he was also in the film.

"Oh, yes," he said enthusiastically.

"What part do you play?" I asked.

"My head is the head in Idi Amin's freezer." He was very proud of his role.

"We'll look for you. Come sit with us?"

"Oh, no, I'm not going in. I can't afford a ticket." So Jock bought him one and never have I seen anyone more thrilled about the role his head played.

Since our cook and gardener and the *syce* for Rick's horses had never even heard of a movie but had watched it being filmed at our house, Jock and I thought it would be a big treat for them to go see it, so we gave them money for their tickets, a beer, and transportation to town, and tried to explain to them what a film was. We got blank expressions in return, but they set off for their big new adventure with great excitement, but when they returned a few hours later, they were very glum. "How did you like it?" we asked.

"Oh, it was terrible," they all answered, shaking their heads in sadness.

"Why?" we asked, surprised.

"Because Bwana Rick was killed. We are very sorry." We actually had to call Rick at work and ask him to drive home so they could see that he was alive. When they saw him, they laughed and laughed and slapped Rick on his back, and thought the film was not only splendid but real magic.

The next film Rick and McDonnell did was *Quest for Fire*, then *Savage Jungle*, with Tom Skerritt.

The night the film crew left, Rick, Dancy, McDonnell, and Jock and I were eating dinner, and they were telling us about the insanity of film making. Rick said, "This film company brought plastic human arms and legs from Hollywood to strew around the ground in some ghastly scene, and you can imagine the terrible time they had explaining the bloody limbs to the terrified customs man. The poor African had never heard of such a thing."

"Did you hear about the vultures?" McDonnell asked us. "They decided they had to have some vultures for the last day of filming, so they spent thousands of dollars to get a bird person to catch some, but by the time they were ready to shoot on their last day, it was dusk and the vultures, which had been struggling to escape all day, fell asleep and refused to fly—five thousand dollars down the movie drain."

"And so it goes in the movie business!" Rick shook his head and laughed.

"You know," Jock commented, "movie making is like a military operation. The logistics alone are like preparations for an invasion. Two hundred people have to eat, relieve themselves, get from here to there. The four-star general arrives (the producer), and then the three-star general (the director), then the sergeant (the production manager) arrives and screams at everyone and is loathed by all. Making a film is like being in battle—egos and temperaments fly like bullets."

"If I had only three words to describe movie making," Dancy said, "they wouldn't be 'glamorous' or 'romantic' or 'intriguing' or any of those things I always thought it would be—it would be 'hard chaotic work.'"

"Sure," McDonnell agreed. "Trucks start arriving at five forty-five A.M. and we're still working at eleven P.M."

Rick had traveled from London to South Africa with Otto Preminger, showing him all the locations south of the Equator where he could do his film, *The Human Factor*. He filmed part of it in South Africa and the rest in Kenya. When Otto arrived on the set in Nairobi, he walked right up to his production manager and congratulated him. "Marvelous," he said sincerely, "you've been here only one week and already everyone hates you. Congratulations."

Otto and his wife Hope, a lovely lady, and Lee Remick, another lovely lady (whose husband was assistant director), spent much time at our house, relaxing and playing with the giraffe and having meals, and we all became quite good friends; until Otto walked out of the country without paying a single bill—not to Rick or the Africans or Nicol Williamson, the lead, or any of the other actors, or the Intercontinental Hotel, where he put up the entire crew, including himself (he owed them $168,000—for which they sued). So Rick quit the movie business and got into the safari business and married instead. Bryony, his wife, is a delightful English girl who has lived in Africa all of her life, except for school in France.

When the "Born Free" series was over, Dancy, too, quit the film business and got a job with the Flying Doctors, as Sir Michael Wood's assistant. Together they flew in his little plane to remote areas in Kenya's desert, which might have a population of only twelve people, and she would help him operate.

Flying Doctors is an excellent organization that does tremendous good for the Africans and the tourists. Dancy asked Jock and me if we would help raise some money for them by giving a ball in our house, and of course we said yes. We borrowed a wooden mannequin from one of the local Indian stores, dressed it up in a green cap and mask and gown, put huge wings on it and suspended it from our two-story ceiling in the hall. All the young volunteer bartenders and raffle-sellers wore doctor's operating gear, too, and again the crowds arrived and the band played till four and we raised quite a lot of money for the Flying Doctors.

The next day was Saturday and Dancy had off. The phone rang and it was Rick for Dancy. "Remember Bob, my old school friend? He's just arrived in Kenya for the first time, and I want him to go to the game park. I've got to work, will you take him?"

She argued because she didn't want to go to the game park and finally said, "My car's not up to it."

"You can take my Roho. I'll ride out from town with Jock." So reluctantly she agreed. "Thank you, but I must tell you," Rick said, "Bob's not too happy about going with you. He thinks he needs a white hunter. You know what he said? He said, 'Aren't there lions and tigers in there?' Good old Bob— he doesn't even know there aren't any tigers in all of Africa. He's afraid of animals. The only reason he's here is to see me on his way back from a business trip to South Africa, but he should at least go to the game park. Thank you, dear sister—I owe you. Bryony and I will see you both tonight at seven-thirty at Mother and Jock's for dinner. Bye."

By 8:30 P.M. Dancy and Bob were not back. Jock called the game park, but the ranger who monitors the comings and goings had no report of anyone breaking down inside. At 9 P.M. Jock and I drove to the park entrance looking for a disabled car along the way. Nothing. Where were they? The night ranger at the gate confirmed that no one was inside and let us use the telephone to call home to see if they were back. They weren't. McDonnell and Rick and Bryony had been calling a few friends to see if they had gone there. Dancy is a very reliable person and Bob knew no one in the entire country, so it seemed unlikely they had made some spur-of-the-moment plan to visit friends and not call; but the boys were calling just in case—and probably to give them something to do while waiting the horrible wait. Nobody had seen them.

Jock tried to comfort me. "Perhaps they just decided to go into town to eat at a restaurant."

While we drove around the city to see if we could spot

their car parked near any obvious eating spot, McDonnell and Rick undertook the gut-twisting job of calling around the hospitals to check up on auto accidents. After some agonizing "Hold on a few minutes while I check the ones that have just come in" conversations, they were vastly relieved to be able to rule out a road accident.

As Jock and I were waiting to enter the traffic at a junction, suddenly we spotted Rick's Roho (which looked like a Good Humor truck without the writing or bells) passing. Relief, relief, but as is the way of such moments, we were full of both imprecations and fury at the same time, as we chased it and finally overtook them six miles later. I rolled the window down to yell at them, but it was an African chicken farmer and his wife in their Good Humor truck without writing or bells.

Back to the game park. They must be inside, we told the ranger, so he called the park assistant who appeared immediately in a Land Rover and said he'd go look for them in his car, and for the ranger, with his gun, to come in the car with us. We divided up the park and arranged a series of rendezvous with the park assistant, and the search was on.

At night the park is very spooky. Glowing eyes with no visible bodies moved everywhere; the roar of an unseen lion was too close, the whoop of an invisible hyena was right in our ear. We searched the forest, the Hippo Pool, Leopard Point, Campi ya Simba (lion camp), the open plain, and finally Kingfisher Gorge. Nothing had led us any closer to finding Dancy and Bob, and I was convinced by now, after midnight, that they had been eaten by a lion or their car was in a heap at the bottom of the gorge. Visions of their mangled bodies gored by a rhino danced in my head, and all the grizzly safari stories I'd heard over the years kept coming back to me.

On our third rendezvous with the park assistant at the southern gate, he told us that he had just received a radio call that a lion had been hit by a train just outside the park, and he was on his way to see how badly it had been injured, but he would come back and meet us at 2 A.M. at the main gate. We had driven around for almost five hours, and I was absolutely desperate as we headed for the main gate. Jock was trying to comfort me all along, but he was far too upset himself to console me.

As the gates came into our headlights I could make out a white . . . a white . . . Yes, it was! A white Roho, . . . and along side it two muddy but smiling figures. We all embraced and hugged, and Dancy and I cried too. Everyone talked at once—just a few minutes before, they had been spotted by the park assistant on his way back from the injured lion. They explained that eight hours earlier, at six o'clock, just before sunset, they had turned down a little track in the park to look for lion and got stuck in the mud, from which it is almost impossible to extricate a car without help. For over an hour they pushed in vain, while Dancy assured Bob another vehicle would come by before dark; but none did. Bob, the newcomer, wanted to walk, but Dancy wisely and correctly insisted they stay in the car rather than stumble into a hungry pride of lion as they made for the gate in the twilight. She told him the animals wouldn't approach them in the car, in fact, they'd deliberately stay away if they built a fire, but bumbling about in the bush and surprising sleepy or prowling animals is another matter that just invites an unpleasant encounter.

By chance they found they were beneath the approach circuit for light aircraft landing at Wilson airport, so they flashed SOS to every plane with their headlights but evidently no pilot noticed, or if they did they dismissed the signal as a joke. ("Some joke," Bob commented.) In the back of Rick's car was an old rubber mattress, so they set fire to that, hoping to attract someone's attention, but still no one came. Dancy neglected to tell Bob a fire will keep all animals but rhino away, and a rhino will charge a fire every time. So, on the alert for a rhino charge, Dancy kept telling Bob he was having his harrowing African adventure; and he kept telling her he didn't want one in the first place. No one came. Socks were next; they dipped them into the gas tank to make them burn more fiercely. Then she decided they should burn their underclothes. They were the only things expendable—their outer clothes were too mud-encrusted to put into the gas tank, and besides they were not anxious to be found nude in the game park. (They had just met.) They burned those and still no one came. She told him they'd just have to stay there until someone found them in the morning. Bob was gripped with fear, but Dancy said the worst thing for her was running out of cigarettes.

Cheers went up over the telephone at home when we called Rick and Bryony and McDonnell from the gate. They had food waiting and we all had a grand reunion, then fell in bed exhausted.

The next morning Bob slept late, and after lunch we encouraged him to go for a little walk and headed him in the direction of the river. He was back very quickly, looking very shaken and pale. "I found a dead body in the river."

"Yes," Jock said, "there have been severe floods recently— probably drowned."

"Drowned?" Bob said. "With a burlap bag tied over his head?" We couldn't think of an answer to that, so Bob caught a plane back to the States that very afternoon. (And if you want to go on safari, please do not ask him for advice.)

That evening on our walk through the sanctuary Jock and I came across three huge eland in the forest. Instead of being ecstatic about these new arrivals, I called out, "Go away," and told Jock I had definitely decided in my next life I ain't having no children and no animals.

"Yes, you will. Remember the quote, 'For every mountain you form you also form a valley'? You know that's true—and better than the alternative, which is just remaining bored the rest of your life. The children, and the animals, too, give us many mountains and just a few valleys." He stopped and under a huge fig tree he kissed me, "But Bettyduk, you've given me only a big mountain range."

McDonnell went back to the States to take a film course at the University of Maryland, and Dancy was often away with the Flying Doctors, and Rick was married and no longer lived at home. Suddenly all our giraffe sitters had disappeared, and it was time for us to go to the States again on our lecture tour.

So we hired a woman from Chicago, who had raised chimpanzees in the zoo there and wanted to move to Kenya and work with animals. She moved into our guest house and we worked with her and the giraffe for about a week. She liked the giraffe and the giraffe liked her, and all was well, until the night Jock and I went to Malindi to work on our next book. The phone rang about 3 A.M.: Three Africans had broken into her house and stolen everything—$4,000 she had (unknown to us) in cash, all her clothes, and everything else they could carry—the gas cylinder and the linoleum off the floor in the kitchen, all the sheets and towels and so forth. But the dreadful thing was that she was there during the entire incident.

Jock and I got out of bed and drove back to Nairobi to be with her. She was, astonishingly, all right—certainly better than I would have been; in a few weeks, however, understandably, she went back to Chicago.

(The only humorous thing about the entire wretched episode was when the policeman investigating the crime asked her, "Did they have carnival knowledge of you?")

They never caught the men, and the police gave Jock and me permission to have a gun, unusual because guns are outlawed in Kenya. Little did I ever dream the thing that would frighten me most would be Jock with the gun.

Chapter 16

☆

AN artist friend who works in lucite in Nairobi gave me a lovely, unusual present—a necklace of giraffe droppings. And it really *was* lovely. From our lawn she had gathered some giraffe droppings (which are like raindrops—not in the slightest bit nasty and no odor at all), and encased them in lucite baubles, then strung them into a necklace with amber beads in between each bauble.

The night that Marlon Brando and the Cronkites had come to our New York apartment for dinner, Marlon had picked up a giraffe-shit bauble on a key ring in our bedroom. "What is this?" he asked, puzzled. When we told him, both he and Walter became fascinated and insisted they must have one, so we gave each of them one, and they said they were going to spend the rest of their lives getting rich by taking it into bars and betting everyone $25 they couldn't guess what it was.

Adnan Kashoggi came to Nairobi and we were invited to a reception being given for him at the Norfolk Hotel. As I got to him in the receiving line to be introduced, he took the necklace in his hand and said, "My, this is beautiful. What is it?"

"Giraffe shit," I answered truthfully. And so we got talking and I told him about the plight of the endangered species.

The next night about 10 P.M. Jock and I had just gone to bed. "Do you know you sleep with your eyes open?" I asked him.

"What are you talking about?"

"You do. Your eyes are never completely closed, really strange. But I love you anyway." I kissed him goodnight. "Now open your eyes and go to sleep . . ."

Just then the telephone rang and it was Mr. Kashoggi's financial adviser, who asked us, if Mr. Kashoggi were to donate to the giraffe cause, could we in turn arrange some good Western press for him—perhaps also mentioning his benevolence in the current book we were writing and in various magazine articles we were doing? Jock told him that anyone who saved an endangered species would certainly get good press. Kashoggi's man asked if we would come to town and talk to him about it. Being single-minded about raising money to save the giraffe, Jock and I got out of bed, dressed, and eagerly drove the eleven miles into town and gave Kashoggi's man the whole commercial, explaining the project phase by phase.

"Well, I'm very sorry," he replied when we had finished our pitch, "but I don't think we can help you with the Rothschild giraffe."

"Why not?" we asked, perplexed.

And I swear his answer was, "Because they are Jewish."

Neither Jock nor I could believe what we were hearing. Nevertheless we rallied quickly and assured him that Daisy and Marlon were ardent Christian Scientists, as were all the Rothschild giraffe. He was unimpressed. So then Jock defied him, "Come out and see if you can find one that is circumcised." But that didn't do any good either. To be fair, and it's hard sometimes, he did explain that Kashoggi himself wouldn't mind contributing to the Rothschild giraffe at all, but that many of his followers at home in Saudi Arabia would disapprove and he didn't need that kind of hassle.

Should we have called them the Kashoggi giraffe? After all, the only reason they're called the Rothschild, instead of the "five-horned giraffe" as they were originally called, is because one of the Rothschild family went to Kenya to hunt, saw it was a different species, and registered it in his name.

Later Jock and I thought maybe Kashoggi's man was right all along—maybe our giraffe were Jewish. They drank only

imported powdered milk from Israel, and if we tried to sneak
in the equivalent local product or real pasteurized cow's milk,
they turned away with the offended expressions of dowagers
being offered bad fish. The Israeli powdered milk, on the
other hand, disappeared as if siphoned off by a suction pump.

Suddenly our life was filled with Arabs. The phone rang and
guess who it was? The Sheikh of Araby's private secretary,
who said, "The day before the Sheikh was due to have flown
to Kenya last year, there was a major political crisis here, a
big power struggle, and that is why he didn't come to stay in
your house and why you haven't heard anything. Now he is
interested in negotiating for the land again. His Excellency
requests that you dine with him at his Palace next Saturday."

Because we were on our way back to the States for our
lecture tour and going to Arabia was only a slight diversion,
we accepted with undue haste, and, like everyone else, dashed
off to get our hands on some Arab money.

Admittedly the timing could have been better. Not only
was September the hottest time of the year in one of the
world's hottest places, but it was also the month of Ramadhan,
the strict religious fast that precedes Id, which is roughly
the equivalent of Lent. Now to those of you who, like me,
aren't Middle East buffs, Jedda is the airport that serves
Mecca, and Ramadhan is the time when the faithful the world
over make their pilgrimage to the tomb of the Prophet.

Thus we found ourselves the only infidels aboard a crammed
707. Strict Muslims are on best behavior when embarked
upon the *hajj* (pilgrimage) and have nothing to eat or drink
all day; the ultra-strict won't even swallow their own saliva
until the sun has set. Only at night may they eat or drink.
Just before takeoff, about 8 P.M., a stewardess in a flowing
pink sari passed around a basket of what I thought were
candies, but as I opened and chewed mine I noticed that the
other passengers were delicately sniffing theirs. I had eaten
the sachet. No one seemed to notice, thank God (except Jock,
who thought it was *so* funny), for the rush was on to stuff
themselves with all they could eat and drink before dawn. A

huge and delicious vegetarian dinner was served and, as it was cleared away, breakfast was immediately presented, so everyone gorged himself until 3 A.M., when we landed in Jedda.

For connecting flights, which we needed, there is an interesting system. We had to submit to full immigration treatment, health documents, visas—the works. Customs inspection was very thorough. We had to unpack everything, and they confiscated a film we had made of the giraffe in the sanctuary, which we were taking to show the Sheikh. We were then told we had to leave the building, walk two hundred yards, and check in through immigration, health, and customs all over again. Two ragged little boys insisted on being our porters, and as we stepped out into the night, I thought we had unwittingly been projected into the shooting of Cecil B. DeMille's biggest ever. Arabs in white robes were sleeping on the ground or cooking pre-dawn snacks on little stoves, or praying or arguing or walking about. They stretched in every direction as far as we could see, and we had to pick our way for the two hundred yards through this teeming white-ant colony of humanity before taking a right turn back into what was the connecting side of the very building we had just left. Inside once more, the crowd was even thicker, and without exaggeration, there must have been 5,000 people, all men, all in white, lined up at each of about a dozen airline counters. Our flight via Riyadh and Dubai was due to leave in an hour, and there was no way we could possibly reach a desk with our ticket.

To walk, we had to search for a place to put our toes, and to maintain our balance, we clutched the tops of shaved Muslim heads. They were very courteous and kept propping us up as we tripped over them and the sleeping bodies on the floor. Some were even cooking inside the terminal and little plumes of smoke spiraled up to the ceiling. It was strangely quiet.

"No sense in both of us trying to storm the ticket counter," I told Jock. "I'm plotting a maneuver to the ladies' room."

"Fine. I'll head for the counter. I'll just leave our luggage here on the floor."

"Leave it?"

"Of course. No one steals in Saudi Arabia. They cut your hand off or something."

With much difficulty I planned my strategy and navigated my way to the ladies' room. It was filled with men. They were shaving their heads and changing from their standard white robes to white turkish towel robes worn off one shoulder. (This, I was to learn, is the kit in which a true zealot walks the 123 miles to Mecca. The heat goes over 120 degrees at times, and there are no Howard Johnson's to step into for a lemonade.) My arrival in the ladies' room didn't seem to bother anyone, so I figured what the hell, and with a brave smile made my way into the little booth. This is when I discovered that instead of loo paper the Arabs have a hand shower fixture like those sometimes found in bathtubs. They think our system of paper is not only unsanitary but revolting and, come to think of it, they do have a point.

When I left the men's ladies' room, I couldn't see Jock. I scanned the crowds for him, but as it turned out my not locating him was the best thing that could have happened. I was now alone—the only woman among 5,000 men—and Arab men love Western women, especially blondes and especially if they are, as they always say, "round and white and full like the moon." Their own women cover their faces and their bodies with black robes called *bui-buis* (the Swahili word for spider), which give them the appearance of spiders or black bats. *Purdah*, this state of being unseen, has its advantages, because since only your eyes show all you need to dress for a party is a tablespoon of mascara. You can forget the dress, the hairdo, the makeup, the holding your stomach in. (And I'm told if you want to have a secret love affair, all you have to do is change your shoes and toddle off to your assignation because the only way anyone can tell who you are is by the shoes you are wearing.)

So there I was, standing alone with my blonde hair and

painted face, exposed to the world of Arab men, when a swarthy, intense-looking one in a long white *dish-dash* and flowing white *kaffeyah* approached me and said in a sort of English that he was an airline official and could he be of any assistance? (All Arab men look swarthy and intense, and there is something romantic about their dress.)

I explained that I was trying to get to Dubai, but that I would obviously have to abandon the thought for the present because of the impossibility of reaching the counter to check in.

"Come with me," he commanded.

We wove in and out of the masses of people, through a "No Admittance" door, down winding corridors. Through a window I could see the first signs of dawn.

"Your sunrise is beautiful," I said.

"So are *you*."

Uh-oh. Was he really an airline official? The little badge he was wearing on his robe could have said "rapist" for all I could read of that spaghetti writing. I was just recalling a novel I had read about modern white slaving when he stopped in front of a door. Relieved, I saw it said "Staff Only" in comforting English, and suddenly there I was behind one of the airline counters, looking at Jock and all the masses.

I flirted outrageously with the Arab official and in a few minutes everything was arranged for our flight; even the confiscated film was miraculously returned. If I had been in *purdah*, we would never have made it.

My rescuer was miffed to find a husband showing up and he barely acknowledged Jock; however, he did lead us back to the departure lounge (which was right next door to where we had gotten off the plane). I started to ask him if it wouldn't be easier on the passengers, the customs officials, the airline ground staff, the baggage handlers, the sleeping people we had trodden upon—on everyone in fact—if we had simply been shown to the transit passenger's lounge while our baggage was being transferred to the new flight. I started to ask, then I stopped. We were, after all, in Jedda, and it was the time of the *hajj*.

As we boarded our flight, Jock said, "I'm glad you're so attractive, but I hate it, too, because I get jealous. Jealousy reared its ugly head just now when you were with 'Omar Sharif.' "

"Good," I told him. "If you didn't have a twinge of jealousy every now and then, I'd think you didn't care. The opposite of love is not hate, it's indifference. But you know you have no reason ever to be jealous because you are the only love in my life—no one else even exists."

Middle East Airways offered no one liquor (forbidden in all of Muslim life) but landed nicely in the Arab Emirates. Two of the Sheikh's emissaries were waiting for us and drove us to the Hilton, where we had a suite awaiting us because, since I was but a woman, I could not stay in the Palace.

"My God," I said to Jock. "This is where they really need women's rights."

"Well, you know I have always believed in equal rights."

"I don't. I see no reason why men should be allowed to become the equal of women."

"No wonder no one likes you." Jock laughed. "Remember what Jack Paar said, 'If God wanted man and woman to be the same he would have made one.' "

We waited for the call about dinner, but it did not come.

The following morning, Martin, Jock's brother-in-law, or former brother-in-law, I do not know which to call him, came to see us and said not hearing from the Sheikh of Araby was quite normal. What's the hurry, this is the Arab world.

I would like to tell you about Martin, but I don't think all you American men should know about this, so this paragraph is only for women to read: Martin and Jock's sister, who lived in Kenya, split up, and Martin, a pilot, moved to the Arab Emirates and got a job with Gulf Air. After he had been there a few months, he learned that if an Englishman became a Muslim he would be paid $3,000. No messing about with missionaries, no proselytizing of any kind, just sheer cash. Since Martin was an Englishman, needed money, and as an agnostic couldn't care less what religious label he had, he did so. And now that he was under Koranic law he could take up to four wives, so he married a pretty Arab woman and had two children, and never divorced Jock's sister—no expensive divorce case, no alimony, no nothing.

Martin lent us a car, and Jock and I drove 100 miles to an oasis through the land of Cadillacs and camels, which used to be called the desert. But now empty whiskey bottles litter the sand like cactus—forbidden fruit, I guess; and apparently fine modern American cars, many of them Cadillacs in showroom condition, were abandoned, some left by owners for nothing more than a new set for plugs or a fan belt. Just buy another in the oil-rich state.

We still heard nothing from the Sheikh, which was fine with us. We were having a lovely time—romantic dinners by candlelight, dancing, sleeping late—another honeymoon, all on the Arabs. Three days later we were summoned, not to dinner in the Palace, but to his office. No explanation or apology. We were received courteously in the sumptuous surroundings with a great French crystal chandelier over a priceless table, on which was a plastic green lace tablecloth with a bowl of cheap artificial roses. A perfect monument to bad taste.

We told the Sheikh, who was pleasant and spoke English, about the sanctuary and showed him the photographs and film of the giraffe and warthogs in the forest. He was very enthusiastic. Picking up a picture of Walter Warthog and looking at it carefully, he said, "Yes. We will fly to Nairobi now, in my 707, and I will buy the place."

Jock kicked me in glee under the plastic tablecloth. We were so pleased. One house on the edge of the primeval forest would be fine and now not only would the forest be saved, but we could build Jock's dream. Then the Sheikh of Araby added, "I have just been pig sticking in Germany—it is a wonderful sport, wonderful. So my friends and I will hunt the warthogs and the giraffe."

"But . . . but," Jock and I stammered, again unable to believe what we were hearing.

" . . . This is not exactly what we had in mind," Jock said, aghast.

"This is a sanctuary . . . to save the animals . . . ," I pleaded.

"And anyway," Jock interrupted, "hunting has been banned in Kenya. No hunting of any kind is allowed anymore . . ."

The Sheikh waved his hand, dismissing the thought. "A high-up politician there is a friend of mine. There will be no problem for me to hunt, I assure you."

We figured he was probably right, so we thanked him for his time and told him we'd think about it, folded our tent, and stole away into the night, never to contact him, nor he us, again.

So, not a nickel from the Sheikh. Realizing we were such miserable failures with the Arabs, we gave them up forever and had to find another way to get a nature sanctuary and educational center and to save our Jewish giraffe.

Chapter 17

☆

So we did some more Giraffe Galas—this time in
Houston, Dallas, San Antonio, and Baltimore—and
raised enough money to translocate more of the giraffe to safety, and decided just to let the house be mortgaged,
but *had* to get the educational center.

After our lecture tour, we played in New York and saw
lots of Paul, and went to Kirk Douglas's birthday party—by
mistake. Lewis Allen, who is on A FEW's board and produced
Annie and *My One and Only,* had asked us to the preview one
morning of his film *Never Cry Wolf.* Afterwards he asked us
to lunch with him and suggested Elaine's and called for a
reservation. In the cab Lewis said to us, "Elaine said a funny
thing just now. She said, 'Everyone is here.' I don't know
what she meant . . ." As we walked in, Kirk Douglas was
standing at the door in his dimpled chin, greeting everyone.
He put his hand out to me, looked me in the eyes, and said,
"I'm so glad you could come." Never having seen him in
person in my life I was startled, so I just sort of nodded and
went on in. What Elaine had meant was that all Kirk Douglas's guests were there for his private birthday party, and she
had just assumed, since he had been in one of Lewis's films,
that Lewis had been invited which he had not. Kirk Douglas
was very nice about it—what else could he be?—and gra-
ciously insisted we stay. We did and had an unexpected birthday lunch, complete with Henry Kissinger and many other
celebrities.

Jock and I were incident-prone. Our lives were always overflowing with unexpected events. We were so lucky—it seemed we were always in the right place at the right time. We were in Kenya, for example, when Lord Mountbatten was there, so we had lunch with him; and one night a young minister friend of Rick's telephoned and said he was anthropologist Margaret Mead's aide on her visit to Kenya and she wanted to see the giraffe. Daisy and Marlon were becoming the wonder of the animal world, she had said, and could Earl bring her out? So he did, and she put on Jock's gum boots and sloshed down to the *boma* in the rain and thrilled at feeding the giraffe. It was indeed a fascinating evening. She was very positive and adamant in her views. We would be telling her something we thought was a correct theory, but she would interrupt with "Fiddlesticks" (that is, until the third martini, when she'd interpolate "Bullshit"), then tell us what was actually what.

Somehow the subject of euthanasia came up. "It means 'good death' in Greek, you know," Margaret Mead said.

"I believe adamantly that those who are terminally ill and want to die should be allowed to do so," Jock said.

"Correct," she agreed.

"With death control through life support systems, medical science has posed questions we've never had to face before, not in all of human history," Jock said.

"It was a whole lot easier when God made the decisions," Earl, our young minister friend, agreed.

"Graham Greene put it well—he said, 'I really don't want to survive myself. I don't want my body around after my mind has departed,' " Jock commented.

"No one does," Ms. Mead agreed, "but clearly the choice must be made before the crisis occurs."

"We should all get Living Wills," Earl said. "We can always change our minds if we want to—if we decide we do want to live because of changing ideas or conditions."

We all agreed on that subject at least, and then dinner was served and the conversation changed to other interesting topics. We enjoyed her and the entire evening immensely.

I remembered my promise to Jock and thought how we should get Living Wills on our next trip to the States.

Jock and I were also lucky to have just arrived back in Kenya another time, just when Candice Bergen was there. We had dinner with her and she agreed to be on our board. Cheryl Tiegs, and Judy and Hal Prince, and Steve Sondheim all came to us for a few meals. Also Gloria and Jimmy Stewart came to lunch one day. They are both very concerned about and big supporters of wildlife; they are also Africa-philes and good friends. They had given us a lovely dinner party at their house in Los Angeles, and one of their daughters and Rick had dated. After lunch and feeding the giraffe, they wanted to walk in the primeval forest. Like all the others, they were filled with wonder, but with Nairobi being almost a mile high, it is a long, strenuous walk, and when we arrived at the stream Jimmy said apologetically that he could not go on because he feared he was having a heart attack. Panicky, Jock ran back to the house, got our 4-wheel drive, and bashed it through the bush as far as it would go, which was only a few hundred yards for Jimmy to walk. We got him back to the house and he was fine—never once complained, only apologized for the inconvenience and concern he had caused everyone.

"I'm so glad it wasn't a heart attack and he's all right," Jock said after they had left. "He's such a nice person. Gloria, too. I feared we might have a nasty incident. It's lucky I could get the car close to him. We are so lucky in so many ways, Bettyduk, but mostly because our love not only remains magical, but grows."

Jock and I would say "I love you" to each other many times a day. But what is love anyway? What does it mean when you say you love someone? You can love your mother and father and children, you can love baseball and your dog and ice cream and opera and travel, but you're not *in* love with any of them—you are not romantically or sexually involved with any of them. To complicate matters even more, you can love your mother or your brother, but not only are you not in love with them—you may not even *like* them.

Then what is love? I think to have total love you must have four parts: mind, heart, body, and soul. The least complicated and the least important is the body—the sexual attraction; but you can certainly be attracted to someone sexually and not be in love with them, or love them, or like them at all. (Although sex is the least important, to make a marriage work you must have it; it is like transportation—the car is the important thing, but it won't go without the gasoline, which is sex.)

The heart is romantic love—the irrational, the magic, the orgasm of the heart, the *in* love.

The mind, which is probably the most important because it's so lasting, is enjoying someone, having the same standards and values. This does not mean you have to agree all the time. As someone said, "If two people are exactly alike, one is superfluous," but you have to at least "speak the same language" and agree on the basic values.

The soul, for lack of a better word, is where the respect and admiration come in. You can like (enjoy) someone without admiring or respecting them; and you can respect someone but not admire them. For example, most people respect the Pope, but many don't necessarily admire his philosophy. Camus said, "Admiration is the rarest gift of all," and he is right.

Pheromones are important too. An entomologist told me that insects still have this strong chemical substance that produces a reaction to other insects, and although we humans have lost much of our pheromones there are still enough left in us that we do react chemically to people. This is not sexual but chemical, and it exists between two people of the same sex as well as with the opposite sex. Who has not walked into a room of strangers and seen someone you would like to talk to, and another whom for some reason you would like to shove down an elevator shaft?

So to be able to say I love you, you have to like someone

(mind), be in love (heart), feel admiration and respect (soul), and be sexually attracted (body). And the pheromones have to be right in all departments too. No wonder people are confused about love. You may have two out of the four parts and, understandably, think you love; but then you discover you really don't *like* each other—and what you thought was true love may even turn into true hate.

It's a miracle anyone ever gets all four parts, and Jock and I had that miracle. We liked each other, we enjoyed each other, we had the same standards and values and sense of humor. And we were desperately *in* love—the chimes within us never subsided; we admired and respected one another, and the physical attraction and the pheromones were also splendid. So we had it all. We *LOVED*.

We melded. We were together twenty-four hours a day, talking, working, laughing, and being silent; it was almost as if we were the same person—we didn't feel whole without the other one. I never tired of just looking at him: his blue blue eyes and great mass of hair, the two white spots on his front teeth, and his tall lean body. I loved the way he walked and talked, what he said and how he said it in his British accent and excellent vocabulary. Also he taught me so much, made me think . . . and laugh. And I loved my Tuesday presents and all his romantic ways and his total absorption with me. I also respected his casual authority and confidence and elegance and gentleness. I never worried about him with other people, for he was comfortable with everyone and found something to enjoy about even the most awful people. I admired his honesty and his ability to write and his lack of anger and his easygoing manner and his great gift for finding delight with even the little things in life, like banana bread and Fats Waller and butterscotch sauce and snow.

We had had a good spell cast on us.

Speaking of spells, the promoter of the Baltimore Orioles baseball team came to Kenya to ask a witch doctor to cast a spell on the other team in the World Series that year. I guess he had read how, in soccer games in Kenya, one team would

release a white dove (a bad omen to some tribes) right before
the game and freak out the opposing team so badly they would
lose. Anyway, the Oriole promoter did everything the witch
doctor told him to, including not having any sex for two
weeks. Fortunately the Orioles lost the pennant anyway, thank
goodness. If they had won I could just see us having to organize witchcraft safaris.

However, witchcraft does work—if you believe in it, which
of course we did not. (It is no more difficult to believe in
witchcraft, a term always used pejoratively, than in any other
supernatural system, such as Christianity.) One day a Giriama tribesman, who worked for us at Malindi, came to the
house trembling. Someone had buried a carrot in his path,
God forbid. He went totally to pieces and was unable to eat
or work or do anything, until we sent him to the good witch
doctor to remove the bad spell he insisted had been cast upon
him. I feel certain the good witch doctor and the bad witch
doctor work in cahoots; but we paid the fee and the spell was
removed and all was well again. (Just remember not to bury
a carrot in a Giriama's path.)

Then suddenly it was as if someone had buried a carrot in
our path of life. A lovely young Italian woman who had worked
for Jane Goodall and her chimpanzees in Tanzania returned
to Kenya and wanted to work with animals, so she came out
to see if there was anything she could volunteer to do for the
giraffe. We told her, of course, that we had so much to do
running A FEW, which was all volunteer work, and we
needed all the help we could get. She offered to come out a
few days a week when she returned from seeing her mother
in Rome, to type thank you letters to our supporters and help
us plan different projects to raise money and so forth. We
were very appreciative and said how grateful we were and
looked forward to having her work with us upon her return.

When she got to Rome she went to the zoo on Sunday,
when most Italians take their afternoon siesta, and was therefore alone in front of the tiger cage. Because she thinks she
communicates with all animals, and no one was around to
stop her, stupidly she climbed over the rail and put her hand

inside the cage to pet the tiger, which ripped her arm off.

She ran out onto the street, and a passing car stopped when they saw this woman with blood gushing from her shoulder. In a state of shock she said to them, "Would you please go to the tiger's cage and get my hand, because I've just had my fingernails done." They took her to the hospital, but nothing could be done. The tiger had torn all the muscles from her shoulder.

In the next six months, twelve of our friends died tragically and four more were murdered. Two good friends of ours were killed in a plane crash, along with Gordon Parks, Jr. (the American photographer); and four other close friends were killed in road accidents, two more drowned fishing, two others committed suicide, and a young couple just married were burned to death in a nightclub fire. And in *one* month the four friends were murdered. It was unbelievable. Allard Lowenstein, who had been to see us with his children (and his Christmas card had been a picture of his children with Daisy), was shot in his New York office by a former protégé of his who had mental problems. A husband and wife, longtime friends of ours, were brutally murdered in the Virgin Islands by a gang, and Joy Adamson, who had just been at our house for dinner, was also murdered. All four in the same month.

Then Rutherfurd was shot (but not fatally). He had worked with Joy for eight months, helping her take care of her leopard, and just before she was killed he had left to pan gold in a remote region of northern Kenya. He was the only white man among hundreds of Turkanas and Pokot.

The government had asked Jock and me, since we had been so successful in saving the endangered Rothschild giraffe, if we would help them with the highly endangered black rhino, so of course we said yes (conservation is a form of insanity), and we were having a Rhino Rescue party at our house to raise some money to move the rhinos to safety. Rutherfurd put in a radio call to us and said it had been six months since he had seen civilization and had heard from someone who had visited him about the rhino party and he was flying down for it.

"I don't know what makes you think it will be civilized,"
Jock told him, "but we'll be delighted to see you and of course
you will stay with us." But he never showed, not too unusual
for Rutherfurd, so we didn't think too much about it.

The night of the party we had a full-sized papier-mâché
rhino suspended from the hall ceiling, and all the kids were
volunteer bartenders wore bands around their heads with a
papier-mâché rhino horn attached to it, so we had horny
bartenders. And once again the guests ate and danced till
dawn and a grand time was had by all, and we raised some
money for the rhinos.

The night after the party Rick telephoned and said that a
nurse at a dinner party he was attending had just told him
Rutherfurd was in intensive care. Jock and I rushed to the
hospital and learned that while Rutherfurd was sitting in his
camp chair after dinner the night before he was going to fly
to Nairobi, he heard a shot. He looked around and there was
a Pokot standing behind him with a smoking gun. Rutherfurd
jumped to his feet, but with no gun on him he picked up his
camp chair, and hit the African with it, then began wrestling
him for the gun. Finally the Pokot dropped it and fled. Rutherfurd looked down and saw that the first shot had gone into
his back, right through his chest and out the front.

The other 200 Africans had run off when they heard the
shots, assuming Rutherfurd had been killed. Because there
was no one to help him and because he had been a major
during the Mau Mau uprising and knew a lot about gun
wounds, he judged he had about twenty minutes to live. He
leaned over and dumped the blood (so it wouldn't fill his lungs)
from the open hole in his chest, on the ground, then sat down
and waited to die. An hour later he was still alive but growing
weaker all the time and almost unable now to continue dump-
ing the blood to keep him from drowning.

Finally one Turkana came loping back. Rutherfurd told
him there was a Catholic mission fifteen miles away, and for
him to go and get help. Through the bush in the night, amidst
buffalo and elephant, the Turkana ran. A few other Turkana
finally appeared and got Rutherfurd onto his cot in his tent,

then sat on the floor with their bows and arrows, waiting for him to die.

Four hours later Rutherfurd was slipping into a coma, when the tent flap opened and he saw "the angel of mercy coming to take me." But it wasn't the angel of mercy; it was a wet, fifty-four-year-old nun whom the Turkana had summoned, who had driven in a Land Rover to the other side of the river, then, carrying drip bags high above her head, crossed the river and climbed up to Rutherfurd's tent—and saved his life. She radioed the Flying Doctors, who picked him up at dawn and rushed him to the operating room. His shoulder bone was gone but other than that he was almost out of danger.

Two days later he was operated on again, and the very next day he telephoned us and said he was leaving the hospital, he couldn't stand it anymore. "Rutherfurd," I pleaded, "you can't leave the hospital. You were just operated on yesterday and . . ." But I was wasting my time and knew it. "Okay, stay there, we'll pick you up." Jock went in for him immediately, but by the time he got there, fifteen minutes later, Rutherfurd had gone. Jock knew where to find him—at his favorite local bar, and there he was at 10 A.M., drinking his warm beer and happy as hell.

So Rutherfurd survived, and other good things started to happen again, too, which is typical of life. The tide goes out and the tide comes in. Life is joy and it is sadness. We felt we couldn't complain about our sadnesses because we certainly had had more than our share of joy, and there was more to come. The first joyous event was Daisy producing a baby.

Jock and I were upstairs writing, waiting for some tourists to arrive in an hour. We heard someone calling from downstairs and it was one of the tourists, saying she was sorry they were so early, then added, "Daisy's having a baby."

"We think she's pregnant," Jock told her as we walked down the stairs, "but the vet told us last week she is not."

"But I mean Daisy is having a baby *now*," she said excitedly. "The legs are hanging out."

We raced onto the lawn and just standing there were John Paul, June Murphy, and Daisy with two little limp legs hanging from her. I knew something was wrong—giraffe always, always hide to have their babies, and anyway the head should come first in birth. So I ran to the phone and hysterically called the vet, who said: "Betty, in giraffe the feet always come first."

"But something is wrong. The legs are just hanging limp. Please come right away, I'm sure you're going to have to do a cesarean."

"All right, Betty," he comforted the distraught parent, "but I bet you by the time I get there it'll be born and fine."

I tore outside to find the tourists fascinated and Daisy totally unconcerned, acting perfectly naturally, not at all as if she was giving birth. The little limp legs still hung there. The baby must be dead. Daisy and the others chewed their cuds.

Our camera had no film in it and we did not want to leave to find some, but fortunately the tourists were all clicking away.

Then the little legs started moving—getting longer, coming out more. Where was the vet? Why wasn't he here? After all, I had talked to him two minutes ago. Daisy glanced back once, as if a fly were annoying her, then continued to ignore events. In about ten minutes there was a plop and a great mass of jelly lay on the ground. Daisy looked around, quite surprised, and touched it with her foot.

"It's dead," I said sadly, and everyone nodded solemnly in agreement.

After a few minutes Jock said, "Wait, it looks as if a foot is moving."

"Reflex," someone muttered.

"No, look. The other foot is moving," Jock insisted.

"The whole thing is wiggling," I cried.

"That's the head coming up, Betty!" Jock told me happily.

"It's alive, it's alive!" everyone was shouting.

Daisy bent down and licked the little baby, the head came up, and the cutest little wet face with big brown eyes looked around its new world. It seemed very pleased. Soon it flopped down again, but up came the head for another happy look around, and flopped back down. All the other giraffe were standing around watching it, intrigued.

Then the little legs began to try to stand up. They tried so hard, but they'd buckle; then try again and buckle again. Finally at 6:04, forty-one minutes later, the little giraffe managed to stand. Everyone cheered and clapped and cried, and one of the tourists gave me a cigar.

The vet arrived with that "I told you so" look on his face, but he said he would have given anything to have seen the calving. He had never seen one nor heard of anyone else who had. And he had never heard of a giraffe giving birth in the open. So Daisy produced not only a beautiful baby but a historical event.

The tiny thing (six feet tall) looked like a little duck with big furry ears and crossed horns. Adorable! We loved her and named her Daffodil. But I must tell you that she is a half-caste. Daisy fell in love with Tom (of Tom, Dick, and Harry), and so Daffodil is not a pure Rothschild.

"She doesn't have pure white legs," I told Jock. "Shame on you, Daisy."

Jock smiled. "But she *is* a brand-new species."

Chapter 18

W E were almost finished our third book and wanted a chapter on South Africa. We also wanted to see what our safariers got up to there, so we accepted their tourist board's invitation for a two-week free trip and flew down.

Although we knew very little about apartheid, we had heard horror stories about it: An Asian friend of ours, who had lived in South Africa before she moved to Kenya, told us when she was pregnant she went into a department store in Johannesburg to shop and needed to go to the ladies' room. She was told there was a ladies' room for whites on all floors, but "For you it's on the fifth floor." She got on the elevator but the white elevator operator told her since she was not white she had to walk. Then a friend of hers was having her baby delivered by a colored (as Asians are classified) doctor when she had a complication and needed a emergency cesarean operation; but her doctor was prevented from entering the white operating room, the only one available at the time, or from using the services of the skilled white staff. The qualified white doctor who came to take a look at her said he could do nothing because she was not white. She died.

The official government comment was, "Non-white doctors are not permitted to work with white staff. This would create all sorts of problems."

When we arrived in Johannesburg we realized that *everything* is separate. As a white woman, I was not allowed to get into a cab along with a black male driver. There were separate buses and taxis, post office counters, benches, libraries, and, of course, living quarters. Black Africans can't own land, and they have no rights or privileges.

I would have failed the trivia game question if I had been asked what the third largest city in Africa is? Cairo? Johannesburg? Lagos? No, Soweto—where the Africans who work for whites in Johannesburg are forced to live, and without their families. Of course, the objective of the whites is to create a situation to have all the black labor available to them, and they ship the Africans out to "homelands," which simply become supply centers for cheap labor.

South Africa is a terrible place. Apartheid, the Afrikaans word for "segregation," is condoned by the South African Dutch Reformed Church (known in some circles there as the "Dutch Deformed Church"), which states, "The Church allows no equality between whites and non-whites," and goes on to quote the Bible, "Be ye not unequally yoked together— as an ass with a camel." The Afrikaners are a believing and churchgoing people, and this church teaches them that apartheid is moral. As Edgar Brookes says in his book *Apartheid*, "To change, the Afrikaner would have to undergo an experience no less extraordinary than a miraculous religious conversion. Apartheid is more than a law, it is a fundamental premise, a philosophy of life, in which the prejudices are rationalized and apartheid becomes moral principle."

From Johannesburg, Jock and I went to Durban, where tourists were being pulled around the city in rickshaws by an African acting as a horse. Next was Cape Town, which is beautiful, but because of apartheid is also the most depressing place we'd ever been. We learned the whites in South Africa had the highest standard of living in the world; we learned that censorship is rampant. (Even the book *Black Beauty* was banned because of its title.) We learned what a total police state it is; we learned many terrible inhumane things.

One evening Jock and I were having a glum dinner. "I'm learning how little I know," I told him.

"Few people ever get that far, Betty. But you know that out of every experience comes something awful."

"Every minute of every day would be awful if I weren't with you. You make life bearable even when it's not—like being around these Afrikaners. They're dinosaurs in their mentality. Do you want to stay here? We've got eight more free days."

"I feel like reaching for my parachute and bailing out now."

"Let's . . .," and we were on the next plane back home.

"I'm glad we like living in the same forest," I told Jock as we entered our driveway and greeted Shirley Brown and the giraffe.

Our children came for dinner. (Our new cook roasted a chicken with the feathers still on it.) "Did you enjoy yourself in South Africa?" McDonnell asked.

"We had to, there was nothing else to enjoy," Jock told them. "Those Afrikaners are not only terrible people, they are outstandingly dull. One is indistinguishable from another. The only concern these people have is for their electricity bill—not a humane bone in their bodies. There isn't a hope. It's inevitable the blacks will soon be under military siege by the whites—it's coming."

"But they were nice to you, weren't they?" Dancy asked.

"Niceness to whites only is not an attribute which appeals to me," Jock answered.

We wrote a chapter about South Africa, called "The Cruel Paradise," for our book, and when it was published we were banned by its government.

The next morning we were just about to celebrate the joy of being home by walking in the sanctuary, when Pierre Trudeau's two little boys arrived to feed the giraffe. The new servant came up to me and asked me if I wanted my "knickers for uppers" ironed?

"Knickers for uppers?" I asked, puzzled.

"*Ndio.*" He nodded his head patiently.

It took me a few seconds to realize what he meant. "Knickers" are what the British call underpants, so "knickers for uppers" had to be my bra. The Trudeau children thought this was so funny—they were delightful, beautiful-looking children. The Prime Minister had planned to come with them but got held up in a meeting with the President of Kenya; however, he wrote the nicest letter afterward, thanking us and saying how disappointed he was to be unable to share the most marvelous experience his sons claimed they had ever had.

꜒ After lunch Jock was just saying, "How about going for a long walk—I just love walking alone with you," when our friend Peter Beard, well-known photographer and Isak Dinesen buff, who was married to Cheryl Tiegs at the time, arrived at the house. Having heard we had some of Karen's furniture, which he had been searching for, he had come over to gawk at it. Because possessing something of hers was so important to him, we offered to give him a piece he could put in his tents, which he lived in on the land we had acquired for the sanctuary. He was so thankful and then asked us how we were certain it was her furniture. "I don't have any proof," Jock said. "Only that I knew her and her house, and she was a good friend of my mother's, and I know which pieces she gave to Mother, but there is no documentation. And you're right, it should be verified if they make her house here into a historical site and we give it there."

Suddenly Peter said, "Kamande! He'll verify it for us." Kamande was Isak Dinesen's beloved cook, who worked for her for years and whom she wrote a lot about. Peter brought Kamande, who didn't even know we had some of her things, over to the house. First we pointed out everything of hers to Peter, all of them mixed in with our belongings, and now we wanted to see if Kamande could identify the same things. We asked him in. "There are some things here which belonged to Memsahib Karen. Do you see any of them?" Peter asked him in Swahili.

Kamande, an old man now, shuffled around the drawing room, slowly looking at each individual object. *"Hii ni yake"* (This is hers), he said, pointing to her writing chair, then

at a vase. He said it again in a bedroom, pointing to her twin
beds, and when he got to the chest of drawers, he pointed
to the top drawer and said that was where she kept the payroll,
the bottom drawer was where she kept medicines. In the
twenty-two rooms he didn't miss one thing. We could tell
that Peter really wanted the twin beds, and when we told
him they were his, he was delighted and certain now they
were the ones that had belonged to Karen Blixen.

As he and Kamande were going out the front door, Jock
poked me and whispered, "Now our walk."

But Peter asked, "What are all those nuns doing walking
around the lawn?"

"Oh, that's my good friend, Helen," I said, stifling a laugh
and waving to her. "She's in a convent here in Nairobi now.
Some of the nuns have been in Africa for twenty years and
have never seen an animal. They don't have any money for
safari or even game parks, so we told her she could bring any
of them out here to see the giraffe and warthogs any time she
wants."

"The nuns are terrific," Jock added. "I've stayed with Helen in her convent in Rome and frequently go to the convent
here. Helen's become a good friend of mine, too—I adore
her."

We said goodbye to Peter and Kamande and greeted the
nuns, and the minute they left, Jock and I were putting on
our walking boots in the kitchen when we heard the most
terrifying screams out front. We had hired some Africans to
refinish the floors, and among them was a woman. She was
the one screaming. Fearing a giraffe had kicked her, we ran
toward the front of the house and were glad to see her race
into the front hall, for at least she was ambulatory. Trembling
and crying, she shouted, "The biggest dog I have ever seen
just chased me into the house."

It was Daisy. Sweet, gentle Daisy had ambled along, following the woman toward the house, thinking she could get
some carrots from her. Everyone else who came to the house
gave her carrots. Daisy put her head in the hall and looked
very perplexed at the woman's reaction. The fact that she

had never even heard of a giraffe *is* startling—that is, until you consider it and then it makes perfect sense: Africans have no money for game parks, children's books, or television, and there are no zoos—how *would* they know what a giraffe is?

After we calmed the woman down, it was time for us to fly to Lake Naivasha with some of our safari clients and our friend Iain Douglas Hamilton, the elephant scientist. He is a wild pilot, and at least we knew what was coming, but the luckless tourists with us were in for the scare of their safari. Hell's Gate is a small Grand Canyon, which only two people in the world are crazy enough to fly through. One is Iain and the second, another of our crazy friends, is Alan Root, the brilliant film maker. This day, as always, the tips of the wings of Iain's plane were almost scraping the rocky sides of the narrow canyon. The passengers, astonished he had flown in there in the first place, were the perfect example of the white-knuckle flight. "Don't worry," Iain called back to them, beginning his routine. "No one else ever flies in here except Alan Root, and we have a bargain that if he and I happen to be in here at the same time, when we see each other we've agreed that I'll go up a bit and he will fly down," and as if that were not enough to petrify them, he always adds, as if he's trying hard to remember, ". . . or is it that I am supposed to go down and he up . . . ?"

Before dinner at Naivasha Jock suggested, "Let's just sneak off alone and take a little walk around here."

I feigned exhaustion. "I'm too tired to walk now," I teased him. He looked so disappointed that I burst out laughing, and on our walk we talked about the wonderfully crazy bizarre life we led. "We ride the waves together."

"Wouldn't you like a more peaceful sea every now and then?" he asked.

"There's enough time for peace when we're dead. If we weren't in the fast lane of life, we might miss something."

"Well, there's more madness coming up with our trip to Ethiopia and Teheran on our way to the States," Jock said.

The children came to dinner the night we were leaving and gave us a bottle of Scotch for our going-away present.

"Wow, thank you," exclaimed Jock, pouring a drink for us in the library. "Scotch is almost forty dollars per bottle here . . ."

"Don't worry," Rick said. "We didn't pay that for it. We always buy the stolen booze from the gas station—it's half price. They steal it, from us probably, then we buy it."

"I wish we were going to Ethiopia tomorrow with you," Bryony said, sipping her drink. "I lived there for quite a while. I wore long dresses and ate with my fingers, like the Ethiopian women. They don't eat with the men, but their custom is to stand behind the men and feed them with their fingers."

"I know," I said. "I went there the first time in 1960, when TWA delivered Ethiopia's first jets. I was invited to the Ambassador's house for dinner. I had no idea what Ethiopians ate, and was appalled by the *injera* and *wat*."

"I love it," exclaimed Bryony.

"How anyone can love raw chicken and rancid butter dumped in a pie crust that looks and smells like an old gray sponge is beyond me. I had met the Ethiopian Ambassador to the United States, and he invited me to his house in Addis for dinner. I had to stand behind him as he sat at a little sort of wicker birdbath on a milking stool, and tear off a piece of the sponge with my fingers to use as a scoop for the *wat*—the chicken stuff—and put it into his mouth. It ran all down his chin and onto his shirt. I was a total failure at feeding him. But I was intrigued with the country. It is so different from Kenya. The Ethiopians do not even call themselves Africans, they call themselves Ethiopians." I got up and stoked the fire. "They've had two thousand years of religion and historical roots—from the Queen of Sheba to the Lion of Judah, Emperor Haile Selassie. I knew him well. That's an exaggeration—I met him only a few times—the first time on the inaugural flight our group had an audience with him, and he gave us a dinner party at the Royal Palace that night. The second time was when I was associate producer of the TV documentary "City on a Mountain." I had an audience with him about it at the Palace again, twice as a matter of fact. Mostly I remember his blue eyes, and the fact that he spoke

English but always had an interpreter. Guess it gave him time to consider his answers. . . . Your father is the only white man I know who speaks Amharic . . . and Arabic, and Maasai—how many languages does he speak, Bryony?" Dancy asked.

"Sixteen." Dinner was served, so we went into the dining room.

Jock said, "Bryony, I remember your mother telling me that when she was secretary to the Governor in Saudi Arabia and met your father, she thought he was an Arab."

"He still wears his Arab garb occasionally," Rick put in.

"Umm, when Mother found out he was an Oxford graduate, an Englishman, they got married. They had the entire Arab wedding—a four-day feast in the desert with galloping horses and guns and sheep's eyes—all of it."

Jock asked, "Didn't he get the CMG and the OBE* from the Queen for stopping a war in Saudi Arabia?"

Rick said, "Brian, waving the Union Jack, galloped his horse in the desert between two warring tribes. He's a true Lawrence of Arabia. Not many people left like him today."

"Then he decided he wanted to be a Maasai," Bryony said. "He's a full blood brother of the Maasai, you know."

"He's a true-life Walter Mitty," Rick added. "After becoming a Maasai, he decided he wanted to become a Somali—so he did. But he's a very substantial person—he's *the* camel expert of the world, and an excellent agriculturist. He's saved countless people from starving. He says there's going to be a real famine in Ethiopia—it's avoidable, but it won't be because of political reasons. There is one province in Ethiopia that is so fertile it will feed the entire country, but the politicians won't give them enough money for irrigation and so forth. They spread it around, uselessly, because they need votes from all the provinces. Brian claims there's going to be such a disaster there, and that it could be prevented."

"Of course, the only real problem in Africa is the population

*CMG, Companion of St. Michael and St. George; OBE, Order of the British Empire.

growth rate," Jock said. "There are just too many people to feed. Look at us—Kenya is number one in population growth in the world."

This was my soapbox subject. "Before, one in every forty-two babies lived. Now one in every three does—because the missionaries brought in medicine. But when we have death control, which is medicine, we must also have birth control. We cannot leave to nature what is no longer a natural situation. We have to go all the way. Bringing in medicine means we have to have birth control too."

"Mother," Rick interrupted, "this is not your lecture audience. We're all aware of this."

"My father's been fighting popualtion growth and destruction of the environment for years," Bryony said. "Uganda is the worst."

"Everyone and every organization in the world has pulled out of Uganda because it is so dangerous," Rick interrupted. "All but Brian. When people see him when he comes to town, which is about once a year, they don't say hello, they say. 'You still alive?' "

"I just don't how he survives," Jock commented. "He eats nothing but the rations the Africans get."

"But he's the happiest person I know," I added. "He's adviser to Oxfam now, isn't he, Bryony?"

"Yes, he's just gone to Ethiopia—he loves the bush so much. It was Mother who coerced him to leave. We had lived in the bush ever since they were married, and when I was thirteen and my three brothers were fifteen, nine, and three, she thought we should be vaccinated, and go to school—and she wanted some civilization, so reluctantly my father gave in and we moved to Devon."

"You call that civilization?" I asked.

Bryony laughed. "We did. I hadn't seen electricity or running water before."

"How do you like it?" Rick asked. "Do you think it's here to stay?"

"By the way," I said to Bryony, "I know your godmother is Vivien Leigh, but I don't know why."

"Well," she answered in her gentle British voice, "Vivien Leigh's real surname was Hartley—my maiden name, and she is my father's cousin. He used to carry her around on his shoulders when she was a child, so that's how it all came about."

The conversation turned to other things and then we said our sad goodbyes to them and Shirley Brown and the giraffe and headed for Ethiopia.

After a few days there of going to Axum, birthplace of the Queen of Sheba, and organizing other exotic spots for our safariers to visit, we went to Teheran and had tea with the Prince in his palace, which I spilled all over his priceless Persian carpet. He got down on his hands and knees with me and helped me wipe it up; I was so embarrassed. I remember Teheran's terrible traffic, and the fact that there were snowy mountains where we could ski, and that Bebe, with whom I had gone to Africa the first time, and who we were staying with, had a maid named Noose Rat, and that when we said goodbye to her we said, "We just don't know how to thank you," and she answered, "Well . . . try."

On the flight to the States, with our finished manuscript in hand, I was reading the paper and said to Jock, "It says here that every American Nobel Prize winner is an alcoholic."

"Betty"—Jock squeezed my hand—"you better start drinking."

Jock was particularly excited about going to America this time, because he had spent a year preparing to become an alien immigrant of the U.S.A. It had taken him all that time to meet the requirements of the American Embassy. He had to take original copies of his birth certificate, marriage license, divorce decree, and a police statement from everywhere he had lived in Kenya and England saying he had no police record. Furthermore he needed chest x-rays and endless forms, and finally when everything was accomplished, he was sworn in by the Consulate in the American Embassy in Nairobi.

As we went into Immigration at JFK, Jock had his papers at the ready. When he rather proudly handed them over, the

Immigration man jumped up and shook Jock by the hand and said, "Congratulations, Mr. Leslie-Melville. Welcome to the United States of America. Report to your draft board on Tuesday." Not once in the entire year had there been a mention he would be eligible for the draft, and of course I feared that, despite his paralyzed arm, with his training at Sandhurst they would need him for something special in the Vietnam War. But fortunately when he reported Tuesday, they told him he was 4F.

Paul laughed so hard when we told him this story. He thought it was the funniest thing he had ever heard. He had come to the apartment for a drink, and as we all got in a taxi to go to dinner, suddenly there was blood everywhere. It took us a few seconds to discover it was from Paul's finger, which he had caught in the door of the cab, and because he has no feeling in his hands he didn't even know it.

After a few days of fun and seeing family and friends, we were about to land in Dallas for our first lecture. "I'm looking forward to eating some Texas chili carne."

"Chili *con* carne," I corrected him. "Stupid foreigner."

Jock smiled his lovely smile and adjusted his sling as he got up to disembark. "Someone told me that Dallas airport is bigger than Manhattan."

"Texas is big and rich. You know, I think the rest of the world looks at America as Americans look at Texas—sort of big and vulgar."

"I love Texas, except it always makes me nervous how everyone talks to you. Even in an elevator, Texans always say, 'Hi—where you going?' when actually it should be obvious that you are either going up or down."

"They're just friendly. The Brits always look embarrassed to be in the same elevator with you."

"Well, here we are," Jock said as we walked into the airport, "off on our lecture tour."

"Nothing ever changes. I'm still selling eggs, only now I'm calling them safaris."

"I don't care what we do as long as we are togther. We make our own music."

"I love you so much, you make everything and everywhere so good for me, but best of all I like writing with you. When we go back, let's write another book."

"What about this time?" Jock asked as we waited for our luggage.

"How about writing about the famous Lord Errol murder case in Kenya? Your mother was his best friend and she told me a lot about it."

"Excellent, because writing together in our ivory tower in never-never land with Shirley Brown and the giraffe is my favorite thing too. And after that I think we should write a novel, a saga of a family in Kenya."

And so we did.

Chapter 19

WE had owls in our roof. In the evenings, after writing all day, Jock and Shirley Brown and I would go down to the *boma* and feed Walter Warthog and the giraffe, then sit on our front steps and marvel at the speckled giants and little Daffodil ambling across the lawn, with Walter running after them, his tail standing straight up in the air like a mast. The giraffe would go to the fish pond to get a drink of water, then dance around the lawn playing with Daisy's baby; finally they'd come up to us for a final carrot and a goodnight kiss before going off into the woods for their all-night feast.

Putting his arm around me, Jock said, "Oh, Betty, we lead such a heavenly life, the kind most people only dream about. Living in both worlds, here and in the States." He patted Shirley Brown and lifted her up to her feet by her tail. "Our only sadness is Shirley Brown." She was now sixteen years old and very frail. She could walk only if we held her up by her tail, but her enthusiasm for life never wavered, so we just helped her walk into the sun room with us, as we did every evening, to watch the sun fade in pinks and blues behind the snow on Kilimanjaro and the Ngong Hills.

For the last few weeks, just as the sun quickly disappeared, we would hear gentle footsteps right above us, many of them, like soldiers marching on parade. Then through a hole in the sun room's roof we would see the owls fly gracefully away.

Although we enjoyed watching them, we could imagine what was accumulating in our roof and were not delighted with the idea that one night, while we were sleeping comfortably in our bed, our pasteboard ceiling might give way and we would be covered in owl poop, not to mention baby owls and broken owl eggs and dead mice and other awfuls that had got hung up in the vines on our house one day when the drainpipe under the roof gave way and dropped this macabre load.

So wanting to get rid of the owls. Jock told Ronald, our gardener, to get them out, and Ronald, always so sweet and accommodating, said no. I was astounded, but Jock explained, "The Kikuyu think owls are a bad omen. I thought perhaps Ronald might have been sophisticated enough by now not to have this superstition any longer—you know, as we walk under a ladder comfortably; but obviously I was wrong."

Ronald was looking desperate. *"Ndege hii ni kufa—kabissa."* (Owls are a sure sign of death.)

"Don't worry, Ronald, it's all right. I'll get someone else to do it," Jock told him kindly.

Ronald was relieved he wasn't going to lose his job, and we got a European to rid the ceiling of the owls.

A week later we put Shirley Brown in the car with us and drove to Malindi. Jock was unusually quiet. Finally he said to me, "Betty, we have to put Shirley Brown down." I was appalled. But with tears in his eyes he insisted. "She can't get up unless we lift her, she can't walk alone, she can't swim or chase her ball or birds anymore, she's lost control of her bladder. She's had such a good life. Let her have a good death."

I cried and argued, but I knew he was right. So, sadly, the next day I made a pan of fudge and let her eat it all, as we sat on the floor with her and talked to her and played with her, then tearfully we carried her into her beloved ocean and held her while she paddled around for her last swim. The vet arrived and Jock and I held our dear constant companion for sixteen years in our arms, and I sobbed as he jabbed her. She looked up at us with her soft brown eyes and seemed to understand, even to be grateful, as she died.

We buried her with her ball under a frangipani tree and put a little plaque over her grave, which read SHIRLEY BROWN. Standing there, clinging to each other and crying, Jock reminded me, "You must remember to do the same for me, Betty, when my time comes." (Little did I know that in exactly four years' time, to the day, it would be Jock's funeral.)

We were so sad and exhausted. It had been a hectic safari season and we had been engrossed in our latest book, our fifth, *Bagamoyo*, the long generational saga of Kenya from colonization to statehood. When we got back to Nairobi, after feeding the giraffe every evening we would eat our supper on trays in the library in front of the fire and reread our manuscript. One of those nights, uncharacteristically, Jock fell asleep as he was reading, and the same thing happened each night for the week before we departed. He said he didn't feel well; he was afraid he might be coming down with the flu.

When we got to New York, he seemed unusually lethargic—strange because New York invariably exhilarated him. I attributed it to a combination of virus and jet lag. A few mornings after arrival, he went out to the neighborhood market for provisions, and I went into the kitchen to find all the gas burners blazing, but nothing on the stove. Then, when he returned from shopping, he had only half the items on the list we'd drawn up. Over the next few days, when I asked him to do this or that errand for me, more often than not he would return empty-handed, saying he'd forgotten completely. I began to grow irritated with him, even complaining to my good friend Colleen that Jock was behaving so oddly and seemed so vague; then at a board for A FEW, where Jock was always so attentive and alert, I grew alarmed when he nodded off to sleep.

A few nights later, driving back to New York after visiting the Paars in New Canaan, Jock said, "Betty, the strangest thing happened tonight. While you and Miriam were in the kitchen after dinner, I was talking with Jack, and I kept losing my train of thought. It was odd—I'd start to tell him something and then completely forget what I was talking about."

"I lose my train of thought fourteen times a day," I smiled.

"No, this was different," he said seriously.

"You're going to a doctor tomorrow."

We went to a specialist in tropical diseases. His diagnosis was sleeping sickness. "Your symptoms are classic," he told Jock. "It will be a long haul—three months in the hospital, a year to really get over it, but we can cure it these days. You'll have to have a spinal tap to confirm it, but that's what it is."

"What a nuisance," Jock said. "But I'll be fine, Bettyduk, don't worry."

Don't worry—I was distressed. As we left the doctor's office, I told Jock, "But I just can't believe it's sleeping sickness. . . . We haven't been in any infected tsetse fly areas. I'm going to put in a call to Adriano." So I called our own doctor in Nairobi, and over the transatlantic line he barked, "Bullshit. We haven't had an infected tsetse fly here in two years. Get him to a neurologist."

I called a highly recommended neurologist, Frank Petito, at New York Hospital, who sent Jock for a spinal tap and a scan and made an appointment to see Jock in three days' time, when the scan result was back.

During those three days we had friends in for dinner, and I grew progressively worried, because although Jock remained cheerful he was always falling asleep—even at the dinner table.

The tropical medicine doctor called and, chagrined, said the spinal tap came back negative, it was not sleeping sickness. We were very relieved, and our spirits were high as we packed the car to go to Philadelphia for a big party Colleen was giving for us there, then on to Baltimore to see the family; but first we had Jock's appointment with Dr. Petito. It was Halloween and a beautiful crisp and sunny morning as we walked hand in hand down the street, laughing on our way to the hospital.

We did not know it was the day all the laughter would die.

It's a good thing we don't have crystal balls, that we can't see the road that we are about to travel on, for if we could we might decide not to take it.

We stopped in a bakery and ate fresh doughnuts along the way, then tried to wipe our faces so we would look serious for our appointment with Dr. Petito, but we bumped into him in the corridor with powdered sugar still on our lips.

Sitting in his office, he told us that the scan showed something, he didn't know what, but Jock would have to be admitted immediately. Could I go home and bring him his bathrobe and toilet articles? Jock and I just looked at each other. Everyone was silent for a few moments. I was staggered, and later Jock told me his only reaction was concern for me. On my way home I forced myself to be hopeful, because Dr. Petito said what he had seen on the scan could be just a lesion from one of the high-temperature diseases Jock had had. I cancelled our trip, returned to the hospital, and tried to sound optimistic. Jock took me in his arms and kissed me. "Oh, Bettyduk, I feel so sorry for you. You'll have to cope with my being in here alone, and you'll be all alone. I'm so sorry, but I'll be out soon."

Jock spent the day being examined by ten different doctors. "What diseases have you had?" they all began, and ended up being astounded when Jock listed typhoid, tick typhus, malaria five times, brucellosis, polio, and cerebral meningitis. Because he was so tired by the arrival of the tenth doctor, I said, "Look, his history *is* on the chart—the same thing— nine times already. Do we have to go through it yet again?" And then he explained to me that in neurology they use many doctors there on the same case, so that if one misses something, another may pick it up—ten brains being better than one. They would all have their conference in the morning.

That evening I stopped Dr. Petito in the corridor and asked him about Jock. "What I really think," he answered casually, "is that it's a brain tumor. If he weren't from Africa, where he might have picked up something strange, there wouldn't be a doubt in my mind. Of course it may not be malignant. I'll keep you posted as the tests come in." He nodded politely and continued on his rounds.

A brain tumor. A brain tumor! I went cold. It was the first time that thought had ever occurred to me. When someone doesn't bring home the loaf of bread you asked for, you don't think it's because of a brain tumor. As I walked home, I felt as if I were in a dream or a play. I had no sense of reality, and everyone's walking around the streets as skeletons and Donald Duck and bears for Halloween didn't help.

Jock had not been sick one day of our seventeen years together. And hospitals scare me and doctors irritate me—why couldn't they at least be more humane? Angry at what I considered offhand treatment of what was the most important thing in my life, I telephoned Dr. Petito the next morning and said tersely, "I'd like to get you in Africa, out in the bush in front of a herd of elephant, then I'd say to you, 'That bull elephant may or may not charge. If he does, he may kill you— I'll let you know when I come back."

Of course, he had no idea what I was talking about, and when subsequently I learned what a sensitive, caring person he is, I apologized for my hostility, but at this moment I wasn't sorry.

I spent the weekend in the hospital with Jock and my sister (whose husband died of a brain tumor when he was fifty-one years old) and the many friends who came to visit. Jock was extremely cheerful. Monday Dr. Petito said all the tests were negative; they would have to operate to see what was going on. The surgeon came in and set the date for Wednesday. I went into his office and asked, "What is the alternative to operating?"

He made a steeple with his hands and answered emphatically. "You don't have one."

I liked his answer because it was so definite I didn't have to make a decision about something I knew nothing about. Dr. Petito told me there was good possibility that if it were a tumor it would be benign, and Jock would be out of the hospital and his old self in ten days' time. How I clung to those words and repeated them to myself and everyone else over and over. How I prayed.

McDonnell, the only child who was in the States at that

time, and my sister came to New York to be with me during
the operation. Just before they took Jock up to the operating
room, I started to cry.

"Don't cry, Bettyduk, don't cry. I'll be fine. I don't mind
this at all."

For four hours McDonnell, Evelyn, and I sat in the waiting
room and waited and waited and waited. Finally the surgeon
appeared and said, "It's a tumor all right. I couldn't get all
of it."

"Malig—?"

"I couldn't tell—sometimes I can, but I couldn't this time.
The biopsy results will be back Friday."

The nightmare started.

Jock was wheeled down, his head a helmet of bandages,
and as he came out of the anesthesia he smiled his lovely
smile and muttered something incoherent. I was glad he wasn't
conscious enough to see my pain. The next day he was still
incoherent, and I stayed with him, holding his hand and
stroking his forehead and telling him how much I loved him
and how sure I was everything was all right.

Friday morning Dr. Petito and another doctor came into
the waiting room where I was with McDonnell and sat down
next to me. "We are repeating the biopsy. The second opinion
won't be in until Monday," Dr. Petito said.

"What was the first result?"

He patted my shoulder. "A glioblastoma."

"What's that?"

He put his hand on mine. "The worst kind of malignant
brain tumor." Then he added softly, "It is rated on a scale
of one to four; four is the worst. Jock's is between a three
and a four."

I felt sick. I felt crazy.

"Does pathology ever make a mistake?" McDonnell asked,
but it didn't sound like his voice.

"No," he answered quietly. "The tumor is near the frontal
lobe. Jock won't be able to do much. And, Betty, I don't think
there is any point in telling him the truth—unless you want
to. Because of the damage to the frontal lobe he'll believe

anything you tell him." He left a pause, then added sadly, "He'll be like a child."

McDonnell took my hand and we were silent for a moment. Then I whispered, "How long can he live?"

"Six months," the other doctor answered somberly.

It was as if lightning had struck me.

"But he's only forty-seven years old," McDonnell muttered to no one and put his arm around me.

But I wasn't me anymore—I was pain, all pain. Six months . . . Jock dead? . . . gone forever? Jock . . . dead . . . ? This extraordinary man I loved so much, who was at the core of my being . . . gone forever? I felt as if my heart and mind were strangling. Horror. Torture. Fear. All of these were growing inside me as unstoppably as the lethal growth destroying Jock.

It was unbearable.

I was too stunned to think, to translate my feelings into words, but somehow I knew I would not tell Jock the truth. Why have two of us feeling this despair? There are things more important than truth, and in this case the most important thing was for Jock to be as happy as he could his few remaining months. So somehow I walked back to Jock's room and leaned over his bed and looked into his blue blue eyes and managed to say, "You're fine. They got all of it. It's not malignant—you're fine."

He squeezed my hand and smiled his lovely smile. "Thank God . . . it would have been so terrible for you if it had been malignant," and fell back to sleep.

Chapter 20

WHEN Jock awakened again he was incoherent and gradually he grew more so. The first few days I attributed his dimness and confusion to the anesthesia and operation, but then I realized it was brain damage. I had no idea it would be so severe. He could not walk, and worse, he was acting like a two-year-old.

I knew he would rather have died on the operating table than be alive like this; he definitely would not want to "live" this way, not if Jock were Jock.

Vividly I remember his insisting on putting Shirley Brown down, and the incident with the impala when we were first married and I had first made my promise to him. I remembered three other similar incidents when he had put animals out of their misery and had made me vow again to do the same for him if he ever became incapacitated.

I also kept thinking about another incident. Bob McIlvain had been American Ambassador to Kenya, and he and his wife Alice were friends of ours. Bob retired and they returned to D.C., and one morning Alice's father telephoned her from Florida and said her mother had been taken to the hospital. He was so upset she couldn't get much from him, so she flew down. About fifteen minutes after she arrived in her mother's hospital room, her father asked her if she would step into the corridor—he wanted to be alone with his wife for a few minutes. As soon as Alice was in the corridor, she heard a shot. Her father had shot her mother dead in bed. Her mother was eighty-four years old, had suffered a stroke and was totally paralyzed, unable even to speak; her father was eighty-five. He had Alzheimer's disease and knew he would be unable to take care of himself, much less her, and they had a pact that if either of them became terminally ill they would both walk out into the sea together to end their lives. After the first shot her father had immediately turned his old World War I pistol to his head, but the recoil from the first shot made his hand shake and the bullet went through his throat instead of his brain, as he had intended. He fell onto the bed and took his wife in his arms, then pulled the trigger a third time, but unknown to him there had only been two bullets in the gun. Nurses and doctors racing in, found him holding his dead wife, rushed him to the operating room and his life was saved.

He was then charged for murder.

The evening Bob and Alice were relating the story, Jock had told them, "What an act of love. That's certainly what I want Betty to do if ever I become incapacitated. I've made her promise." And then he turned to me, "Never forget it."

Sitting there now on Jock's bed in New York Hospital, stroking his face, my promise to him haunted me. Especially I remembered his own mother. She was seventy-two years old, with cancer so widespread that surgery would not have helped, and the increased dosage of morphine had ceased to dull her terrible pain. Jock had said that when the morphine stopped working it was time to end it. So, knowing his mother would not want to prolong her agonizing death, he called a doctor friend who was passing through Nairobi and asked him to come to his mother's house and put her out of her pain.

Frankly, I was horrified. Here was I, a person who puts spiders out of windows, unable to kill anything—married to a "murderer?" Intellectually I understood, but emotionally I was very upset. Inculcated in me was the belief that life is sacred. "I don't think you should play God," I told Jock.

"But Betty," Jock said patiently, "this assumes there is a God in control of each life and death. So when a life is saved that God has stricken with incurable cancer, or mortally

injured in some way, isn't that playing God as well, interfering
with the Divine plan—prolonging a doomed life by artificial
means? We can't have it both ways."

I thought a minute. "But people say God gives us our minds
to cure diseases . . ."

"Fine, but if this is so, then can we not also use our minds
to reason in behalf of dignity and humaneness?"

"But you are ending her life . . ."

"No, that has already been determined. I am merely ending
her pain and suffering." It was his honest conviction, and it
was his mother, so the doctor arrived and gave her a jab, and
she died peacefully.

Now, as I touched the two white spots on his teeth, I could
hear the words he had spoken later that day. "There are many
things worse than death, Betty. If ever I am terminal and
suffering, if ever I don't have full use of my mind, if ever I
lose my dignity, remember you have promised me you will let
me go."

A nurse came into Jock's room and interrupted my thoughts.
I leaned over and kissed the forehead of the pathetic figure
lying in bed. I looked at this man whose mind had always
been so clear, whose dignity had always been so great. I
thought of how he had never used the "Esquire" after his
name that he was entitled to use—twice, as a matter of fact:
once as the grandson of an earl, and also as an officer in the
Coldstream Guards. But he never used it because he didn't
have to. He needed no props: His elegance and dignity were
so obvious. But now . . .

Had he been capable of realizing what had happened to
him, he would have taken his own life—of that I was sure.
And he certainly would expect me to do it for him now. Right
then I made up my mind. After all, it wasn't my decision—
I had promised.

I walked out in the corridor and went up to the resident
on duty and said as clearly and rationally as I knew how, "If
you don't kill my husband right now, I am going to." Looking
extremely alarmed, he took me by my arm and got me into a
little doctor's office and telephoned Dr. Petito, who arrived

quickly with a few more doctors. "I am not going to let my intelligent, dignified husband deteriorate into a helpless, retarded child. I've promised him I would not let him live if ever he became this way, and I am going to keep my promise. Now."

They all talked and talked, trying to calm me, assuring me Jock's dementia was mainly due to the swelling from the operation, that it would go down and he would be better, much better—at least for a while. Finally they convinced me enough that I changed my decision to not making a decision, at least for the time being. And the doctors were proved right, but only up to a point. For the rest of Jock's short life he was a 40-watt bulb instead of the 150 watts he had always been before.

In the next ten days he did improve quite a bit mentally, and slowly and with help he began to walk again. Therefore, knowing our insurance covered only a $100 a day, and that the cost in the hospital was about $1,000 a day, Dr. Petito let Jock go home. Since our apartment was very close to the hospital, Jock and I walked there every day for his radiation. The chemotherapy he took in pill form at home made him sick, and that doctor said the one thing that would stop the vomiting was marijuana. Doctors had discovered this when everyone in a cancer ward got sick from the chemo except a seventeen-year-old boy. Test after test of the boy showed nothing different from the other patients. Finally the doctors asked him if he did anything the others were not doing. "Only this," he answered, opening his bedside table drawer, and there were the joints he smoked. They tried it on others willing to smoke it, and sure enough it prevented the nausea. Jock was willing, and not only did not get sick again, he enjoyed it very much. For an experiment I tried it with him one night but didn't like it all, but if my only alternative had been throwing up, I guess I would have smoked it, too.

Because of the damage to the frontal lobe, Jock didn't read or write or even open his mail. But he was never happier. He was like a child. It was as if he had had a lobotomy—he didn't have a care or worry in the world. His great mass of hair fell out, which normally would have devastated him, but now he was merely excited about getting a wig and had great fun picking it out and having it cut in his special way.

As for me, I looked forward to going to bed at night to get away from the nightmare of the day.

Friends shattered by Jock's six-month sentence to death came to see Jock constantly, but every one covered up his distress and put on a good act. When Betsy and Walter Cronkite saw Jock, Walter, with a hearty handshake and a big smile, said, "Don't *do* that again, Jock." When the Paars came to visit, despite being called the terror of the late-night show, Jack is so caring and sentimental, his eyes filled with tears and he started to break up; but he pulled himself together and made Jock laugh the rest of the afternoon. It was his most difficult performance.

I'll never forget the caring support and the love my family and friends gave. They threw me many life rafts and without them I think I would have drowned. Woody Allen has said: "Life is showing up"—and they all showed up.

All but one, that is, and that was our Rolls-Royce friend who became a Born Again Christian. Knowing that Jock didn't know he was dying and that our lies pretending to him that he was fine were an act of mercy, but not aware that Jock couldn't read, he sent a letter to Jock telling him he had cancer: "Your sickness comes from Satan, who is trying to destroy you, Jock. And your cancer will be the victor unless you get before Jesus and ask Him to come into your heart, then He will renounce all the negative things the doctors have said. I have seen a woman who embraced our Lord raised from the dead . . ." He went on and on and on, a four-page letter. Fortunately I opened it and Jock never saw it. I got so angry I wrote him a nasty letter telling him how un-Christian he was.

And I really looked forward to going to bed that night to get away from the nightmare of the day.

But Jock was constantly full of laughter and enjoyment and participated in all conversations; in fact, he talked more than he ever had. One of his favorite stories, which he told again and again, was one Colleen told us, not without a certain glee, about her ex-husband traveling through Wyoming with his new bride in a mobile home. After hours at the wheel in the cab, he asked his wife to come up and drive while he took a shower and a nap in the separate back part of the trailer. As he came out of the shower, she swerved to avoid something in the road and the lurch threw him against the rear door, popping it open, and he fell out—stark naked, without even a towel. She drove happily on for twenty miles, quite unaware he wasn't having his nap, while he stood naked in the middle of Wyoming, clutching himself and panicking. Who would pick up a naked hitchhiker? Eventually his wife realized he was missing and tore back to where he was hiding up a tree. Every time Jock told this story he laughed so hard he could hardly finish it; and I always laughed along with him as if it were the first time I had heard it.

"How do you do it?" friends asked me. "How can you keep on pretending to be so cheerful and that everything is fine?"

"Do I have a choice?" was always my answer. "I have to keep up for Jock."

Then everyone went on to say how strong and brave I was, but I didn't feel strong or brave. I just felt determined to make Jock as happy as possible for what was left of his short life. It was my last, pathetic gift to him.

Chapter 21

*A*FTER a month of radiation and chemotherapy, there was nothing more the doctors could do and Jock wanted to go home, so I decided to take him back to Kenya for Christmas, where we could be with the children and the giraffe, and at Malindi.

Dr. Petito told me, "Watch for symptoms of the tumor's growing."

"What might they be?" I asked.

"We don't know which direction that tumor will move. Jock could just get so weak he couldn't walk at all, he could have convulsions, he could start slipping into a coma."

"Great choice."

"Betty, you will be responsible for Jock's dignity. That's the biggest job. . . . Oh, and one more thing—watch your money."

How would I, alone, be able to take care of Jock, finish our book, run our safari business and A FEW, and lecture—all of which we had always done together?

How would I cope?

Someone suggest Valium, but I have an aversion to pills, so although I had given up smoking for two years I started again, figuring it was better than tranquilizers or booze.

But how would I cope?

There are organizations for spouses of alcoholics, of drug addicts, even gamblers, but nothing for the loved ones of the brain-damaged. I was on my own, knowing death, with its incomprehensible finality, was on its way.

I tried to convince myself there was a Heaven, or that death might in fact even be fun—perhaps that's why no one comes back—maybe it's a better party where they are. Or, I wondered, if there is a life after death, perhaps we are already through with death—but I didn't succeed in believing any of these things. The only things I clung to were practical axioms—"Cooperate with the inevitable," some wise person once said, and you might just as well; also, as my father always used to tell me, "Life is like a whiskey bottle—it depends on how you look at it: It's either half empty or half full." And I know it is attitudes in life that count, not circumstances. So I kept telling myself that Jock and I had had a perfect, magical life together for seventeen years. How many people could say that? I should just be thankful for what we had had. I was; but I wanted more.

Dancy and Rick and Bryony got special permission to board the plane when it landed in Nairobi. When they had last seen Jock, just three months before, he was robust physically and mentally; now not only was his luxurious mane of hair gone, his mind was dim and his frame bent and feeble. Watching them feign joy as they greeted him, when I knew their hearts were breaking, was so terribly sad. He was overjoyed to see them.

When we got home Daisy ran up to him and gave him a kiss, as did the other giraffe, and with a cane and help from the children and me, he was able to get to the *boma* to feed them. Then Jock and I sat side by side in the sun room as we had always done and watched the sun go down behind Kilimanjaro. I don't think I'm superstitious, but I was glad there were no more owls in the ceiling.

"Isn't this wonderful, Bettyduk? It's so good to be home. I'm so glad I'm all right."

"I'm so glad too." I kissed him and ran my fingers over the two white dots on his teeth. Agony. "I love you so much."

For the first time in my life I was now responsible for tending to everything—Jock, all our jobs, all the taxes and rates and insurance and the masses of other bills and problems. Jock ignored them all and couldn't even remember his bank manager's name. When finally I tracked down who it was, I discovered Jock was $60,000 overdrawn. I was shocked. Jock said, "Oh, don't worry about it, Betty, in a few weeks I'll be working again—I'll sort it all out. Just forget it." I smiled and hugged him. "I know you will. We won't worry about anything boring like bills." How would I pay them all?

We all drove to Malindi for Christmas, which all his doctors had told us would be his last one. The children and I tried to feign " 'Tis the season to be jolly," then knowing it would be the last one we would ever spend together, we ran into other rooms to weep. It was the saddest day all of us ever had, except for Jock, who claimed it was his best Christmas ever.

After we had opened the presents and the children had walked, sadly, down the beach to visit Bryony's parents, Jock said he wanted to go swimming. So I helped him down to the beach and told him, although he was an excellent swimmer, not to go out over his head; but not realizing how debilitated he was, he did so immediately and was too weak to cope with the tiny waves. He began to flounder and call for me. I had swum after him and he grabbed for me, pulling me under. We struggled, flailing about violently. Frantically. I tried to move him into shallower water, but he kept grabbing me and we both went under time and time again. Desperately I looked for someone on the beach to help. It was empty. We continued to struggle, each of us getting water in our lungs and growing more alarmed and weaker each minute. We both came very close to drowning, but somehow I managed, with that extra strength one gets in an emergency, to pull him back into shallow water and he crawled to the beach. Then I got him to bed and fell exhausted and trembling next to him.

When he awoke, we made love for the first time since he was operated on. I clung to his naked body and pretended it was as wonderful as it had always been, but all I could think of was that Jock, my lovely Jock, would not be around for long and therefore we would soon never make love again. My suffering negated the joy of it—for after all, sex is between the ears. But Jock enjoyed it and never knew.

Later on the children and Bryony's family arrived for our big turkey dinner, and in the evening Jock and I picked some pink and orange bougainvillea and put it on Shirley Brown's grave. Jock said, "Poor Shirley Brown. She loved Christmas so much. Remember how she used to get so excited and rip open everyone's present? She had such a good life, and we gave her a good death." He squeezed me. "Bettyduk, she wouldn't have wanted to be alive, not being able to run after the birds or her ball. If I thought I wouldn't ever be able to swim properly and jog down the beach again and do all the things I used to do, I wouldn't want to be alive."

He thought my tears were for Shirley Brown.

My promise to him loomed large. Just because he was happy and in no pain, should I not keep my word? Should I have just let him drown? He would have said yes, of that I was sure. But he was having such a good time.

And he was going to have even a better one. We had always talked of going to Venice but had never managed to do so. I was determined to get him there, while he was still able to travel, and after Venice I'd take him to England to see all his family and friends. I'd have his funeral for him while he was alive, so he could enjoy it.

Venice thrilled us. Our interlude there was for me one of the most romantic, if poignant, we'd ever had. It was lovely, it was tragic. I felt I was in a beautiful dream and a nightmare both at the same time. How unreal reality can be, but somehow despite my broken heart I carried on, pretending to him that everything was fine and that he was getting better. He was confident that he was and his spirits remained buoyant, but for me life was an endurance test.

In London we stayed in Jock's family's flat and saw all his cousins and friends there and enjoyed the theater almost every night, including the revival of Abel Gance's *Napoleon*, the triplex 1927 silent film classic, which had the London Symphony Orchestra playing at each performance. We ate butterscotch sundaes in Fortnum & Mason and walked hand and hand in Hyde Park and Jock laughed so hard at a sign on a newly painted bench that said, "Wet Paint, Darling."

After a week in London, we were to be off to raise funds at Rhino Rescue in Texas the next day. Everyone said to me, "Don't you have more than enough to do already? Why did you agree to have this Rhino Rescue party in Dallas?" Work was what kept me sane and Jock loved the parties, and McDonnell, who was participating in the gala, would be there to help me with Jock, so from London we were flying directly there. But the day before we were to leave, Jock began insisting he wanted to stay an extra day to get a video machine for us to take to Kenya, and I mean *insisting*. Rick and Quentin Crewe, a good friend of ours, happened to be staying in the apartment at the time and none of us could convince Jock to come with me, which was odd, for Jock never wanted to be away from me a minute; but he was adamant about staying.

Rick and Quentin said for me to go on. They'd go with Jock to get the video, put him on the plane the next day, and I could meet him in Dallas. So I did, but when I went to Dallas airport to meet him, he wasn't on the plane. I called London, and Rick and Quentin were staggered—they had gone with him and bought the video, but then Jock had insisted he take the cab to the airport alone. "Why are you going with me?" he had asked, insulted. "I don't need an escort." All their arguing was in vain, so they put Jock in a cab headed for the correct airline and, since they hadn't heard from him, assumed he was in Texas.

Where was Jock? Three long, wretched hours later, I got a call from Rick—Jock had just walked into the London flat. "Bettyduk," Jock said cheerfully over the phone, "I went to the airport. I got there two hours ahead of time, but they never called the flight." Of course they had called the flight, he just didn't realize it. "So you know what I did? I took a taxi back to London and went to see *Evita*—it was wonderful, I loved it. Then I went to Langan's for dinner and had lamb and creme brulée—delicious meal. I wish you had been with me . . . Oh, but I lost the video—wait till you see it, I got the best one. It was $1,500, but I'll go get another just like it tomorrow and bring it with me."

I tried not to holler about his not letting anyone know where he was, or about his spending $3,000 we didn't have; I tried to enthuse about *Evita* along with him and tell him how much I loved him; then I told him he would miss the rhino party, so he might as well fly right to Baltimore, far less air fare, and I'd meet him there. Then I explained it all to Rick.

So Jock took the plane to Dallas anyway. Fortunately he called me from Dallas airport and caught me just as I was leaving the hotel to fly to Baltimore, but he said he was too tired to fly anymore that day, so I collected him and we stayed that night in Texas.

I understood immediately what Rick and Quentin had had to deal with. Jock, in three days, had changed considerably. He was adamant about what he was or was not going to do or eat or wear—about everything; he was totally inflexible and unalterable. He said he had never felt better in his life, he was extremely enthusiastic, but adamant and determined to do whatever he wanted, even if it wasn't in the slightest bit logical.

Since I was still in Texas, I needed to go to Houston for a day to talk to the A FEW committee there about a Rhino Rescue fund-raiser they were organizing, but Jock refused to come with me.

"But Jock, we'll stay with Jane—you like her so much. If it weren't for her, we might never have gotten together. Remember how she called you all those years ago at Parliament and asked you to come to a party that I made her have so I could see you again?"

Although Jock could not remember what day it was, his long-term memory was superb. "Of course I remember, I had no intention of taking you to her party, but I want to go to Baltimore now. I want to get some yogurt."

"But they have yogurt in Houston."

"No. I want only the kind in Baltimore." And so it went. Finally McDonnell said for me to go on to Houston, he would fly with Jock back to Baltimore and they would stay at his house until the next day, when I arrived. He called a friend, who filled the refrigerator with Jock's favorite kind of yogurt.

The next morning at Jane's, the phone rang and it was McDonnell, hysterical. "Mother, you have to come right back now. I am going to have a nervous breakdown—Jock is lost."

"What do you mean 'lost'?"

"Well, he got up and insisted he wanted more yogurt. I told him there were ten of them in the refrigerator, but that wasn't enough, he said—we might run out and he wanted more. So finally I gave in and told him I'd drive him to the store to get some more. No, he was going to drive himself . . ."

"But he's not allowed to drive," I said, alarmed.

"I *know* that, Mother, but he simply would not let me drive or go with him. He left in the car—and hasn't come back. So since he has my car, I called Evelyn, and she and Dick have been driving around looking for him, and I'm here waiting by the phone in case he calls. I was hoping maybe he had called you. I'd better not tie up the line any longer. I'll keep you posted."

About an hour and a pack of cigarettes later, McDonnell called back: "Well, we have him. Evelyn and Dick found the car at the shopping center, but no Jock. They kept on driving around, and finally they found him walking in the wrong direction about a mile from here. I had told him the car wouldn't start without the seatbelt fastened, but he forgot, so he couldn't get the car going again after he bought all the yogurt in the store, so he decided to walk back here. It's only three blocks and he knows this area so well, but he got lost. Whew, we're all wrecks—that is, everyone but Jock. He can't imagine why anyone was concerned. Mother, please take the next plane back."

I did, and found Jock ecstatic, but wild, when I got there. He told me, "I can do anything, I've never felt so powerful in my life—I feel like a sixteen-year-old Napoleon." Then he talked on and on of the silent film we had seen in London about his hero, and within a few days he decided he was, in fact, Napoleon himself.

Chapter 22

I CALLED Dr. Petito, who said to get Jock to New York Hospital—either the tumor had started to grow in the direction that was unbalancing him or, if we were lucky, it could be just a reaction to the steroids.

Getting Napoleon to the hospital was no easy task. "Hospital? Why, I'm fitter than I've ever been," he said, opening a file which he entitled "Napoleon's Commands." For six grisly days Napoleon was impossible—totally manic, omnipotent, infallible, and given to abrupt outbreaks of rage at the most inconsequential imagined slights. One morning I wouldn't give him more than twenty dollars (he only wanted to buy some gum) because, as in the video affair, he was spending money foolishly or losing it. Furious, he stormed out of the apartment in a rage, and only later I learned, when the salespeople in the drugstore, the cleaners, and the liquor store said to me, "Oh, by the way, your husband borrowed a hundred dollars," that he was getting money from them, which he then gave away or lost.

Deciding he was also a beneficent millionaire bent on curing all the world's blight, starting with New York's traffic problems, Jock telephones Lewis Rudin, an important man connected with the city whom we knew only slightly: "Lewis, this is Jock Leslie-Melville. I have the answer for New York's traffic problems. You are to send me a check for two hundred million dollars for my idea. Now I'm not going to tell you what my idea is, for you might steal it, but as soon as I receive the check I'll tell you my great plan"—which was putting up signs at every entrance to New York saying there would be a $500 fine for anyone stopping their car in an intersection. I could only imagine Lewis's reaction.

Friends who came to visit tried and tried, in vain, to convince Jock his traffic idea wouldn't work. "But I *know* it will," he insisted, obsessed with it. "In fact, I'm going to call Lewis tomorrow and tell him he must send me *four* hundred million. Now, I'd like to give you all a little present . . ." and he wrote everyone a million-dollar check.

I snuck over to a nearby friend's apartment, called Lewis Rudin, explained the situation to him, apologized, and suggested he just have his secretary say he was out of town for a few weeks. He was sweet and understanding.

Again and again I tried to get Jock to go see Dr. Petito, but he was having none of it. "No. Napoleon wants to go to the hardware store and then the movies, *now.*" I agreed and, walking up the street, I suggested, "Let's buy the movie tickets first, so we won't have to stand in line, then go to the hardware store."

Jock went into a fury, grabbed me by the neck, and began choking me on Second Avenue. His voice changed as he hissed, "Don't you *ever* say that again." People stopped and stared at my head flying back and forth. Somehow I managed to indicate to Jock we would go to the hardware store first, and then he was fine. I just could not imagine gentle Jock choking me or causing a scene. The line was long at the theater, but since Napoleon doesn't wait in lines, he merely pushed in front of everyone, right to the box office, and bought two tickets. I was afraid some New Yorker would poke him right in the nose, but they merely looked startled.

The next day he choked me again in the apartment over something equally unimportant. This time I was upset, and since patience is not one of my virtues, I hollered and screamed at Jock, the usual all-I-do-for-you and you-never-think-of-me speech, and then I stormed out and walked up to the corner, hating myself for losing my temper and being so terrible. I kept telling myself it wasn't his fault he was sick, but hell, it wasn't my fault either. Then who did I see riding his bicycle down Second Avenue? Frank Petito. I told him what had happened and said I wasn't frightened, but I was concerned. "You *should* be frightened," he told me. "You can never tell where that tumor is going and Jock could become very violent. You have got to get him over to the hospital."

Colleen, who had stayed with us the first two days we were in New York, called from Philadelphia and said she was worried. Jock was dangerously manic, yet she had noticed he was concerned about a slight cough. Could I use that as an excuse to get him to his internist? If he agreed, she could call him from Philadelphia and explain."

Jock coughed. "Oh, that cough sounds bad," I said sincerely and hoped he wouldn't detect the lie.

"Do you think so?"

"Oh, yes. You don't have to go to the hospital, but perhaps we could go to Dr. Rosenbluth's and get an X ray." I held my breath. He agreed. Surreptitiously I called Colleen and she called Dr. Rosenbluth and explained.

Dr. Rosenbluth whispered to me that it was very obvious Jock was manic. He was wonderful, going along with the ploy —listening to his chest, taking an X ray, and saying, oh, yes, it was pneumonia and if he went to the hospital immediately, he would be fine in a few days. Then Dr. Rosenbluth went to another room, called Dr. Petito, and told him we were finally on our way, but Petito said there were no empty beds in neurology's intensive care and for Jock to go to the accident room and wait.

While we waited five hours, for someone to die, I imagine, Jock talked to everyone with great enthusiasm, telling them how he was going to cure all of New York's traffic problems. Finally a young resident called Jock into a little examining room. "I understand you are having some mental problems."

I shook my head no at him behind Jock's back.

"Mental problems?" Jock asked, as if the doctor were crazy. "Of course not, Napoleon doesn't have mental problems."

"Oh, I see," said the doctor, catching on. "What do you do?"

"I raise giraffe," Jock said proudly. "In Africa."

I could see the "Sure you do" look on the doctor's face. I nodded my head yes at him behind Jock's back. He looked more confused than Jock. "Well, I'm going to put you in intensive care."

"Wonderful," exclaimed Jock, "I can entertain everyone there."

The doctor smiled. "We sure could do with some entertainment in intensive care." Jock talked on and on, telling him all about Daisy and the New York traffic solution and wrote him a check for a million dollars. The resident told me aside how charming Jock was. And he was. He was so cheerful and happy and generous, but that he would not stay in bed—he kept getting up and running to all the other patients in the intensive care unit, and when he didn't get much of a response from any of them, he ran down the hall into other rooms.

The staff told me they could not keep him there, he was causing too much havoc, but first they would try a private nurse to see if she could control him.

I went home for supper, and when I got back to the hospital Jock told me, "There is this one nurse, Betty, who is crazy about me. She follows me everywhere and hangs on to my every word."

"I'm jealous. I'll scratch her eyes out."

"Would you mind going home now? I have a lot of people in here who want Napoleon to visit them."

Exhausted, I was delighted to fall into bed, but Jock, and his admirer, walked around all night long.

Dr. Petito explained that first they were trying a lower dose of steroids, but it had to be reduced slowly. If they just took Jock off them altogether, he would die in about three days; but in case that wasn't the cause I should shop for an institution for Jock.

Institution. A horrid word. This intelligent, vital man I loved so much in an institution? I felt sick.

I spent the next few days in the hospital with Napoleon, who I thought began to get less manic, but perhaps it was only because I wasn't having to cope with him. But Petito agreed. "I think he's better. It may be a reaction to the steroids after all."

"When all this started," I told Petito, sitting in his office, "if we had stayed in Nairobi, where they have no scan, Jock would have just died naturally—you say a glioblastoma is a fast-growing tumor. But we were in the States, so first he is operated on and brain-damaged and left feeble and unable to read or write or work or do anything, and then he is devastated by the radiation and made sick by the chemotherapy and all his hair falls out, and then he becomes physically decrepit. He has drugs that turn him manic and make a fool of him. Sometimes I wish we hadn't come here for all this advanced medical science. Do you guys ever wonder what you're doing?"

"All the time" was his solemn answer.

"I tell you," I went on unfairly, "if ever you tell me I have a glioblastoma, I'm walking right out of here. None of your marvelous 'advances' for me. Some advances." I got up to leave and he put his arm around my shoulder as we walked out. "You're doing a great job. That's probably why Jock is still alive, because you give him so much love and joy and hope."

I decided that if it wasn't the steroids but the tumor and Jock would be totally irrational for the rest of his days, I would not put him in an institution, I would not allow his dignity to be totally destroyed—I would kill him. How would I do that? Well, Dr. Petito said if he were taken off the steroids suddenly, he would die in three days. I could just not give him his pills. But what if it didn't work? Would I be capable of shooting Jock? Someone once said a bullet is the fastest death. After the rape of our giraffe sitter, the firearms department had given us a license for a .38 revolver, which I carried in my jeans pocket all day in Nairobi and slept with by my bed all night. Did I love Jock enough to shoot him?

Then one morning, after Jock had been in the hospital a week, the telephone rang and it was Jock—the first time he had called me.

"Bettyduk," he said, in his old sweet voice with a touch

of sadness, "I'm not Napoleon anymore." So I brought Jock, not Napoleon, home. "Let's go to the movies tonight," he suggested.

"Fine. But I'm not taking you to see *Jesus Christ Super Star*. Being Josephine was bad enough, but the Virgin Mary is out."

Chapter 23

*A*FTER another sad Thanksgiving and Christmas with the family in Baltimore, all of us once again certain that it was the last time we would ever spend the holidays with Jock, I took him back to Kenya because Telecom, a film company, was going to produce two documentaries for Westinghouse TV—one on lion, which was to be narrated by Ali McGraw, and another on rhino to be narrated by Richard Thomas. I was hired as associate producer and, not believing in sacrificing kindness for truth, I told Jock we both were. Michael Lepiner, the producer, had had us at his house in New York to dinner with Richard Thomas, who was not only charming but brilliant, and was currently excited by his newborn triplets.

The first day as I was walking in downtown Nairobi with Richard, he kept turning around all the time looking at the passersby. The Swahili greeting is "Jambo," and every time someone said hello to someone else as they passed on the street, Richard thought they were greeting him, saying, "John Boy" (his role in the TV series "The Waltons").

We didn't meet Ali McGraw until she got to Nairobi, and she was also charming and bright. She arrived with her eight-year-old son, a delightful child, and also Willie Nelson's delightful harmonica player. We gave them and Michael and the crew a Welcome to Africa dinner party at our house, and they arrived in time to feed the giraffe, which of course thrilled them all. As I always explained to people that Jock was terminal and brain-damaged but thought he was fine,

Michael had explained the situation to everyone, and they not only went along with the ruse, they were particularly attentive and nice to Jock. At the dinner table he got up and gave them a toast and a little speech. Although he was bent and tottering and nowhere near as articulate as he used to be, everyone was so touched by his effort and great spirit that the applause went on and on. He was so proud.

For the filming of the lion documentary it was decided to shoot first at George Adamson's remote place in Kora. George lives there in a large wire compound, and the lion wander about outside in the bush freely until feeding time, when they come to George's cage in the evening for their camel meat. So on Ali's first day in Africa, they chartered a little plane, flew to George's, admiring the snow on Mount Kenya, with the Equator running right through it on the way, and landed at dusk. Everyone collected his belongings, but where was the food? It turned out the mini-bus driver who took them to the airport had forgotten to put it in the plane. So they had nothing to eat; and when they arrived at George's there was only one available room in his "house" in the cage, so Ali and the three crew all had to sleep in the same room on camp beds. She was a very good sport, no star stuff, no complaints whatsoever. The TV crew loved it and said when they returned to the States they were going to tell everyone they had slept with Ali McGraw.

Richard dashed off on a hair-raising rhino capture and translocation, then went on to film one of A FEW's projects, the Camel Corps—an anti-poaching unit that is highly successful, because while the poachers can hear a vehicle approaching, they cannot hear the camels approach, and therefore many poachers are caught.

Ali and Richard and Michael and the crew kept passing through Nairobi and always came out to visit. We had a wrap-up party for them, and Jock enjoyed it all so much.

The morning after the filming was finished and everyone had left, about 6 A.M. Jock started making a very peculiar sound in his sleep. Thinking he was having a nightmare, I nudged him and shook his arm gently to waken him, but he didn't wake up and the terrible noise grew louder. I switched on the light and saw his eyes staring glassily into space, his mouth foaming, his body rigid and convulsing violently. "Jock, Jock!" I cried, but he could not hear me. I hollered to Dancy and she came running just as his convulsing stopped, so she raced downstairs to call the doctor.

I was sure he was dead. His eyes were still, his body was still, and he did not respond to anything. That electric shock of the terror of death raced through me. I was sobbing and holding him in my arms when I heard a moan, then another, a grunt, then another. Next his arm moved, and his eyes moved. Dancy ran back into the room and said to give Jock some more Dilantin immediately. (He took it every day as a precaution against convulsions.) We got him to swallow the pill, and finally a few incoherent words came forth. Then he sat up and said, "Let's go feed the giraffe."

"Jock, you've just had a convulsion."

"Oh, really? My father used to have them as a result of a fall playing polo. Come on, we're all awake, let's go feed Daisy."

Dancy said the doctor said convulsions look worse than they actually are, and I will admit nothing looks worse. How often would Jock have convulsions?

So a symptom had come forth, and brought Jock's death back into sharp focus. The year of Jock's relative well-being had shielded me from the reality of his imminent death; also, pretending all the time that everything is all right had made me almost believe it myself. Then too, as Huxley said, "The entire philosophy of life can be summed up in five words, 'You get used to it,' " and there is some truth in that. Of course I was anguished by it, but I had gotten used to Jock's being the way he was now, and his sweetness and charm were still there. He was still Jock to me, we still loved each other so much, and I would rather have him alive like this than dead.

But now once again the fact of his death was no longer

diluted. I spent days trying to figure out the meaning or meaninglessness of death, and of course came up with no answers, only the hope that just because I didn't understand something—a life hereafter in this case—didn't mean it didn't exist.

We drove to Malindi and along the road saw ninety-six elephant and herds of zebra and many giraffe, but they weren't as pretty as ours. We stopped in Mombasa for Jock's favorite *samosas* (small crispy Indian meat pie) at his favorite Indian restaurant, which is closed at lunch and dinner time, and in Malindi we watched the *dhows* sail, as they did in Biblical times, back and forth from the Persian Gulf with the monsoons. Mostly we just loved. One night, sitting on the terrace, holding hands and watching the moon come out of the Indian Ocean, Jock said to me, "We are to each other what the sun is to the moon."

"We found the Holy Grail." I kissed him, and then, like every night, we went to bed in our large mosquito-netted bed and clung to each other all night long as the soft breeze from the ocean rippled softly over us. The first thing I would see in the morning were Jock's blue blue eyes looking at me adoringly as he held me close, and for that second upon awakening, before focusing on what day it was or where we were in life, I would assume we were "back there." Then reality would crash in. The morning we were leaving to go back to Nairobi I was lying there wondering if we would ever be in Malindi together again, when Jock awoke and kissed me and said his usual, "Good morning, Bettyduk, I love you, and now I'm going to get you your orange juice and coffee."

I lay there and watched him struggling to get out of bed. It was so difficult for him, but he always refused help. This morning he tried time after time to push himself up with his weak legs, but he would fall back onto the bed, then try again and again, and when finally he was able to stand, he looked at me, smiled proudly, and shuffled, stooped, into the kitchen. It was the smile that did it—he was so heroic; it was heart-breaking. Suddenly I was filled with rage. Why did all these atrocities have to happen to such a wonderful man? I was so angry with God, or somebody, that I sat up in bed and grabbed the nearest thing, which happened to be a book, and threw it across the room; but that didn't do it, so I threw the ash tray against the wall and smashed it to bits. That helped, but not enough, so I jumped up and kicked the mattress and hollered every obscene word I could think of.

"Did you call me?" Jock called from the kitchen.

"Is your name 'O'Shit'?"

"What? I can't hear you."

"Nothing."

That evening when we got back to Nairobi we were strolling down to the *boma* at sunset to feed the giraffe. We had called them and they were ambling along, following us; Walter Warthog was already standing in the *boma*, anxiously awaiting his food; Kilimanjaro loomed in the distance; birds were singing; the resident eagle was sitting on his favorite tree limb—it was idyllic. Except Jock was dying.

He said, "I'm so glad I'm better, because next month in the States I'll be able to raise the money for the educational nature center. I know I can do it, Betty, and by this time next year it should be built and filled with African schoolchildren." He was so enthusiastic. He grinned. "I just can't wait to see it go up."

Not having any idea where we would get the money, I said, "Let's call an architect tomorrow and get started." Somehow Jock just had to see his dream come true.

Just as I walked ahead a few paces to prevent a warthog fight, which was about to happen, Jock fell and just lay on the ground. Now, one can never lie flat around wild animals. I don't know why, but every vet and all animal people have always told us this is true, and sure enough the giraffe grew very excited and began dancing very close, too close, to him. It was so dangerous—just one unwitting, powerful giraffe leg hitting him would have killed him instantly. I shouted for him to get up, but he cried, "I can't, I can't." The giraffe, sensing the tension, became even more excited, so that I

feared if I got in close enough to pick up Jock we might both
be killed. Nevertheless, I took a deep breath and plunged in
through giraffe legs and managed to pick him up, and all was
well (except that I had pulled my back and could hardly walk
for two weeks).

"Oh, Betty, you saved me—you are so wonderful, but I
worried so about your getting kicked or killed."

"Good. I love it when you worry about me. But I'm fine."
I smiled at him and took his hand as we both walked, bent,
to the house.

"Thank God you're all right Betty—I couldn't live without
you."

Rick and Bryony came for dinner and told us a hunter we
knew who had developed terminal cancer had recently driven
himself to a remote animal-filled area, got out of his Land
Rover, and merely walked out into the middle of the bush,
never to be seen again.

"That's awful," I said.

"No, that's good, Betty," Jock told me. "He didn't want to
be kept alive by artificial life-support systems with life and
death no longer distinguishable. Medicine should be used to
prolong life, not death. He always controlled his own life, he
certainly wanted to control his own death. I do, and you do
too"—he turned to Rick and Bryony—"but we decided long
ago we're going to live forever. But if . . ."

"Didn't your grandmother live to be ninety-six?" I interrupted, trying to change the subject.

"Yes and happily too—she booked horses every day."

"Your grandmother was a bookie?" Rick asked.

"Lord Portman's wife?" Bryony asked. "How wonderful.
Or do you mean she bet with a bookie?"

The subject switched to horses, and I was relieved I wouldn't
have to make my broken promise yet again. I felt I had failed
the ultimate test. I was shamed by my observation that I must
love myself more than I loved Jock or I would have carried
out his wishes. If only we could get the educational center

built and he could see it. This would not only delight him, but I could justify to myself my keeping him alive.

The following week Betsy and Walter Cronkite arrived. Walter was filming his "Universe" series then, and they fed the giraffe and Walter's namesake Walter Warthog, and we flew back to the States on the same flight with them, talking all the way, which Jock also thoroughly enjoyed, but every minute of every day I was now also watching for a convulsion.

Life became even more of an endurance test.

One evening, a few days after we had settled into our New York apartment, Jock was in the bedroom and I was in the living room, when I heard the terrible noise. I raced in, and Jock was standing, rigid and convulsing and foaming at the mouth. Somehow I got him to the bed, but he was totally stiff and convulsing so violently I could not turn him on his side, which I had been told to do to keep him from swallowing his tongue, so I tried to hold him.

Petito had said he might break his back convulsing, and I was sure he was going to. It was hideous, lasting much longer than his first one, and again that electric shock terror of death went through me, for when it was over, again I thought he was dead. Holding Jock in my arms, I dialed Dr. Petito. I was trembling and he talked to me a long time, calming me down and assuring me Jock would be all right; and twenty minutes later he was fine, but I wasn't. The convulsions affected me much more than Jock—he merely shrugged them off and hardly seemed concerned or even aware he had had one.

What if I hadn't been there? What if I had been at the store? I realized I could no longer leave Jock alone, not even for five minutes. Although I could do most of my work at home, there were times I had to go out for a business appointment, for food, to the bank . . . so I telephoned Nairobi and told Rick to send Mwangi, our faithful major-domo, to the States to help me with Jock. Of course, Mwangi was delighted, never having been out of Kenya.

Jock and I drove to JFK to meet him. He was amazed at

New York. "It's a city of diamonds," he cried, looking at the
lights. We drove him around, showing him the Empire State
building and the UN and the Twin Towers, but what impressed Mwangi most was the toll booth, where we threw in
a quarter and the pole went up. "Magic," he claimed. He
was thrilled with the States, and I was thrilled to have some
help with Jock.

The Brits Mwangi had worked for before had found him
herding goats. Seeing how pleasant and alert he was, they
brought him into the kitchen to help their cook. Soon they
promoted him to a full-time servant because he was so bright,
and then his employer sent him to electrician school so Mwangi
could help him work his ham radio set. Learning so quickly
to be an electrician, his employer then sent him to plumbing
school, carpentry school, the Cordon Bleu cooking school
(taught in Swahili), and to picture framing and watch-repair
classes. Along the way Mwangi learned to speak English in
addition to the Swahili and three dialects he already spoke.
When he left them and we hired him, Jock taught him how
to drive. Imagine being able to have a cheerful intelligent
man cook the most delicious gourmet meals, repair your roof
and your watch, build a house, sew a hem in your dress,
drive to town and pay the bills and do all the shopping and
other chores, keep accounts, wire your lamps, paint your
living room, and fix the leaky bathtub. But still he had not
reached his potential, so we decided to make him Director
of the Educational Center if we ever got it. I could not have
survived without Mwangi's helping me in the States with
Jock. We took him to the movies with us, to our friends'
houses, to Baltimore—where Jock fell all the way down my
sister's cellar steps, but Mwangi, who was in the basement
doing some laundry, heard him coming and broke his fall.
Another brush with death. That evening, as we were sitting
around my sister's dinner table, she asked Mwangi, "You're
a Christian, aren't you?"

"Oh, yes," he answered proudly. "I'm a Catholic."

Knowing he had three wives, so far, I asked, "Catholic,
Mwangi?"

"Well, half Catholic."

"What's the other half?"

"African."

I could hardly wait to tell my nun friends.

The next day was McDonnell's wedding. He had met Eve, a delightful young American woman at the American University in Nairobi. Her father was a nuclear physicist and her mother was the pathologist at Kenyatta Hospital. She wanted to be a doctor, too, and had come back to the States to go to medical school in Baltimore, which I am sure is the real reason why McDonnell had come back to the States. Rick's young minister friend, who had brought Margaret Mead out to our Nairobi house, married the couple in their flower-filled garden. Then we had a lovely reception with lots of champagne and good cheer, and a big smoked sailfish from Kenya.

I feared U.S. customs would prohibit the fish, so I hadn't told Mwangi there might be a problem when I asked him to bring it, figuring they might let him, an innocent first-time visitor, get away with it, but they'd know I knew better. Also in his luggage—in fact, the only other thing in his suitcases (we were going to buy him new clothes)—were one hundred black candles, cast in the shape of rhinos, each about six inches high and ten inches long, which we gave to everyone who donated $500 to "adopt" a rhino. The customs man in New York thought the contents of his luggage very odd and suspected the candles were filled with dope. Suspiciously he cut a rhino in half, to find it was indeed wax, so he gave Mwangi a form to fill out and send in if we wanted the customs department to pay for the damage they had done. Feeling sorry about poaching a rhino, I guess, they let him through with the fish.

(I wrote to customs and explained the purpose of the candles and therefore they owed $500 to A FEW. We would be glad to name their adopted rhino "U.S. Customs Department," I assured them, but they never answered.)

The night of the wedding Jock kissed me and said sadly, "Oh, Bettyduk, isn't it awful that I haven't been able to make love since my first convulsion?"

Knowing he would never be able to make love again (because of the large dosage of steroids which he could not live without), I lied, "But it's just your Dilantin medicine. As soon as they get that regulated, you'll be fine again. And anyway, it isn't awful—we love each other just as much. Sex is only a very small part of love, and we have so much of all the other parts, the important parts." I kissed him. "To me, romance—your holding me and telling me you love me—is better than sex anytime." I kissed him again. "Oh, I'm going to miss you. I wish I didn't have to go to Ethiopia tomorrow."

The country had just opened up for tourism again after the revolution, and I was to check it out for sending our safari-ers. I was sorry the Lion of Judah was no longer there ("Harry Selaski," as McDonnell, age seven, had called him). I had been fond of him and his country, and knew how different it would be this time under Communist rule. Jock and Mwangi were going to Philadelphia the next day to stay with Colleen for the two weeks I would be gone. We said our sad goodbyes—how I hated to leave him—and I went off to JFK to catch my flight to Addis Ababa.

That night Helen and her nun friend Marie were being given a Welcome Home from Africa party at Helen's father's house in Baltimore. Jock and Mwangi went over early in the afternoon so that Mwangi, an excellent cook, could help Marie with the food for the thirty guests.

An hour before everyone was to arrive, Marie asked Helen and Mwangi, "Where's Jock?"

"He's in the living room watching television," Mwangi said.

"No, he's not, I just looked. I've looked everywhere for him—he's gone," said Marie excitedly. (And Marie can usually cope with anything—she's had lots of practice—she didn't have a bath for thirteen years in Uganda, and anyone who can deal with that must be able to cope with almost anything.) They drove all around, looking for him, but he was nowhere to be found.

"Why didn't you tell him not to go out?" Helen asked Marie.

"I did, of course, but asking Jock that is like asking a paraplegic to get up and walk."

232 BETTY LESLIE-MELVILLE

"What do we do? Do we page Betty at the airport?" Helen said. "I don't know how to tell her."

"I'm sure we'll find him. It would be terrible to call her back and in the meantime have him turn up," Marie said.

The guests had already started to arrive when the telephone rang, and it was a man saying he was walking down the street when Jock came up to him and said he was lost and didn't remember where he was visiting. The man was from South Africa and knew nothing of the area, so he took Jock to the house where he was staying and looked through Jock's address book. When the man go to Colleen's name, Jock said yes, to call her, in Philadelphia. Why he didn't call Helen or McDonnell or my sister or anyone else he knew in Baltimore, we'll never know. But fortunately Colleen was home and knew Jock was supposed to be at Helen's party, so the man brought Jock back there, and all was well. And fortunately I didn't even know about that drama until I returned from Ethiopia.

Chapter 24

Jock, Colleen, and Mwangi were waiting for me when I landed at JFK, and I had never seen Jock happier to see me. He was beaming like the sun and sporting a dark blue beret instead of his wig, and after hugging and kissing each other, which normally would be far too British for him to endure in public, I told him how much I liked his beret. He was so pleased. "I fancy myself in it no end. . . . I've missed you so."

"How glad I am to be back with you." We sat in the back seat of Colleen's car, holding hands and whispering how much we loved each other, and just gazing at each other all the way to the apartment.

Colleen and Mwangi said Jock had had no convulsions, but there had been a few difficult times. Diane Fossey, the woman who lived with gorillas in Rwanda, had spoken at the Natural Science Museum in Philadelphia. Jock, normally the most gentle, quiet-mannered man, stood up in the audience at the end of her talk and in a loud and rude voice said, "What you said isn't true. I want to tell you a few things," and he went on and on, contradicting her and wouldn't let her or anyone else in the audience speak. Colleen was powerless to stop him, and described it as the most painful evening she had ever had, agonizing for the loss of Jock's great dignity.

Jock's brain damage manifested itself oddly: He had always been extremely articulate, and that remained—in fact, he was still more articulate than most people; but it was *what* he said and did that was so out of character and unlike Jock.

And how he would have hated it, if Jock had been Jock. But he was sure he was brilliant, and he was still so happy. Is there more? Certainly Jock would have said yes, and I couldn't stop agonizing about my promise to him. I kept hearing the words he had said to me, time and time again, "Betty, one thing we never get out of alive is life—but we can choose *how* we get out of it." Shouldn't I exert every effort, every wifely and familial prerogative, to see that his life ended as he would want? Wasn't I failing him by not keeping my promise and letting my wishes override his?

But again my decision was not to make a decision. This time my rationalization was that I only had to keep him away from situations where he might lose his dignity. And he just had to see his impossible dream come true; I *had* to raise the money and get the educational center built. Or was I merely copping out?

We thanked Colleen, bid her goodbye, and spent the next month in New York. We had such a lovely time together that it justified my decision. Except Jock began to fall frequently; once getting the mail in the lobby, twice in the kitchen, and once knocking himself unconscious in the bathroom for ten minutes, when again I was sure he was dead. Every time he'd thank me for picking him up and tell me how much he loved me and how he appreciated everything I did and he would be perfectly fine soon and able to manage everything so I could do nothing. I invariably told him that I was fine, but I often dreamed I was choking to death. He tried so hard to help me in every way he could. *Bagamoyo*, our saga of Kenya, was due at the publishers soon, and Jock was working on it too. I pretended everything he wrote was brilliant, then threw it away, but he felt he was contributing, which was what was important.

Luciano Pavarotti was going to be at Lincoln Center and Jock wanted to go. Of course, I was petrified he would have a convulsion, but it meant so much to him to see the great tenor that I took him. We were in the middle of the middle row of the theater—no easy exit in case of a convulsion, which would ruin everyone else's evening, too. It was one of the worst evenings I've ever had—I sat there digging my finger-nails into my palms—what if he has a convulsion during one of Pavarotti's arias? I was convinced the night would never end—but it did, and without incident.

The next day Dancy landed in the States. She had worked for the Flying Doctors for two years, and before we had left Nairobi she had said to me, "Mother, I wish I had been a doctor."

"Go back to the States and go to medical school," I had told her.

"Mother," she said rather impatiently, "in seven years' time I'll be thirty-four years old."

"Dancy," I told her rather knowingly, "in seven years' time you'll be thirty-four years old *anyway*."

So Dancy arrived to attend medical school and stayed a few days in New York to be with us, and we had a lovely time together.

The time on Mwangi's excursion air ticket was running out, and I still had lectures to do, so Mwangi took Jock back to Kenya the end of June; I would arrived in Nairobi the end of July. But when I called to see if they had arrived safely, Mwangi told me Jock was fine, except he had insisted they have separate rooms in the hotel in Athens where they spent the night to break their trip, and then had fallen in his room in the early morning and had lain on the floor for two hours until Mwangi had found him.

I talked to Jock every day and he seemed all right, but two weeks after their arrival in Nairobi, the telephone rang at Dancy's new apartment in Baltimore, where I was spending the night, and it was Rick saying Jock was very sick, he had just been taken to the hospital, and was slipping into a coma— I should come immediately.

That plane ride was the worst ever, "Oh, dear God, please don't let Jock die without me, please." From Nairobi's airport I raced right to the hospital and met a cheerful Jock walking down the corridor! He had insisted upon taking his steroids by himself, but then he had begun to forget. The minute the hospital regulated his steroids, he was all right again.

One neurologist in Baltimore has what I think is a fairly good solution for terminal brain-tumor patients. He lets them take their life-giving steroids as long as they are able to remember the dosage properly, but when that time passes the doctor feels that is the time to let them go, so he just lets the patients continue ministering to themselves, and when they can no longer do so they just slip into a coma and die. I considered that, but I just couldn't do it and merely insisted from then on Jock be given his pills. It was a difficult situation—Jock thought he was perfectly fine and alert mentally, and we didn't want to let him know he wasn't. But to my surprise he accepted this, as he accepted everything—happily.

Although I had left a lot of work undone, I was glad to be back home with Jock. One reason was that just after my arrival Daisy produced her second baby. He looked like an adorable sea horse, and we fell in love again and named him George Pew, after our friend in Philadelphia who adopted him.

Then another good thing happened: We had a call from London, saying the video Jock had lost had been found at the airport and returned to the flat. Our friend Quentin Crewe would bring it to Nairobi next month, when he was coming to stay with us a while to write his book about crossing the Sahara. As if that feat were not extraordinary enough, what made it even more so is the fact that Quentin has muscular dystrophy and has been totally paralyzed for thirty years. Wilfrid Thesinger crossed the empty quarter of the Arabian desert one way, but Quentin had crossed it both ways—in a wheelchair. Of course, he had Bedouins to lift him in and out of the truck, but it was a historical journey. Now he wanted to write about his new feat of crossing the Sahara, and we had invited him and his pusher (as we always called the man who pushed his wheelchair) to come out from London and write at our house. My sister asked me didn't I have enough responsibility with Jock, wasn't I taking on an added burden? Of course I wasn't. Anthony Armstrong-Jones had designed an electric wheelchair for Quentin, who drove it all over the house. He had to be carried downstairs in the morning and up at night, but all day he was totally self-sufficient. Quentin, who looks like Beethoven, wrote "Letter from London" in Vogue magazine, was a gourmet food critic in London, but his real love is the desert. He is brilliant and sensitive, and it was a comfort as well as a delight to have someone to give me some rational feedback.

Quentin arrived with the video, and with no television in Nairobi, we now had the fun of watching films at home. I was particularly pleased for Jock's sake because, unable to read, he watched it many hours a day, and it warmed my heart to see him sitting there in front of it, laughing at a film.

The first time Quentin had come to stay with us, he had gone to an enormous amount of trouble to bring us some grouse. He spent hours having it packed correctly, then he went to the airport two hours early to make sure the airlines would fly it in a special place under the wing—the only place where the temperature is correct. When he arrived at the first stop, Cairo, he made the crew take the grouse out so he could check that they were traveling all right. After presenting his prize present to us with great aplomb, Quentin then explained to our cook, for about a half hour, how to cook them. The following day we all drove to Malindi, and when we arrived, Quentin asked when we were going to have the grouse. "Oh, I didn't bring them here—I left them in Nairobi—I froze them."

He was appalled. "Grouse in a freezer. Dear God."

"You know," I told him, laughing, "it really is a pain having a gourmet like you around—just relax and enjoy your peanut butter and jelly sandwiches."

"Betty, you're the only person in the world I know who is secure enough to serve me such dreadful food."

"It's good for your character, Quentin—you'll know how the real world eats."

"Well, the grouse will certainly be almost ruined by freezing, but they'll still be better than anything else I'll get to eat in Kenya."

A few days later McDonnell telephoned and said, "Oh by the way, Mother, Sunday I was here alone and hungry, so I opened the freezer and saw these really funny looking little chickens in there—they were really shriveled up, but there was nothing else to eat, so I put all of them in the oven, but they smelled so weird, I threw them all out. Why did you ever buy those things?"

So Quentin didn't bring any grouse the next time. Instead he brought caviar. "What is this?" asked the custom man at Nairobi airport.

"Caviar," Quentin told him.

"What is that?"

"Fish eggs."

"How many are you bringing in?"

Quentin looked at the medium-sized tin and said, "Oh I guess about 6,000."

"I will have to charge you duty on each egg."

So we never got another present, but this time he did bring the video.

About a week after Quentin's arrival, we had an earthquake—.5 on the Richter scale. We were having dinner and there was a thunderous noise and then the entire house began to shake. I thought we were being bombed—no one had ever told me there was loud noise when an earthquake approached. We all raced outside, and found a stricken night guard—he thought it was the end of the world. He had never even heard of an earthquake, so we tried to calm him and explain it to him quickly. He told us the giraffe had started racing in circles in alarm around the lawn about a half hour before the quake. Luckily it lasted only a few minutes, and in the entire country only one chicken was killed.

The following week Jock and I left Quentin and his pusher as giraffe-sitters, and flew to Malindi. Driving was now too much for Jock. The very night we got there was the night of the coup in Kenya. The air force tried to overthrow the government, and they were shooting it out with the army in Nairobi.

"I'm so worried about Rick and Bryony." They were living then in the center of the city.

Jock comforted me. "But Bettyduk, Bryony's on safari with French tourists, stuck somewhere now in the middle of the bush, unable to move, and you know the farther out in the bush, the safer you are, so at least she's all right. And Rick and Quentin will be fine."

"You're right. You're always right, and you always make me feel better when I'm worried."

All roads and telephone and radio communications were cut off, but we learned through bush telegraph that it was very nasty indeed in Nairobi. In addition to many air force and army men being killed, a Japanese tourist was killed, a honeymoon couple didn't stop their car at a roadblock and were shot dead, one African woman went to the morgue to look for her son and found all three of her sons there. The looting was so terrible that Asians were immolating themselves. All Kenya residents were sharpening their knives and getting their wagons in a circle, but fortunately the coup was put down the next day, and eventually I got through on the telephone to learn that Rick, Bryony, and Quentin were all all right.

When we got back to Nairobi, our giraffe John Paul had disappeared. Mwangi had searched our woods, in vain—he must have gone to Olalua Forest, an enormous forest eleven miles away, where some air force insurgents were still hiding out. We knew the forest well but were told we mustn't go, for the soldiers would kill us to steal our car; but we decided to risk it to find John Paul. Quentin's pusher was too frightened to go, so he lifted Quentin onto the front seat, and I drove with the loaded .38 and Quentin in the front, and Jock in the back. We drove and drove on the dirt tracks through the thick forest and saw nothing but monkeys and antelope— no John Paul, no bad guys.

There is one place a car is unable to go—the far end of a *vlei* (glade), where animal tracks lead down a rocky path to the river. About halfway down I knew I could get a view of the entire river and the surrounding terrain where it is easy to spot giraffe; once when Daisy had wandered over to Olalua we had spotted her from this vantage point.

I stopped the car. "I'm going to climb down and have a look. I'll be back in ten minutes." I left the gun for their protection and proceeded cautiously down the rocky slope but found no giraffe in sight, so I climbed up again. The car was gone. Had the air force kidnapped them? It was dusk and in Africa the sun sets so quickly it would be dark in half an hour. There I stood, in the middle of Africa, eleven miles through the spooky woods from home—surrounded by hungry killers? What should I do? I need not tell you how happy I was when in just a few minutes our car appeared.

Quentin later told me that the minute I had disappeared Jock scrambled into the driver's seat, and despite Quentin's protestations that he was not supposed to drive, and especially not now with convulsions, Jock drove off—first into a rock and then to another *vlei* to see if John Paul was there. Quentin had no choice but to go along for the petrifying ride, and try to remember how to get back to me.

That evening after dinner Jock picked up the .38 and began twirling it. "Don't fool with the gun, Jock," I said.

He ignored me an began peering into the barrel and twirling it some more. Quentin looked appalled.

"Please give it to me," I said.

Jock got angry. "I know more about guns than you."

"I know you do but . . . I want to see it . . ."

"When I'm finished," and we had that kind of conversation for a while, with Quentin and me ducking every time he'd point the gun in our direction.

Finally Jock grew bored with it and wanted to go to sleep. When I got him to bed, Quentin and I had a brandy by the fire. "Betty, I am a wreck—how do you stand it? I would be totally mad. I'm nearly certifiable now. Why haven't you become unhinged?"

"What makes you think I'm not?"

"I certainly could not cope with the situation; I don't know of anyone who could. Yet you never even complain." Quentin shook his head.

"Would it do any good? I guess I learned a lot from my mother when my father died. She never complained, and as she told me it makes sense—if you whine and are gloomy, friends feel they should sympathize and that it is not appropriate to be happy or tell funny stories or cheerful news to someone who's in agony. If you're reasonably jolly, they do, and some of the joy is bound to rub off on you."

"But you don't have to be a superwoman . . ."

"Yes I do," I interrupted. "There's no one else to assume the responsibility, and even if there were I'd want to. I love Jock. I want to be with him every minute I possibly can."

The next day when we went looking for John Paul again, Quentin refused to come along. This time, when we got into Olalua, Jock pleaded with me to let him drive. He had always been an excellent driver and loved it so, and not being able to drive was the only thing he had ever complained about. I told myself there were no people there for him to run over; the terrain was flat so he couldn't drive us over a cliff if he had a convulsion—I could not deny him. His great pleasure over such a small thing was so poignant that when he got into the driver's seat, as pleased as a little boy being allowed to drive for the first time, put the car in reverse by mistake, and went smack into a tree, I didn't even mind.

To our delight we found John Paul in the *vlei*, with four large Maasai giraffe. We called him and he swung around from the tree he was nibbling and looked at us with recognition; the others looked at us with suspicion. I had brought a bowl of his food with me and when I got out of the car one of the Maasai giraffe grew alarmed and ran off. I advanced one step and another giraffe ran off, then the other two, and then there was only John Paul left. He just stood there looking at me, wanting his food; but suddenly he too took off after the others.

"I know you're disappointed he decided to go feral, Betty," Jock said, patting my knee when I got back into the car. "But we always wanted them to have the choice, and he's well and not in a snare. But I'm sorry for you, because I know how much you'll miss him."

The next morning we were packing our car to go up-country to visit friends—and who came walking onto the lawn? John Paul, exhausted from his eleven-mile walk through African farms surrounded by barbed wire. We greeted him elaborately and unpacked our car and fussed over him all day long. He has never left since. I guess he learned he can't get any carrots out in the bush.

Chapter 25

CANCER is not only the worst disease, it is the most expensive, and expenses began to worry me seriously, even though Dr. Petito, who had taken such good care of Jock, and me, for almost three years now, had shown great concern and tried to keep costs down. (How many doctors are that good, caring, and generous?)

There were other large doctors' bills, however, and hospital and drug bills, plus airfares and everyday living. Financially things were tough, so I decided to build a little house attached to ours and move us in there so we could rent the big house and get some money. Bryony and Mwangi built the little house quickly, and when Quentin left I rented the big house, and just as Jock and I were moving into the new little house, which was almost finished, Jock got sick. His temperature was 105°—he couldn't even sit up in bed. I got him into Nairobi Hospital immediately. It was pneumonia. I stayed with him until midnight, then went home alone to the little house. Although there were bars on the windows, there were no panes yet, nor locks on the doors, and the people in the big house were away. I listened to a lion which was roaring in the distance but getting closer and closer, and I eyed the windows and waited for a lion paw to come in—or a black mamba to slither in or a hand to reach in.

People kept telling me how brave I was to move in with such little security, but I wasn't brave—I was scared to death. Our only neighbor, a sweet eighty-two-year-old widower, had just moved away because he was attacked by burglars who broke in, tied him to a chair, then put all his valuables and clothes into his car and drove off. His dog came over to us right after it happened, and we knew something was wrong because it was Colonel Rowe's habit to walk his dog every evening to sit by our fish pond and watch the giraffe for a while. When his dog appeared at 10 P.M., we hurried over and found the mess. Colonel Rowe, who was very bruised and shaken, went to live with his daughter. So now there was no one to even hear my screams, and of course the phone was out of order.

I went to bed and lay there feeling sorry for myself. I was tired of trying to be strong, brave, a "survivor." I didn't want to be a survivor anymore; I wanted someone to take care of me. But finally I fell asleep, and when I awoke I was a survivor again.

Jock got better and the day he came home we had a letter from the J. N. Pew, Jr. Charitable Trust, the foundation I had approached to fund A FEW's educational nature center, saying they had approved it and would give us a grant for $90,000! I couldn't believe it. "Jockieduk, Jockieduk," I called as I drove in from the post office with the letter. "Guess what? Your dream is going to come true! We got the grant! We can start building your sanctuary immediately!"

Never have I seen him so pleased. "Oh, Betty, we are so lucky . . ." His eyes filled with tears. "Imagine having my dream come true." We called the builders immediately and, with the plans two young architects had drawn up as their contribution to A FEW, we began. Every day I'd walk Jock down to the building site just below our house and he would sit there watching, thrilled with each stone as it went up. "It's wonderful, Betty. The plans are perfect. I just can't wait until the first African children arrive. Just think how they'll not only enjoy this but will learn about conserving the animals so they can get jobs. Oh, Betty, I've never been happier."

Soon the roof was going on, but it was the first of September, time to go lecture, and Jock was too feeble to travel to the States this time. What was I going to do? I had to go, but Jock could not stay alone—he was a twenty-four-hour-a-day job and neither Rick nor Mwangi could assume that responsibility. Although it broke my heart, I had no choice—I must put Jock in a nursing home. I found one in Nairobi, which did not please me at all, but Jock thought it was fine. I was to be gone only a month, and Rick and Bryony and all our friends, bless them, organized themselves to take Jock out each day.

It was pitiful leaving him there, but he said cheerfully, "Bettyduk, it's only for a short time and I'm going to start writing my autobiography. And what better place? I won't be interrupted. It's fine, I actually like it here . . . but I'll miss you . . ." His blue blue eyes looked so sad as I kissed him goodbye, and I sobbed all the way to the airport.

I telephoned him almost every day and had a hard time finding him in. He was being more social than he had ever been. When I did reach him I'd ask how he was and his answer was always an emphatic "Every day I get better and better," and I knew every day he was getting worse and worse. I had a letter from him, the first time he had written in two years. His typing was not what it used to be but readable.

Rick and Bryony took me out to see the center and it's is superb. My beautiful dream is beautiful. I can't wait for you to see it—we'll have the official opening when you return. I've never been more excited and pleased. So you see I am making my fun outside the hospital. My God this nice place is a mortuary for geriatrics. Never let me get to that stage Bettyduk—never. If I get there before you do just pull the plug. Preferably we go together. I love you.

Jock

Oh, God . . . The recurring question haunted me constantly.

After I had been in the States only two weeks, Rick telephoned and said, "Mother, I hate to tell you this but Jock has deteriorated badly. Suddenly, he's unable to walk and the doctors here say he must come to the States immediately for a scan. There's no way Mwangi can cope traveling with Jock alone, but Bryony will come with them."

Dreading the condition I would find him in, I was surprised when he walked through from customs at JFK, but Bryony told me later he got out of his wheelchair only at the last minute to walk through for me. We hugged and kissed but I could see he was a lot worse, so it was back to New York Hospital, where he was admitted for a few days for a scan and tests.

Much to Dr. Petito's amazement, the scan still showed no change in the tumor since the operation. Three years had passed, but Petito still would not let me be encouraged. "Betty, that tumor must have fingered out so we just can't pick it up on the scan. Jock just can't last much longer. All I can do is adjust his drugs to try to make him feel a little better."

Jock came back to the apartment, but he was weak and more confused, and took to calling everyone he knew on the telephone. One of those people was Candice Bergen, who was on our A FEW board. I came in one afternoon after work, and Jock was very excited. "I called Candice—she's in town and wants us to have lunch with her tomorrow."

"You've always had a sneaker for her," I accused him playfully. "She's so pretty and bright and pleasant—I hate her." So we gave Mwangi the day off and met Candice and her mother in a very elegant restaurant on East 63rd Street, a half-hour before her other guests were to arrive as planned, so we could catch her up on what was happening to A FEW and wildlife and Kenya.

Jock sat between Candice and me, and told her and her mother all about Africa and the educational center and what A FEW was doing for wildlife. Just as the others started to arrive and I turned to meet them, I heard that dreaded, awful, never-to-be-forgotten sound: *ug-ug-ug-ug-ug* . . . I spun around and Jock's glassy eyes were staring unseeing into space and he was trembling. Thankfully the convulsion was a *petit mal*, not a *grand mal*. Panicky, I grabbed his hand but said calmly, "Jock, you're having a little convulsion. You'll be all right, don't worry, you're fine."

Candice and her mother were naturally very alarmed, and the others arriving didn't know what to think or say or do. The noise went on for what seemed like ten minutes, but it could only have been three, then suddenly he was silent. I explained to everyone that Jock had had a little convulsion, not to worry, convulsions seemed worse than they were but he was all right now, and . . . just then his head flew to one side, his face contorted grotesquely, the sounds grew louder and louder, and his entire body began to convulse and convulse violently—worse than it ever had.

A man lunching at the table behind us jumped up and, with the help of Candice's guests, got Jock onto the floor. The five men had to hold him down to keep his back from breaking. Everyone in the restaurant grew silent. An Indian woman rushed up and knelt beside him. "I'm a doctor," she said, "get a spoon." She thrust it into his mouth, as he convulsed violently, his head still wrenched to one side, saliva pouring from his open mouth. Finally he went rigid and still; he was comatose.

Candice ran to get an ambulance, but I called after her. It wasn't necessary for him to go to a hospital, just call a cab, I'd take him home—he'd be all right. The five men lifted Jock onto a chair and carried him to the cab. I jumped in first and they put Jock in next to me, and the man at the table across from us jumped in the cab on the other side of Jock. Candice's four men were all saying they'd go with me, but this man was insisting he'd go, and I was saying I didn't need anyone—Mwangi would be back soon and the doorman would help me get Jock into the apartment (and the cab driver was wishing he didn't have this fare). But the man at the next table won, or rather lost, and as the taxi started he leaned across catatonic Jock and we introduced ourselves. I kept thanking him and he told me, "That's all right, if it ever happens to me—probably from being so drunk, I just hope someone brings me home."

He and the doorman and I got Jock onto the living room sofa, and the man said he would stay. But I told him since he had been in the middle of his lunch and had just abandoned his wife, and Jock had had convulsions before, he would be all right, and I was all right, I finally convinced him to leave.

Slowly Jock began to make sound, speaking a word here, a word there, but again, as in the other two times, I couldn't understand anything. It was as if he were speaking backwards. The syllables were clear but they didn't make any sense. He said things like "ainuflew" and "edkay," then grew impatient because I didn't understand him.

"I love you so much." I stroked his forehead. "Do you want some soup?" He shook his head yes.

"What kind?"

"Tralew."

I hoped that meant chicken, because it was the only kind we had. I fed him the soup and some toast and ice cream, still not understanding anything he was saying. Then I telephoned Dancy to tell her of the drama and, in the middle of the conversation, Jock reached for the phone and finished the story in perfect, understandable English.

He hung up and said, "Let's go to the movies. I feel fine."

Well, I didn't feel fine, and for once I denied him his wish.

Candice called from the restaurant to see how Jock was and told me that when the man at the next table left with me and Jock, she invited his abandoned wife to join them, and when he returned she asked him to join them too. So at least they got to have lunch with Candice Bergen. Candice, her usual kind and thoughtful self, called again later that evening, too, to inquire about Jock, and so did the manager of the restaurant. People are so good.

But wait until you hear this: The next morning the doorman delivered an envelope and inside was a nice note from the man at the next table and a check for $100. Candice had told him about A FEW and the work we did for wildlife, and he said he wanted to contribute. Both Jock and I were so touched and agreed that people go up in our estimation every day.

But this awful episode was the rape of every part of Jock's dignity.

Mwangi had to leave the next week. What was I going to do now?

Chapter 26

$\mathcal{A}$GAIN my only choice was a nursing home. I decided on Baltimore—Dancy, McDonnell, and Eve were there, my sister and niece and nephew, and lots of our friends, and I could spend part of the week and every weekend there with Jock. It was also less expensive than New York.

I found one in the suburbs of Baltimore; it was a friendly, comfortable place, a big old Victorian house with ageless oak trees towering over a porch where he and I frequently had a picnic lunch. An affectionate dog ran in and out of the residents' rooms. He loved it. I told him he was there just temporarily, until the doctors could sort out the proper dose of Dilantin, and then we'd go back to Africa. We covered the walls of his large cheery room with his favorite photos of friends and family and the giraffe and our houses in Africa. He had a television set and a typewriter to work on his autobiography, which was mostly incoherent, but at least kept him busy and gave him a purpose.

Most of the other patients were victims of Alzheimer's disease, or just painfully old and senile. Many had to be strapped into their chairs, drooling, just waiting to be dead enough to bury. Some would cry out all day and night, "Oh, dear God, please take me." One woman was 108 years old; she had been there for twenty years, and in a coma for two. They fed her with an eyedropper. I asked one of the staff, "She's helpless and hopeless and devoid of all dignity—she wants to die—why do you feed her?"

"It's illegal not to," she shrugged.

After Jock had been there about a week, he took my hand and said, "Betty, I'm really happy here. It's giving me time and privacy to write, the food is excellent, and I know I am only here for a few weeks, but don't you ever leave me in a place like this. Ninety-five percent of these poor people in here should be shot, put out of their misery. If I ever get like them, it's bullet time for me, and if I am unable to do myself in, you've got to do it for me."

And I would agonize all over again.

I went back to work in New York, arriving late at night. Early the next morning the nursing home called. Jock had fallen and broken his hip; they were sending him to the hospital in an ambulance. Dancy had gone to Kenya for Christmas with Rick and Bryony, so I telephoned McDonnell and Eve and they raced to the hospital to meet him when he arrived, and I got on the train back to Baltimore.

Not only was his hip broken, but he had pneumonia, and the doctor could not operate until it was cleared up. They put his leg in traction, dosed him with penicillin, and when I walked in he smiled his lovely smile. "Bettyduk! Isn't this a nuisance? I was almost entirely better and now this had to happen, but they'll put a pin in my hip and I'll be fine in just a few weeks." The next few days his temperature went higher and higher; he got sicker and sicker. Colleen drove down from Philadelphia, and after seeing Jock she took me aside and said gently, "Betty, I've seen people die and I don't think Jock is going to last the night."

That terrible electric shock feeling of death surged up in me again. This was the fifth time I was sure Jock was dying. It was as if he had been tied to a railroad track for three years now and the train was on its way but it kept breaking down. Every minute of every day I waited for the "train" and waited, knowing it was getting closer and closer, yet praying it would never arrive.

He got through the night (better than I did), and the next morning his temperature started to drop. The penicillin was working, and five days later he was well enough for the operation, scheduled for 4 P.M.. The surgeon told me his hip was no problem, but there was a chance he would not survive the anesthesia because of his weakness. That terrible feeling of death started in the pit of my stomach again and encompassed me. I sat on Jock's bed trying to be cheerful, but as 4 P.M. approached I broke. I put my head on the pillow next to his and sobbed.

Surprised, Jock asked, "Betty, why are you crying?"

"I always cry when people have anesthesia," I lied. "Don't you remember when you had your brain-tumor operation I cried before you went up to the operating room?"

"Betty"—he patted my hair—"this hip thing is nothing, and as for my brain operation—you know I'm not afraid of death, you know death doesn't bother me. The only thing that bothered me about that operation was that the tumor might have been malignant and then you would have had to watch me die slowly and I couldn't have stood that. Thank God it wasn't."

I bit his pillow to keep from crying out, and it took every bit of strength I had to sound lighthearted, not as if my heart was breaking, as I said, "Well, maybe you don't mind death, but I think you're really terrible not to have cared about leaving me alone."

"But Betty, that's why I got better—so I could take care of you."

If he had stabbed me it wouldn't have hurt as much. Just then they came for him and put him on a stretcher. I walked down the corridor holding his hand and wondering if I would ever see him alive again. There were so many things I wanted to say . . . We got to the operating room and I kissed him and all I was able to say was, "I love you."

"I love you too," he said and with a cheerful wave disappeared through the swinging doors.

McDonnell, Eve, and I waited the terrible wait. Every time the operating doors swung open we feared it was someone coming to tell us Jock had died. Finally the surgeon came out and said Jock was all right and that he had decided not to give him anesthesia after all, they had given him a local. Why hadn't he sent someone to tell us that and saved us two hours of misery?

Jock survived the operation, but the doctors told me he would never walk again. Never walk again. But Jock didn't know it and wanted a physiotherapist. Although I knew it was useless, a wasted bullet, I got him one to come to the nursing home every day, and it was pitiful watching him do his exercises, relentlessly trying over and over to take a step. "I'll be jogging by the time we get home to Africa."

"Let's go discover the source of the Nile," I said, wheeling him onto the porch. He was gaunt and withered, his body enfeebled, brittle and bent, his once beautiful features aged like an old man's. A nurse guessed his age as eighty-two, nowhere near the fifty he had just turned. The irreparable brain damage became more evident. Step by regressive step, Jock had become a half a man living in a half a world. Only his blue blue eyes and lovely smile remained of the man I had married. But when I looked inside I saw the same Jock— his sweetness, thoughtfulness, and cheerfulness were still there. I hated to talk to him on the phone because his voice sounded exactly like the old young Jock—I dreaded hearing his voice.

One of Jock's doctors urged me to "let him go." "Betty, I definitely believe in the quality of life. Five years ago I would have taken away Jock's steroids and let him die, but now, if some nurse doesn't report me, some cleaning woman would. I could be sued, I could lose my practice. I'm sorry, I really am—you should take him home and withdraw his drugs. He'll slip into a coma in a few days and have a very peaceful death. We can't do it but you can."

"I'm not sure it isn't wrong," I said pensively.

"Isn't it harder morally to justify letting somebody die a slow and ugly death than it is to justify helping him avoid it?" he asked.

"I can't—because he has no pain and is full of hope and joy."

"Would Jock want to be alive like this?"

"No."

"Would you want to be alive if you were like Jock is now?"

"No," I admitted.

"Are you going to do it for him?"

"No." Intellectually I agreed with him, but emotionally I balked.

"Then I'm going to keep a record of how many days you're keeping Jock alive, and when your time comes I'm going to do the same with you."

I had long emotional discussions with the children. McDonnell said, "Mother, I can't write Jock's death certificate," and every time we decided that as long as Jock had no pain and was still happy we would do nothing, just continue to fight our losing battle.

Then a nice thing happened: I won a nationwide award as the "most outstanding person in the realm of conservation" and went to the big award dinner in Dallas to receive it. Jock wasn't able to go, but of course I told him the award was for both of us, which it really was. I brought back the medal and gave it to him and he was thrilled. (Jacques Cousteau was the winner the next year, and I, as the previous recipient, presented it to him, but Jock was never to know that.)

That Christmas, Jock's fourth since his six-month sentence to death, was totally joyful for him. On Christmas Eve morning I bundled him up, and as I wheeled him down the corridor of the nursing home we passed the other patients in the recreation room; they were sitting there, slumped and drooling in their bathrobes under the silver tinsel, the living dead, completely unaware of the decorations and the carol the hired piano player was singing, "Don we now our gay apparel" . . . " 'Tis the season to be jolly . . ." It was pitiful.

First we went to my sister's, where Jock joined in the festivities of singing carols and telling the little children how to trim the tree. Then we all went to McDonnell and Eve's for dinner and Jock sipped eggnog and sang more carols and laughed a lot. At about 9 P.M. he got tired, so I took him back to the nursing home. Most of the nurses were off, and there was only one tiny one who could help me get Jock in his wheelchair up the three flights of slippery steps; we struggled and even fell once, but finally made it inside. I got Jock undressed and into bed, then lay down beside him. "Merry Christmas Eve, Jockieduk," I told him, but he was asleep; and so, for the first time in my life, I was alone on Christmas Eve.

Of course, my family had asked me to come back with them, but they were far on the other side of town and the roads were icy, and I was staying in Dancy's apartment near the nursing home and wanted to be with Jock early Christmas morning.

So I just sat in the car and felt sorry for myself. Then I thought, "Damn it, I'm not going to feel sorry for myself—think of the people worse off than you." I thought of Kurt, a twenty-eight-year-old neighbor of Dancy's who broke his spine surfing and is permanently paralyzed. So I drove to a liquor store, another first, bought a bottle of eggnog and took it to Kurt, who was being put to bed by the boy who lived directly next door to Dancy (and who would be my son-in-law by the next Christmas). The three of us broke open the eggnog and had a delightful time talking until 1 A.M. So my Christmas Eve turned out to be pleasant and rewarding, and I vowed to remember that, whenever I felt sorry for myself in the future, I would always go see someone who was worse off.

Christmas Day at McDonnell's was filled with presents and mistletoe and lots of lovely love and more laughter for Jock, but for the rest of us it had to be the most touching Christmas of our lives, for it was obvious there would be no more for Jock.

He was never able to go out again, and by February he was unable to go from his bed to the wheelchair. He was wasting away rapidly; he was a skeleton, a diminished shadow of himself. My promise loomed large. I would have to keep it soon.

Chapter 27

As I wrestled with this terrible dilemma, fate stepped in.

Looking back, I can see that the end started with a rash. "Have you ever had chicken pox?" I asked Jock, kissing his forehead and running my fingers over his face and through his little wispy strands of hair to examine his rash. I really thought he might have smallpox, since he had had everything else, but then I remembered it had been eradicated. The last case was in Ethiopia a few years ago.

Rick and Bryony arrived from Kenya with their four-month-old son Garrick. Jock was pleased to hold his first grandson. He was very interested in their telling us about the education center being finished, and Brooke Shields staying in the house, and visits from Robert Redford, and Mary Tyler Moore, and Mrs. Ed Meese, but he was not his usual self—he was different. The rash began to disappear, but he had lost his enthusiasm, and for the first time he was not optimistic.

But Jock did say he wanted to go to the Rhino Rescue party we were having in Baltimore the following week; and in the next few days he made sure his tuxedo and his wheelchair were in order, and he was planning a little speech. I just could not say no and decided to risk a convulsion, but the very day of the rhino party he said, sadly, that he was just not up to it, and I began to realize he was never going to get out of the nursing home again. Devastated, I decided the time had come. I would have to fulfill my promise to him in one week. Please, dear God, give me the courage.

At 1 A.M., after the party, I went to see Jock and told him
all about it and, as weak as he was, he was so interested.
"Isn't life wonderful?" he smiled. It was unbearably sad.

The next morning the nursing home telephoned me and
said Jock had gotten very sick in the night and they were
going to take him to the hospital for an X ray. I rode in the
ambulance with him, and once again Dancy, McDonnell,
and Eve, bless them, were waiting at the hospital. Jock was
admitted with pneumonia, which used to be called the "old
people's friend." I stroked his face—he looked so ill—and
told him he had to stay in the hospital.

"Bettyduk, please take me home." (He called the nursing
home "home.") "Please—I don't want to stay here, I want
to go home."

The nurse came in to tend him, so I left and called Jock's
internist, Dr. Smith, who said, "There's only a fifty percent
chance that the penicillin will work; the steroids may have
destroyed his immune system. He must be admitted."

Then I called Jock's Baltimore neurologist and discussed
it with him. He said, "Professionally I have to agree to ad-
mitting him."

" 'Professionally' hasn't done much good," I said tersely,
"I think 'humane' is what is important right now. Jock doesn't
want to stay and I think his wishes are paramount right now."

"Betty, professionally I have to tell you to admit Jock, but
I'll tell you personally that if he were my brother I'd take
him where he wanted to go."

I thanked him for his honesty, then called the director of
the nursing home, who said it was all right with her if we
decided to bring Jock back. Then she added, "Not to be
morbid, but if Jock dies what do you want done with his
body?" That electric shock feeling turned my stomach over
and I went cold. For the first time I realized how serious
they all thought it was.

Since Jock had "died" five times before, after the shock of
talking about his body, I actually did not stay panicked as I
had done the other times. (But I was soon to learn that what
Steinbeck said, "I anticipate trouble because I don't anticipate

trouble," was true.) In the waiting room I sat at a little round table with Dancy, McDonnell, and Eve, and we had a conference. "For Jock's sake, I wish the doctors would just let him go," Dancy said. "That's what Jock would want."

Eve, who was now a doctor herself, said, "But it's inculcated in doctors to relieve suffering and prolong life, even if these duties are in conflict—which they often are. And many doctors insist they are healers, not executioners, and we are trained to save lives, not to judge who should live and who should not."

"So the doctors can't decide," McDonnell said, "and we, the family, are too emotional to do it . . ."

"And other families may decide to do so for the wrong reasons," Dancy said. "They may not want the responsibility or the cost and may even be greedy and want the inheritance."

"And what if they disagree?" Eve asked. "The *only* person who can decide is the person himself. That's the only acceptable thing, both morally and legally. But Jock doesn't have a Living Will and he is incompetent now . . ."

"But we know what he wants," McDonnell added soulfully.

"Perhaps the penicillin *will* work," I said. It did the last time and it'll work in the nursing home as well as here."

Dancy interrupted. "The nursing home doesn't have resuscitator machines and other such equipment, but we could bring him back here."

"Or do nothing," McDonnell added.

"But doing nothing *is* doing something," I said, despairing.

Finally we all agreed to take him back to the nursing home. I went to the resident in charge. "I'm taking my husband out."

He was horrified. "He has to be admitted. Dr. Smith says he has to."

"But I say I am taking him home. Will you call an ambulance please?"

"I can't. Dr. Smith says to admit him."

"I don't care what Dr. Smith says. I'll call the ambulance myself . . ."

He looked at me disapprovingly and called an ambulance. I signed the release papers and, much to the consternation of the entire staff, took Jock out. He was so pleased. All the way back he told the ambulance driver and nurse how he had climbed Kilimanjaro and reached the top.

I gave him his first dose of penicillin and fed him his dinner. Almost immediately his temperature dropped to normal, contentedly he fell asleep, and I went to Dancy's and tried to do the same.

At 7 A.M. the nursing home called me at Dancy's. Jock was very bad. His temperature had risen suddenly to 104° and he couldn't move—I should come immediately. I raced to the nursing home as fast as my heart was racing. Jock, as always, smiled when he saw me, but I could tell how very ill he was. I called Dancy who, choking up, said she would call Rick and Bryony, who were in Philadelphia, and the rest of the family to come immediately.

I went back into Jock's room, sat on his bed, and kissed him. I held his hand and talked about going home to Kenya.

He smiled. "I want to stop in London on the way and order a new Citroën. I think I'll order two new Citroëns . . . Shall we go next month?"

"If you're well by . . ."

"Oh, I'll be fine by then," he interrupted and murmured weakly, "This is only pneumonia, I'll be fine in a few days. What color Citroëns shall we get—or would you like another Rolls? That was such a lovely present . . ." He drifted off to sleep.

As the day wore on he grew worse. Rick and Bryony, Dancy and McDonnell and Eve, Colleen and my sister and niece and nephew and the nuns all stopped in, and Jock, though very weak, recognized everyone and greeted them with a little smile, said a few words, somewhat incoherently, then drifted off to sleep again.

Toward evening a nurse said Jock was tired and must sleep—so I should leave. I went with the children to McDonnell and Eve's for dinner. What a gift to see the smiling face of little Garrick; how it helped negate the pain. After dinner I called the nursing home. Jock was sleeping peacefully.

I went to bed, but I could not sleep. I had to go back to Jock. It was 12:30 A.M., April 30th, just three and a half years to the day since I had been told he had a brain tumor and only six months to live. I got up and drove there, and climbed into bed with him, thankful that he wasn't in the hospital for they wouldn't have let me spend the night curled up with him in bed. His temperature was very high, and he was breathing with great difficulty. He hugged me to him and I kissed his burning lips. The penicillin was not working.

Oh, dear God, is it too much just to ask for time, just a little more time? Don't let him die. Not Jock, not my Jockieduk. I don't want him to die—I want him to be just as he was two days ago—sitting in his wheelchair and smiling at me and telling me how much he loves me and we are going to be together until we're a hundred years old. Even if I don't believe it, I want him to tell me.

My heart had trumped my brain. Gone were all my intellectual thoughts that Jock should die because he would not want to be alive like this, that he would never get out of the nursing home, that he would just die cell by cell there on death row now, unable to walk, even unhappy now. Gone were my thoughts that painless pneumonia was a friend that had come along to save him from that horror, and save me from having to carry out that terrible decision . . . all that was gone now. I just wanted him to live, he who was so hungry for life. Would his great curiosity never be satisfied— would he never see the African children at the center, would he never know who would be the next president, when the baby would walk. . . ? I started to cry.

"Bettyduk, why are you crying? I'll be fine." As difficult as it was for him to speak, he still really believed it.

"I'm crying because you are sick again. It's so unfair."

"But Betty, we'll be with the giraffe and in Malindi this time next month." He stroked my hair.

I clung to him and managed to whisper, "We're going to

have such fun watching the African schoolchildren in the center, and the ocean will be so lovely at Malindi . . ." Malindi, that magical place where I knew we would never be together again.

"Will you try wind-surfing with me?" He breathed with such difficulty.

"Oh, yes," I answered, burying my head in his shoulder so he would not see my tears, and held him tighter.

He lifted my face to his, smiled his lovely smile, and kissed me gently, too gently, then whispered faintly, "Maybe there'll be another falling star and we can make a wish."

"What will you wish this time?" I ran my fingers over the white spots on his front teeth and looked into those blue blue eyes.

His voice was almost inaudible, but I heard him say, "The same thing—that we will be together forever." That was the last coherent sentence he ever spoke in English.

We clung to each other all night long and never let go. By morning he was almost unconscious, but his eyes said what his lips could not: They looked at me and smiled. Then suddenly he frowned.

"What is it?" I asked. "Do you hurt?"

"No, no," he mumbled, "the flowers, see the flowers! Aren't they beautiful? And the light—look at that light!"

Bryony stayed home with Garrick, but Rick, Dancy, McDonnell and Eve arrived at 8 A.M. and the nurse told them Jock was now speaking gibberish—but it was Swahili, his first language. The only word the staff had been able to understand was "Bettyduk," which he kept muttering over and over.

All of us stood around Jock's bed, and reminisced in Swahili about all the good times we had had together. McDonnell said, "Jockieduk, remember the time I made my first solo flight and landing, and you all and Shirley Brown came to Magadi to meet me and brought a picnic lunch? And the great times we had when you and Mother came to our school in Switzerland and watched us ski?"

Jock smiled weakly and mumbled, *"Na ogalea . . ."* (and swim).

I was stroking his head. "Remember how proud we were when they won the Kenya championships?"

Rick took Jock's hand and said, "It was always so good to see you at my polo matches. It made me want to win more because you were always so enthusiastic about my playing. But we've all given you a lot of hard times too—remember when I wrecked your car?"

"And when you had to search for me in the game park all night?" Dancy asked, trying to sound cheerful.

"And when I was little and got lost on my first flight to the States alone?" McDonnell said, having difficulty himself trying to cover for Dancy's shaky voice. "You've always been such a good friend . . ."

"And father . . .," Rick added.

"Thank you, Jockieduk," Dancy muttered, "for all the good times you've . . ."

". . . Always given us," McDonnell was just able to finish for her.

"And for our beautiful wedding party," Eve put in.

Rick's voice trembled, too, as he said, "Yes, especially for my gorilla trip and Daisy's capture . . . and Jock, don't worry about A FEW. I'll take over—until you get well, and I'll do a good job too, and . . . ," but his face contorted and as tears welled in his eyes and he couldn't go on.

As I leaned down and kissed Jock's dry lips, the giraffe necklace brushed his chest. I took it in my hand. "Thank you for this, my engagement ring. Remember the day you gave it to me, sitting high on the hill? I never take it off—I love it. Isn't it remarkable, you gave me a giraffe long before we ever thought of having real ones? And all your Tuesday presents did I ever thank you enough?

"And mainly for giving all of us Africa," Rick said.

Dancy, her voice even more shaky, said, "Yes, you gave us Africa, and all the wonderful things about it, but mainly you gave us love."

He was not coherent, but we understood the words he mumbled: *"Furaha . . . niku penda . . . wewe nipe mimi furaha kabissa."* Put together, they translated into how happy we made him and how much he loved us.

With tears streaming down all their faces now, the children walked to the window and stared out. I put my head next to Jock's. "Remember our funny marriage ceremony—and our lovely honeymoon at our Hansel and Gretel house in the woods? Remember trout fishing with Shirley Brown—and how she liked to go snorkeling with us?"

Jock squeezed my hand weakly and smiled.

"And aren't we lucky to live in three worlds really—in our Malindi house with the ocean and the moon, and our Nairobi house with the giraffe, and our pit stop in New York? We live a fairy-tale life in never-never land. And aren't we lucky to have had five books published, and met so many interesting people, and seen so much of the world—Saudi Arabia and Iran and Ceylon and Japan and Singapore—so many places. Except Mexico . . . but we'll go there one day. . . . You've given me so much, Jockieduk, in so many ways."

It was so difficult for him to speak but, still in Swahili, he just managed to mutter, "You have given me life."

O that I could . . . His words broke me, and as I cried I bathed his hot forehead in cool water and kissed him and told him over and over how I loved him. His breathing became faster and faster, he could not hold the thermometer in his mouth, he could not sip the water through the glass straw, he could not swallow his penicillin even when it was crunched up; his pulse was weak, his blood pressure very low. The nurse whispered that he was slipping into a coma. The children walked back to the bed, and we talked some more to the still figure. His last word was *"bagamoyo,"* which means, "Here I leave my heart."

Those blue blue eyes now looked at us blindly, and I knew his life was near the end. He was in a coma, but we kept on trying to reminisce, and I swear there were times when we thought he smiled.

The nurse came in again, took his blood pressure, and said it would be over soon.

Over? NO!

I fell next to him on the bed and sobbed. So for the first time I told Jock—could he hear me now?—that his tumor had been malignant.

"I didn't tell you, Jockieduk, because I wanted you to be happy for the little time we had left together and what was the point in two of us being miserable? You will say how hard that was for me, but Jockieduk, it really wasn't, it would have been harder for me if you *had* known because then I would have had to bear your sadness as well as mine. And we had lots of good times, didn't we? Getting the center built? In Venice? In London? And with Daisy and her baby and the others? And loving each other?

"Pretending to you everything was all right made me almost believe it myself." Tears streamed down my face as I stroked his face. "We cheated the doctors or God or somebody— because all the doctors said you only had six months to live, and we got three-and-a-half years. We can do anything together, can't we? But Jockieduk, the steroids destroyed your immune system and you're going to die, and I don't want you to die . . ." I buried my head next to his and wept openly, but I kept on kissing and talking to the still still figure. "If there is a Heaven you'll be with your family and you'll meet my mother and father and be with Shirley Brown and lots of our dead friends. You'll have a good time . . . just wait for me. And don't worry about me, I'll be fine . . . except I'll miss you so much . . ."

I combed his hair because he liked his hair combed. "You've been so good all through your illness—everyone says so— you've never even complained. And you've been the best husband in the whole wide world." Then I cut a little strand of his wispy hair. "I'm going to bury this next to Shirley Brown at Malindi. And I'm doing what you want—I'm giving your body to medical science." Then I clutched him to me and broke down and sobbed again. "But Jockieduk, you wouldn't want me *not* to cry, would you? I guess I should be ashamed because we've had almost twenty magical years together and how many people can say that? I guess I should be thankful for that, and I am, but I just don't want you to die. I want more . . . more."

He stared into space; then suddenly he took two deep gasps for breath and didn't take another. Rick took his hand, "Say hello to Shirley Brown for us, Jockieduk." Dancy just stood there next to him crying, and McDonnell clenched Eve's hand tighter. I clasped Jock to me closer and cried, "DON'T DIE, JOCK, DON'T DIE!" and after twenty seconds of not breathing at all, he took another breath.

"You called him back," Dancy said quietly and put her arm around me. "Let him go, Mother, let him go."

I gathered him in my arms. "I'm sorry I called you back. It's all right for you to die now if you want to . . . it's all right, Jockieduk. I love you . . ."

And he stopped breathing. Forever.

Epilogue

M y grief was unbearable.
It was as if two people had died—my young, intelligent, and vital Jock, who ran down the beach with his mass of hair blowing in the wind, and that sweet little hairless old man in the nursing home. I loved them both.

The New York Times, The Times (London), the Baltimore *Sun, The Philadelphia Inquirer*, and the Nairobi papers all ran his picture and long obituaries. My instinct was to run to Jock and say, "Hey, look at this . . ." I kept forgetting he wasn't there.

Although I had really had Jock's funerals for him while he was alive, we had a proper one at our good friends the Bouchers seventeenth-century house in the Maryland countryside, which Jock had always loved. Chairs were placed outside, and friends from Baltimore, New York, Philadelphia, London, and even four from Nairobi, sat overlooking the lake, which looked very melancholy that day, and the weeping willow trees surrounding it seemed especially sad. I sat between my two sons, each holding my hand, and Dancy sat next to Rick.

Rick's young minister friend, Earl, presided, and friends gave eulogies: Helen spoke of Jock's noble courage, his kindness and gentleness; Paul said that to have known him was to love him; Bebe told how he had brought so much good and had made such an important contribution to others' lives; Colleen said that he had left the world a better place, that it wasn't a blessing a wonderful forty-seven-year-old man got kidnapped by cancer, but to know him had been a blessing for all of us.

The last eulogy was from Warren, a longtime friend. He stood before all of us and said, "This is a letter to Jock. I'm going to read it aloud, so he can know it comes from all of us:

" 'This is a day that few of us thought we'd ever see: a day when we no longer have to look forward to that most pleasant event of the season—your next visit, your next smiling entrance into a roomful of people eager to feel again a little nobler than they do on ordinary days because they could once more share your grace and elegance, and could believe that some of it, for a while, belonged to them.

" 'With your fine flair for paradox, you'll appreciate the strange idea that this is a very good day for exactly that reason. We no longer have to dwell here in the pedestrian shadows of everyday life, waiting for the excitement you always brought; because now you are always with us, and will be for good. Everything your bright and generous spirit gave us over the years belongs to us now, for keeps. And we'll treasure it. You've fixed forever in our minds the model of what a gentleman should be. The England that bred you out of Scottish roots, the Africa you loved, and the America that loved you, are all richer for the time you gave them. You've left all of us a legacy: the pride of having known you.

" 'Writer, scholar, sportsman, soldier, friend—so long for now. We love you, Jock. You're part of us. And we'll never have to miss you any more.' "

Then we sat silently as Jock's favorite song, "Bridge Over Troubled Waters," was played, and afterward we all tried to have a party, as Jock would have wanted, but we weren't very successful.

The next day was to be Garrick's christening. It had been planned for months, so we went ahead with it. A perfect paradigm of the ebb and flow of life. Earl presided again and spoke of death and life, and sadness and joy; for that is what life is—it is tragic and it is happy.

I went back to Nairobi with Rick and Bryony and the baby, and I certainly did not want to have yet another funeral, but Jock's friends there said they wanted to say goodbye to him, so over a hundred people arrived for the memorial service at our house. (It was the only time I have ever seen Rutherfurd in a tie.) Everyone sat in the entrance hall, where we had all danced and laughed so many times together. Rick stood before everyone and said, "You are all here today as good friends of Jock's. He was my good friend for twenty-one years, and my stepfather for twenty . . ." Just then Daisy put her long head into the hall, as if she too were attending her "mother's" funeral, and I started to cry. Rick, too, had to fight back the tears as he spoke, then looking directly at me, he finished by saying, "So, Jockieduk, remember until we meet again—I love you."

Then a close Nairobi friend got up and said that ours was such a beautiful love story, then said kind things about my caring for Jock with such love over the last three-and-a-half years.

Then an African friend told how he had begun working for Jock years ago when Jock was fighting for African independence and how much Jock had done for Kenya. He said he was speaking for all Africans that day—that so many had called him from Kenya and Tanzania when they read of Jock's death, that Jock was a person who was truly color-blind and how much he was loved and admired by Africans and would be missed by all of them.

The Duke of Manchester gave the last eulogy, and said Lord Leven, Jock's cousin, was placing a plaque for Jock in the family graveyard in Scotland, and let us do so too for Jock, so everyone walked down to Jock's dream, the educational nature center, the first one of its kind in independent Africa, and placed in front of it a brass plaque bearing Jock's name and dedicated the center to him. He will live on there forever.

So there's the story.

Yet there was to be a final irony: Astonishingly, the autopsy revealed no trace of the killer tumor. For the first time in medical history the radiation/chemotherapy combination succeeded in eradicating the glioblastoma, the most deadly of brain tumors. So in that way, Jock will also live on as a medical phenomenon whose unique case may provide science with valuable clues to the final elimination of brain cancer. But the cost was high—the radiation had also destroyed the link between his frontal lobe and his brain center, and the chemotherapy damaged his immune system.

When I told Dr. Petito I often wondered if Jock heard me talking to him in his last few hours when he was in a coma, he said that someone in a coma cannot hear, but someone who is comatose can hear. I asked how to tell the difference, and he said if you pour water in an ear and the eyes fall to one side the person is in a coma, but if the eyes tremble back and forth without falling to the side, the patient is comatose. But I didn't know that at the time, and I prefer to believe Jock did hear me.

And now, quite a few months after Jock has died and I have had time to think and consider, finally I know what I'd do about my promise to him if I had it to do over. I'd do exactly what I did—nothing, because of his happiness and lack of pain. So I am more content with what I did than I am sad for what I didn't do.

So our song is ended—but the melody lingers on. I have endless reruns of our life together and Jock looms before me everywhere. Not only in those special moments that will never be forgotten, but odd, unexpected little things—like a chameleon, or Gravy Train—take me off guard and pierce me. I expect this when I see his sling hanging in the cupboard, or Daisy looking for him, or hear "Just in Time" or a mention of Napoleon or gorillas, but I didn't know that whenever I saw a parrot or a mobile home I'd be stabbed. I am constantly remembering Jock but is he remembering me?

And I hear his laughter everywhere. He has never really left. Most of me is still with Jock; but there is no one to say good morning to.

I could be miserable forever, but I keep trying to remember that it's attitudes, not circumstances, that count in life; and that life is like that whiskey bottle and I always try to see it as half full. I keep telling myself that Jock and I had twenty magical years together, and how many people can say that?

But I think so often how Jock would have loved seeing the hundreds of African schoolchildren we bus to the nature sanctuary every day; how he would love to see their astonishment at feeding the giraffe. We bring out 4,000 children per month; they are the poorest of the poor, and most of them have never seen a giraffe before. If only he could see the delight and wonder on their faces as they walk through the primeval forest and pause on the rocks in the stream where he and I used to. If only he could see their interest when they watch the conservation films in the educational center and they realize for the first time that the animals are their natural heritage and should be saved, not only for the sake of the animals, but to provide jobs for themselves. If only he could see their enthusiasm about it as they drink their orange drink and eat their cookies and discuss it among themselves on the ride back to their cardboard houses.

The idea of selling our house was anathema to me. Leave the giraffe? Impossible. But I didn't want to live there alone, so I worked it out that the house has now become the "Giraffe Manor" and is open for safariers to stay overnight there. When I am there I entertain the guests and give them dinner parties—when I'm not, Rick and Bryony, who run A FEW Kenya and who built a house on our property, act as hosts. All proceeds go to A FEW, so people not only stay in a lovely house with excellent meals and giraffe to feed from their bedroom windows, they are also helping to save wildlife.

But it is so empty, so changed without Jock.

Of course, death changes all things. Outwardly I still appear to be the same person, but I have taken on a different form. Just as a tree is no longer a tree when it has been cut down but still continues in a different form—as a chair or a house or a violin, I, like the tree, continue, but without beautiful leaves or blossoms, without the joyful life that lived within or that lovely life which flew in and out. I do not know what form I will take, for I have just been cut down, but I will be rebuilt again, as trees and life are, into a different design.

But I will never be that Betty again.

And now, just over a year since Jock's death, people sometimes ask me, "Are you still upset?"

And I answer, as I suspect I always will, "Yes. He's still dead."

Yet. . . . I came to realize that my Jock, the Jock I married never did die—he never went through the actual physical act of dying as the sweet senile man in the nursing home did. My Jock never died—and he never will. He is still alive and with me. I hear his voice and his words, and I feel his presence everywhere.

And when I see a star streak across the African sky I wonder—could it be a reminder to me that our wish to be together *did* come true, except for the "forever" part. But could my interpretation of "forever" be wrong? Could death be just an interlude? Could it be that one day Jock and I *will* be together forever? I ponder this often—for after all, I do believe in falling stars.

AN APPEAL FROM THE AUTHOR

Would you like to help?

The African Fund for Endangered Wildlife was formed to aid endangered species in Kenya, and to educate African children. So if you would like to help, please send your tax-deductible contribution to:

A FEW
111 Gwynbrook Avenue
Owings Mills, Maryland 21117

Index